EYES OF DESIRE

RAYMOND LUCZAK, Editor

EYES OF DESIRE

A Deaf Gay & Lesbian Reader

Boston ♦ Alyson Publications, Inc.

Typeset and printed in the United States of America.

This is a paperback original from Alyson Publications, Inc.,
40 Plympton St., Boston, Mass. 02118.
Distributed in England by GMP Publishers,
P.O. Box 247, London N17 9QR, England.

This book is printed on acid-free, recycled paper.

First edition: June 1993

5 4 3 2 1

ISBN 1-55583-204-0

Library of Congress Cataloging-in-Publication Data

Eyes of desire : a deaf gay & lesbian reader / Raymond Luczak, editor.
— 1st ed.
p. cm.
ISBN 1-55583-204-0 : $9.95
1. Homosexuality—United States—Literary collections.
2. Lesbians—United States—Literary collections. 3. Gay men--United States—Literary collections. 4. Deaf—United States--Literary collections. 5. American literature—20th century.
6. Deaf, Writings of the, American. 7. Gays' writings, American.
I. Luczak, Raymond, 1965–
PS509.H57E9 1993
810.8'09020664—dc20 93-1324
CIP

Through the crowds of ghosts we wander still,
Struck yet again by how deaf friends could
Collapse among us, against their will.
They fought, in their drugged weakness, to read
More clearly their doctors' mumbling lips.
As they found themselves more lost at sea,
They dropped their compasses, and their grip
On reality. They held our good
Lost warmth they'd felt in their fleeting lives:
Together like glasses of sweet wine.

—Raymond Luczak

✦

Deafness and gayness are not my problems;
they are those of people who do not accept themselves,
and therefore do not accept others.

—Samuel Edwards

ACKNOWLEDGEMENTS

Without the following people this book would've told a markedly different story: Capitol Rainbow Alliance of the Deaf (CMRA), *Christopher Street* magazine, *Deaf Life* magazine, Michael Denneny, Drago, Jack Fennell, Gene, Robert Giard, M.H. and T.C., Richard Lipez, "James Mackintosh," Ken, Keith R. Mitchell, "Nickolas," A.P.P., Iain Poplett, The Princess, "Ricky," Rob Roth, "Brian Seaman," Ann Silver, Starla Smith, E.T., Frank Toti, and "Victor." I have been very lucky in having had such a wonderful experience in editing this book — let alone my very first book! — thanks to the street smarts of Sasha and the sweet heart of Tom. They are truly angels.

CONTENTS

Foreword

THIS STRONG BEAM OF LIGHT

IN THE BEGINNING, deaf people and gay people existed in freedom. They thrived on the art of gestures and the art of sensuousness until various religions — with religious documents interpreted by people who needed to control their own fears of differentness — swept through human civilizations. Deaf people came to be considered hopeless, warranting pity; gay people came to be considered sick, and were cast out of society's arms.

Such oppression has continued for centuries. Lesbians, considered witches, were tied to burning stakes. Deaf people were considered slow learners and unemployable except for the most menial chores. Doctors and surgeons experimented in unthinkable ways with the sex organs and brains of people identified as desiring sex with their own gender, or as having the inability to hear and speak.

✦

Little by little, the occasional but scattered glimmers of hope for deaf gay people converged into a strong beam of light. This beam has weathered hundreds and hundreds of world-renowned psychiatric experts, whose articles describe homosexuality as a "pathological disease" for which a cure must be found at all costs.

This strong beam of light has also survived Alexander Graham Bell's pervasive obsession with speech as the only viable method of education for the deaf. In 1880, Bell applied his considerable weight at the International Congress of the Educators of the Deaf to make the use of speech, not signs, the organization's objective. This move was shocking, for Bell himself was a fluent signer; he'd married a deaf woman who, it was said, could speak (*and* knew sign language), and he was the son of a deaf mother. Not only that, deaf teachers were excluded from the vote. Fantastically rich from his invention of the telephone (originally an attempt to create a hearing aid), Bell poured money into the oralist cause, and sign language as a method of communication with deaf children in their education was suddenly discredited.

Waiting and waiting, we signed and loved behind closed doors until the 1960s.

✦

The 1960s brought forth tiny rebellions that soon ballooned into signs and banners waving high in the clouds for all to see. Dr. William Stokoe of Gallaudet University, Washington, D.C., showed that American Sign Language (ASL) was hardly "barbarian," that in fact ASL fulfilled every criterion of a natural language, and that ASL was a true language. And if ASL was a language, there had to be a deaf culture. In addition, there was a sudden swell in the number of deaf babies during the rubella epidemic of the midsixties: they would become part of the Deaf President Now movement at Gallaudet in March 1988.

As for gay people, on June 28, 1969, their cloistered history of whispering and furtiveness was thrust directly into this strong beam of light. For a long time, the police had been raiding one gay bar after another in New York's Greenwich Village, alleging that the bars had no liquor licenses to operate. But on that night, something snapped. The drag queens who frequented the Stonewall Inn on Christopher Street fought back and sparked the three-day Stonewall Riots. Their rage was so intense that they even tore out parking meters to throw at the stupefied cops.

✦

Pride became the password for both deaf and gay people in the 1970s. Deaf gay people's pride grew more and more open, in public with both ASL and homosexual desire coming out more and more from the closets of shame. They discovered that the straight deaf community was not too fond of them, so they formed their own chapters of the Rainbow Alliance of the Deaf (RAD); the RAD chapters also helped start the tradition of hosting a national convention every other year.

Technology soon made deaf people less dependent on hearing people when using the telephone: TDDs (Telecommunication Devices for the Deaf) got smaller, cheaper, and easier to use. And the deaf community quickly coined abbreviations to help cut down on the cumbersome typing on the keyboard: GA means "Go Ahead," SK means "Stop Keying," QQ means ?, and SMILE means just that.

And every day closed-captioned television programs, videotapes, and laserdiscs became more common. Deafness is *not* a handicap, but limited information accessibility is. Most deaf people are looking forward to the day when videophones are affordable and clear enough to catch their signs. Too many deaf people are embarrassed by their "broken" English.

In the 1980s, AIDS struck. The number of that first generation of openly deaf gay men shrank horribly, and in some cities, local RAD chapters folded. Misinformation and miseducation was the norm with AIDS organizations in their relationships with deaf people.

✦

All this has been a voyage of self-empowerment. To empower ourselves further as deaf lesbians and gay men, we must question *everything* including whatever our own government, doctors, teachers, and parents tell us. If they don't bother to question enough on their own, we are immediately at risk. What they believe to be truths may turn out to be distortions or even lies. And if we don't question them, we may be hurt by their erroneous truths.

For example, consider the controversy raging over cochlear implants. Because the right education at the right time is so crucial to a deaf child's language development, it would have made sense for the deaf community to be consulted prior to such momentous decisions as the federal Food and Drug Administration's appalling approval of cochlear implants on babies two years or older — even though the procedure is obviously far more *permanent* than hearing aids. (The fact that the FDA did not wait out the required minimum ten-year period of evaluation is even more shocking: They made this decision in a little less than two years.)

At least a deaf person can choose to take hearing aids out and be really deaf in the cultural sense, or put them back in to interact with the hearing world. But cochlear implants mutilate the human head with under 25 percent significant improvement in hearing. That right to choose to be culturally deaf has been summarily removed by parents overwhelmed by doctors and "experts." And in their confusion, parents often don't even think of asking to talk with members of the deaf community for a second opinion. Studies conducted on speech perception among children with cochlear implants and among profoundly deaf hearing-aid users show that implanted children hear much less than even profoundly deaf children with hearing aids.

What's more, a cochlear implant operation costs at least $40,000. A pair of hearing aids — if a pair is needed — costs approximately $1,500. The maintenance of the implant — including visits to the doctor and the audiology clinic for extensive speech and hearing therapy — is far more expensive than sending your broken hearing aids out for repair, as well as being far more intrusive in the life of the deaf child. Moreover, the cochlear implantee is stuck with this *permanent* thing, leading from inside the skull to behind the ear, even though the device could become outdated in a few years. Also, as children's skulls develop, further surgery is required for implant adjustment. The tragedy is that more than 5,000 people, including over 1,000 children, have taken this route. If they're not that rich, guess who's paying? Like many other deaf taxpayers, I don't want my money to support such a questionable enterprise.

✦

And so for us deaf gay people, three big words found their way into our vocabulary. *Paternalism* is the attitude of hearing people who feel compelled to take care of deaf people because the poor things don't know what's best for them. *Homophobia* is the fear and hatred of gay people. And *audism* is the attitude of hearing people who make themselves authorities on deafness but do not allow deaf people to be equals in decision-making processes in deaf affairs, including deaf education. With awareness of these three concepts and their implications, we are that much more capable of greater self-empowerment.

Yes, it's possible for us to rip up that list of injustices — by *questioning* everything. We've proven that already with the Deaf President Now movement at Gallaudet, when we challenged the idea of yet another hearing person running a campus for deaf people. If we are to revel in the prismatic delights of our lives as deaf gay people, we must never give up questioning. It's what guided us forward through the centuries; it has led us to take action one way or another, by coming out to one another, to our parents, and to the world, and by standing up for what we believe.

Oh, it is such a joy to be able to see each other's faces without having to strain our eyes in the dark. We do all have eyes of desire. Let us step forward proudly with our hands and bodies into that strong beam of light and see more clearly a warmer and brighter future with our loved ones. I hope this book will serve as a colorful, grim, funny, and sexy reminder of our past, but also as a prism through which our strong beam of light can create a rainbow.

—Raymond Luczak

NOTES ON THE TEXT

With the exceptions of a few pieces that promote separatism as a means for formulating one's identity, I've chosen for consistency's sake not to capitalize the word "deaf" throughout the book. Such capitalization has been arbitrary too often, and an editor's highest duties are clarity, consistency, and coherence. If the words "lesbian" and "gay" are not generally capitalized, and if being deaf and being gay are to be treated equally in this book, then capitalizing the word "deaf" is not needed. This does not mean that I've rejected the motivation behind capitalizing the word "deaf." Writers who do so want only to emphasize the reality of a deaf cultural perspective, as opposed to the overwhelmingly pathological and medical definitions that have long oppressed the deaf. Given the various viewpoints of both the deaf lesbian and the deaf gay male communities, I feel it is important to be clear and accessible above all, so that readers of all stripes can appreciate — and support — our growing politically diverse pride in being deaf and gay.

Pieces marked with an asterisk (*) come from the interviews I conducted on videotape, and which I translated with the aid of a VCR from American Sign Language (ASL) into English. Without this process, this anthology would have had an extremely lopsided perspective. Many contributors have asked to be listed under pseudonyms (enclosed in quotation marks), and details have been changed to protect their identities. I am forever indebted to these people for their willingness to share so much with me, and for their trust in me as a translator.

ONE

ANN SILVER

SCHOOL ESSAY

ARE THERE ANY SIGNIFICANT EXPERIENCES you have had, or accomplishments you have realized, that have helped to define you as a hearing-impaired person?

During my lunch breaks I fix closed-caption decoders, and on Thursdays after school I repair TDDs free of charge. I translate Deafist slurs for some mainstreamed kids. On school vacations I visit the graves of Clerc, Cogswell, de l'Epee, Gallaudet, Massieu, Sicard, and Veditz. I can fingerspell my ABCs backwards at unflagging speed. I am a connoisseur of Deaf humor.

People worldwide swoon over my line of "Deaf Way" fashionwear. I am a Bi-Bi (bilingual-bicultural) advocate, yet I receive fan mail from Alexander Graham Bell evangelists. I do award-winning ASL poetry. I breed prize-winning deaf cats. I donate ASL textbooks to the school library.

I am the subject of numerous segments on the TV program "Deaf Mosaic." I collect autographs from Deaf trailblazers. I join boycotts against hearing actors performing in Deaf roles. I read Gannon's *Deaf Heritage* and Lane's *When the Mind Hears* in one day and still have time to install a light-signaling system for a friend that evening. I make an I-love-you-sign lapel pin for Vanessa Redgrave, my favorite actress. I contribute half of my summer work earnings to the Center for Bicultural Studies and I read *TBC News* passionately.

My house-pet chimp is currently in training to become a certified interpreter. I become a born-again Deaf woman, thanks to wonderful Deaf role models. I am asked to play Sarah Norman in a community stage production of Mark Medoff's *Children of a Lesser God* and perform the role flawlessly on a half-day's notice. I am an expert at spotting cochlear implantees blocks away. Terms like "deaf-and-dumb," "deaf-mute," and "hearing-impaired" do not appeal to me whatsoever.

On weekends I hurl dead hearing-aid batteries from a great distance at tiny, fast-moving metal objects with deadly accuracy. I win prizes in hearing dog shows, ASL storytelling competitions, and fingerspelling bees. I save all of my National Theater of the Deaf ticket stubs and programs from its early years as collectibles. I can recite nonstop the name of every single Deaf school superintendent in America. Hearing parents of Deaf kids trust me. Whenever it comes to Deaf-style good-byes, I time it efficiently.

Oh. Did I come out yet?

PHILIP J. GORTON*

DIFFERENT FROM THE OTHERS

WHEN I WAS NINE OR TEN, I knew I was different inside as a person. It was a feeling. I didn't know what I was like, but I just *knew* I was different. Then when I turned twelve or thirteen, I started to look at men. It felt so natural to look. That's when I realized why I was different.

At Canius College in Buffalo, New York, I went swimming with my class from my deaf school Wednesdays at their Olympic-size swimming pool. I loved it because there were always men there.

And in the public showers I liked looking at the naked men. I drooled over the ones with nice bodies, and some I just went, "Yuk."

One boy there brought up some gay issues. I don't remember exactly how, but it hit me so hard. I realized that "gay" meant men who look at other men. I realized that I was gay. It scared me, because I knew people didn't like gay people.

Anyway, that's how I knew I was gay.

When I was fourteen, I played around with a boy who once lived next to me in our residential dorm. Umm, we played wrestling, and there was a lot of physical contact.

I told him that it was normal for boys to do that, and somehow we went too far. We played around, you know — we jerked off, but we didn't have ejaculations. There was a lot of touching and rubbing — sort of like "hot steam."

It felt so natural. But we didn't want *anyone* to know, and we got paranoid. We didn't want anyone to know about *this*. (That was in seventh grade, and when I left the school in eighth grade, I never saw him again.)

---

*This interview was conducted by the editor on August 29, 1992.

I was sixteen when I decided to come out. I'd thought to myself, If I keep my mouth shut about myself and if I don't tell my parents, friends, or *anyone,* how long must I keep it all in? What was the point of keeping it in? I felt that if I told someone now, I wouldn't have to worry about it until later, right?

But I didn't know how to go about it. After all, my parents are very religious (they're Catholic), and they had high expectations of me having children, a good marriage, and a good life with my wife.

I decided to do something about it by going to the library. I took out something like ten or twenty books on the subject, and I read *all* of them. I felt a lot better. I realized that I wasn't the only gay person in the world — yeah, I'd really felt that way. I'd never talked about it with anyone. I felt isolated but I read each book and built up my confidence.

Finally I thought, That's it.

I came home. (At that time I was attending a public school in my hometown.) I asked my mother to come sit down. I was scared to death.

She asked, "What's wrong?"

I said, "I don't know."

"You're nervous. What's wrong?"

"I don't know. I mean, something — I mean, something's wrong with me — no, I mean — well, I want to tell you that I am different."

"I know you're different. So what?"

"Oh. Umm, I like men."

"Oh. You like men and you like women. So?"

"No. I like men in a sexual way."

"Are you gay?"

"Yes. I'm gay. I can't believe I said it to you."

Then she got so mad. She said some things I'll never forget. "My God, how can you have a great family? How can you hold another guy's hands? How can you kiss another guy? How can you suck off another guy?" She was so pissed off at me.

I said, "Well, how can you fuck your husband? How?"

She said nothing, and I left the room.

I went into my bedroom, and I was very upset.

I refused to talk to her for one week — not even one word. We passed by each other in the house, pretending the other wasn't even there.

At that time I was still doing more research on gay issues, and along the way I found this one really good book called *Are You Still My Mother?* [Gloria G. Back, Warner Bros., 1985.] A mother had written it because of her gay son, and because of her situation — she knew her husband wouldn't accept their son. It was such a good book and I knew that my mother had to read it.

I went up to her, and she looked at me with a jolt. I showed her the book. "Can you read it for me?"

"Why?"

"If you love me, you'll read the book. Read it."

I left her alone. I gave her plenty of space, which she needed, and I went off.

Two days later she finished the book and came up to me. "I understand you better, and I really realize it was tough for you to tell me. I knew you were gay, but I couldn't bear knowing that you were gay."

"Yes, you're right."

She said she wished that I wasn't gay.

"I know. I can't change. I tried it, but that's it." I explained everything to her.

She hugged me, and she said that she loved me even more because I'd told her the truth.

After that we became closer, and she forgot all the negative things about gay people. We get along great now.

I broke my virginity when I was sixteen. I was very lucky. I broke my virginity with a man I loved. I was living at home at that time, but my home life got screwed up, so I had to live in a foster home under court orders. I had to stay there for two months; after that, it was up to me where I lived. I got depressed and miserable as hell; I ate too little, then I ate too much. I didn't sleep well due to insomnia and bad dreams of my father running after me and laughing at me. My life got really fucked up while I stayed at my foster house after Christmas.

So I decided to go to Buffalo and stay at my friend's house for two weeks during my Easter break. I spent the night, and then my friend left a note saying he had to leave due to a family emergency and that I couldn't stay there.

I didn't know what to do, so I called another friend and stayed at his house. Then I decided to do something for myself. I wanted to be myself, so I went to a gay support group that I'd found in the phone book. I learned its schedule and so I went in. (Lucky that I was on time!)

The name of the group was the Gay Youth League of Buffalo. I loved it, and I was the only deaf person there. There was a great variety of people there, and I liked it. It was different.

While I was there, one boy looked at me, and — that was it. I was lost in his eyes. He was seventeen, and I was sixteen. We kept looking at each other, giving little laughs during a three-hour lecture. After it was over, he stood there with his hands in his pockets. He was macho but really shy. He was so cute. (For your own information, he wasn't my type at all. My type is brown hair and brown eyes, and he had blond hair with hazel eyes. I just happened to be attracted to him.)

He introduced himself as David and I introduced myself. Somehow it went smoothly, and we felt comfortable with each other. We decided to go to his place where we talked nonstop for three days. We never slept together, but the minute we woke up, we'd keep on talking.

I became very curious about what it'd be like to have *real* sex with another man. I don't mean playing around, but *really* having sex — not just jerking off. That night he sat there, and I sat between his legs. One detail I remember very clearly was that a blue lightbulb had been used to replace one broken white lightbulb over him. (It was his friend's place, and his friend had had an epileptic seizure; David knew what to do and made sure that he went to sleep.)

Anyway, I sat there on the floor, and I began to unbutton his shirt. He laughed quietly, and said, "Stop," but I was very stubborn. I wanted to give myself up to him, really. We got to it, and then we got up naked and did it in the shower. Then we did it on the kitchen table, and then *again* on the floor. It was so beautiful.

When I woke up, I forgot for a moment where I was. I was confused because a boy was with me and he's sleeping in my arms. I wasn't prepared for that. I was afraid we'd been going too fast, but when I saw the smile on his face, I just forgot all about my worries. I just held him and fell back asleep.

After that I spent *all* my time with him. I didn't go anywhere else.

Now, at the time I had ignored the fact that he'd enlisted in the Navy, and it was near the end of my Easter break. I was eleven days into my Easter break before I really thought about it. I thought about the fact that in a few days I'd be living three hours away from him, and he'd be in the Navy, and that it was possible I'd never see him again.

That was it — I lost it. I cried and cried. My friend said, "My God, you're really in love with him!" I refused his help. I was so angry at everyone because I thought they were taking David away from me. I just cried.

The next day with David I kept it to myself. But then I asked him, "You going in the Navy?"

"So? We can write letters."

"It's not enough. I want to see you in person."

"I don't know..."

"Fine. Let's see what happens."

Then it was the last day — the day I knew I'd never see him again. Don't ask me how I knew it, but I just *knew* it. I was very quiet, getting depressed. We didn't feel the need to talk about it, because we knew it.

Before my sister came to pick me up to go back to my mother's house, he said, "I will always love you. Good-bye."

"I love you, too."

Then I left. I felt so empty.

I didn't talk to my sister at all; she didn't ask me or anything. She knew something was up, but she didn't say anything.

When we arrived at my mother's house, there was a big family dinner gathering. Everyone sat down, and suddenly my sister came over to tell me that someone named David or something was on the phone and wanted to talk with me. He'd called via the relay service.

"David?"

I was so excited. I turned on the TDD.

"What's wrong?" I said.

He wanted to tell me that he thanked me very much, and that he loved me very much, and that he missed me.

Then the operator said that she was having a hard time understanding him because he was crying, and that made me feel awful. So I tried to calm him down. I told him, "I love you and always will."

When he seemed okay, I hung up.

I refused to eat, just sat playing with my food on the plate and thinking of all the good times we had. I thought of the most romantic time we had, at the Niagara Falls. I remember that night when all those people were watching the waterfalls.

I asked him if I could kiss him in front of all those people.

He said, "No, I'm going in the Navy, and I'm too shy—"

"Come on."

I was stubborn and kissed him anyway. I saw that other people didn't even react to that, and he laughed. So we kissed again. That was so romantic.

Now back to earth, I realized that I couldn't have that ever again. That was it — I just broke into tears and really cried.

And so I've learned what love is all about. David is a treasure I'll always carry with me for a long time. (I haven't had anyone like him since; I just recently turned nineteen.)

✦

I was a freshman in my hearing school, and I was not used to it. (I'd transferred from a deaf residential school to a school near my mother's house.) I wasn't that open in high school. I had already told my mother, but as for my high school, I decided to come out very slowly. I told *just* one friend about myself.

"Oh," she said. That's all she said.

But I still had girls pawing after me. They wrote me love letters and they bothered me a lot, but I turned them *all* down. They were always shocked, asking, "Why? Why? Why?"

I got so fed up with that, so I thought to myself, "What the hell?" I told this other girl, "I'm gay. So?"

"What? You can't be gay."

She freaked out, and the rumor spread around the school just like that.

That was the day I lost *all* my friends.

I was lonely and hurt, but at the same time it made me more determined to do something for myself. I became stronger, and I developed the strength not to give up. I made it through that year.

Then my home life got screwed up again, and I transferred to another hearing public school. I felt very comfortable there because it was such a large school. I was open there, and they accepted me. I saw that, and I became very excited about it. That was so wonderful, and I made lots of friends because of who I am.

It's interesting that all my friends there were straight. Gay students there were afraid to associate with me because they didn't want to be identified as such, so I had no gay friends there at all.

After that I moved back to my old hearing school.

It got worse because everyone went, "My God! He's baaack!"

They began picking on me, and started fights. They threatened me with notes in my locker, saying things like "You better leave this school or you'll get hurt." Some boys would wait in the bathroom for me, and whenever I walked in, they'd start fights with me.

So many things happened that year, but there was one thing I really, *really* hated the most: lunchtime in the cafeteria.

Whenever I walked in for lunch, all the people — I mean, *all* of them — watched my every single movement without saying a word to each other. They just watched. I felt hot. I felt sweaty. I felt my heart beating hard. In my mind I thought, "Shit," but I pretended that it was nothing.

Then I had to put up with waiting in line for my tray of food. I tried to hold in my anger, and I was very much alone when I sat down.

When I did that, they broke into whispers about me. I saw that, but I kept quiet, eating my lunch.

Later on they started throwing food at me. They poured soda on my head, and they threw milk at me. And usually, they'd throw some food at me, and I'd throw food back at them. Then they'd lean over the table and grab my shirt, and we'd start beating the shit out of each other.

Of course we got into trouble, but what really pissed me off the most was that the principal always — *always* — blamed it on me. I was so mad, so pissed off over that.

Anyhow, I somehow suffered through the second semester, and at the end, I told my mother, "I'm not going back to that school, period."

"Again? Where *are* you going to go, then?"

"I don't know yet, but let's see. Don't worry."

My mother looked at me and said nothing.

Then I went to a deaf camp and heard about MSSD [Model Secondary School of the Deaf, in Washington, D.C.]. I decided to go there, and the minute I arrived there, I felt great.

I also knew that if I waited until later to come out, it'd be harder. So I thought if I came out right on the very first day, it'd be easier for me in the long run.

It was much easier than I thought, because I was deaf and everyone was deaf. I could speak up and be understood if I talked about gay issues.

✦

My first gay bar was Tracks in Washington, D.C. I went there at the wrong time — that night was a Leather Night. The place was packed with leathermen, and the smell of leather was overwhelming. In the back of my head I thought, "Do gay people like that? Because I sure don't." I knew next to nothing about S&M [sadomasochism] or leather. Yes, I had some idea what it was, but I wasn't familiar with it.

I was so confused, and then I saw a sign saying that it was a Leather Night, a special event of some kind, I think, to celebrate an anniversary of something. I realized that it was only a special event, and boy, was I relieved.

I stayed there anyway and watched everything. It was interesting, but it wasn't my thing.

I decided to go back on Saturday. I looked around, and I thought, "That's it." I loved it. They had a whole variety of gay people — gay youth, black people, older people, and so on. It was so wonderful. (It's become really popular now because they recently set up a new volleyball court with a patio and a few fountains.)

It made me feel so good. I could enjoy myself and have a good time. I could go dancing with a variety of strangers, and I didn't have to know their names. I'd dance with each one until they got tired, and I'd move on to the next partner. I'm a very energetic dancer. And their volleyball court — I just loved it. It has real sand, so I could take off my shoes and play all night long. That's really *fun.*

✦

At MSSD, quite a few students went, "My God, you're gay? Why? Must you fuck another man? My God!" They went blah blah blah with really disgusted expressions on their faces, and kept on saying negative things about gay people.

I said nothing. I was very laid-back about the whole thing.

Finally one of them asked me, "You're not bothered by this talk?"

I shook my head no.

That's when they realized that it wasn't worth their energy, and they shut up. They realized that I'm still Philip.

But later on, a small group of boys tried to spread the rumor that they were going to beat me up.

I just laughed at them. I told the kids I heard this from to send word back that, "If they want to beat me up, that's fine with me. It won't change the way I am. If they stabbed me with a knife or if they tried to crucify me, I will stay gay, period." Those kids didn't quite understand everything I said, but they relayed the message anyway.

That's when they realized it wasn't worth it.

Then one day I wore a t-shirt to school that said, "I'm not gay, but my boyfriend is." People really freaked out over that.

Eventually my assistant principal heard about it, and she came over to me. She just laughed. She liked my t-shirt.

Yeah, my assistant principal was so supportive. I just love her.

Later that same day, MSSD had their own Assembly Hall. It's a place and a time for students to air their own complaints, give compliments, or propose suggestions, and they have to get up on the stage to tell the other students.

One student went up there and said, "I don't understand why Philip has to wear that t-shirt." He went on and on, and some students went, "Yeah, yeah, we agree!"

When he was done, I went up there and said, "Have you noticed some black people wearing red, yellow, and green on their t-shirts? It's part of their black culture. Wearing this t-shirt is part of my gay culture, so shut up."

Then later on, in an Assembly Hall meeting, a boy called a person a peabrain. I didn't like that, because I don't like name-calling. This is not related to gay issues, but it does relate to how people call gay people names.

I told that boy who'd called this other person a peabrain, "If you call him a peabrain, you are also a peabrain yourself, because you are both human. So?"

The students were speechless. I made even more friends and I got more respect too.

✦

This year I have a straight — I mean, *exclusively* straight — roommate from Michigan. Yuk! He's macho, but he's very sensitive; he's changed his view about gay people to the point he can share his dreams and feelings about girls with me while I share my dreams and feelings about boys with him.

One wall in our room was full of posters of women, while the other wall was full of posters of men. His part of the room was filled with country stuff while mine was filled with modern stuff. Different, huh? I find it very hilarious.

Many students have picked on him just because his roommate is gay. I was very angry and pissed off about it. One day during the Assembly Hall, he stood up on the stage and threw his words in a rage with large signs at the students: "Being roommates with Philip doesn't mean I'm gay, so why harass me about it? I'm straight and I respect Philip. He respects me, and that's about it!"

The students were speechless.

✦

My mother said something to me once that made my heart warm: "All of my other three children are straight and married, but I've always wanted a child who is different."

That made me feel so good.

This is for every deaf gay high school student still in the closet: "I really want you to work hard and to come out as soon as possible, because it will make your life a lot easier in the long run. Allow yourself to experience all kinds of things by going to gay bars, reading books about gay people, and making gay friends. It's important to realize that being gay doesn't mean that you should have only gay friends, and it's important to get along with everyone, including straight people. Through a variety of such experiences, you'll learn so much about yourself."

"MARY ABERNATHY"*

A COMING-OUT STORY

I WAS LIVING IN MICHIGAN when I came out to my co-worker at the hospital where I was working at the time. She was twenty-four and I was sixteen. We were friends, playing tennis, bicycling, and spending time together at the beach and at her house. She was older than me and I grew attracted to her. I developed fantasies about "what could be."

One day I decided to approach the subject of homosexuality by talking about my high school friend. I said she was a lesbian. It wasn't true, but I used her as an example so I could bring up the subject with my co-worker. I had such a crush on her that I even thought up a farfetched story to tell her about how I was pregnant by my boyfriend. This was to get her sympathy. I knew this woman was developing a life apart from me. She was looking for another job and she was in a new relationship with a boyfriend.

One night I told my mother that I was gonna stay overnight with another friend, but I never planned to go to that friend's house and I never called her up. Instead I went to the hospital to visit my co-worker, who had been switched to the night shift. That was the night I told her the farfetched story about my "problems" with my boyfriend.

My co-worker was sympathetic and gave me the key to her apartment. She told me to go there and wait for her.

I went to her home. I tried to decide where to sleep, either in her bed or on the couch. I finally decided on the couch, and then I waited and waited for her to come home.

She arrived very late as she had to do some overtime at the last minute. During that long wait I had a running dialogue in my head:

* This narrative was translated by Jules Nelson.

"What should I do?" "How do I make a move on her?" "What would she do to me?" and on and on. She arrived home looking very tired, so I didn't push right away. I let her wind down on the couch.

She asked what could she do to help me with my problem.

I told her I had something else I wanted to tell her instead. I asked her if she remembered what I told her about my high school friend.

She said yes.

I said, "She is not a lesbian. I am." I was very scared when I said that because that was the first time I had ever verbalized that sentence to anyone.

My co-worker was shocked, maybe a little bit repulsed.

I felt immediately that I had made a big mistake.

She moved away from me and said, "Mary, I'm very tired. You are welcome to stay longer, but I'm going to bed."

I was heartbroken ... crushed.

After she went into her room, I wrestled in my mind about whether to stay, leave, or ask her to understand.

I left. I drove around for hours and hours before I went home.

Later I saw her again, and she was very distant. Our friendship was never the same. I realized that if this is going to happen every time I told someone ... I felt even more lost. Where could I go? Who could I trust?

This feeling lasted for a couple of months. I became more and more depressed, until one morning...

I got myself a bottle of aspirin and went to school with it. I swallowed them all with Orange Sunkist in my parked car in my school's parking lot. I didn't really want to die ... I just wanted attention and some help.

I went looking for a friend, and I told him what I'd done. He took me to the hospital. He drove my car and he didn't know how to use the stick shift so I did that for him. We went into the emergency room and I saw another co-worker there. He was surprised to see me and shocked that I had tried to kill myself.

They gave me this awful medicine and I threw up over and over again.

Then my mother showed up at the hospital. She looked devastated. Her eyes were red and puffy, as if she had been crying for a long time. She asked me, "Why?"

I couldn't tell her. I didn't want to and I also felt too sick at the time to respond.

I stayed in the hospital for three days. My doctors watched my physical condition, and they also debated about my psychological condition. My mother decided that a private psychological hospital would be best for me.

I went there for two months.

During that time I told my counselors that I was a lesbian. After I got out, I finally decided to tell my mother what really happened.

We were driving home from a doctor's appointment. It was night and the stars were out. I kept looking at them and then at my mother. I couldn't decide how to start this. Finally I just said, "Mom, one of the reasons I tried to kill myself is, I am a lesbian."

She looked at me. Then she asked me about my co-worker: "Is she one of them?"

I said, "No. In fact, she turned me away."

My mother said, "Mary, don't ever do that again — trying to kill yourself. Don't ever do that again. I love you, Mary. If that's what makes you happy, then I am happy. I want you to be happy. Did you know that your Uncle Tom is gay?"

I was surprised to hear that, but at the same time it made sense to me.

My mother continued. "I can send you to Uncle Tom's place as a high school graduation gift."

I smiled at her and realized that I could've turned to her a long time before. I had thought to myself, "I am a lesbian." Today I say, "I am a lesbian and proud of it!"

TOM KANE*

MEN IN PINK SPACESUITS

I KNEW I WAS GAY at eight, nine, or ten years old because I loved going to the movies to watch all those Roman-soldier movies. I loved watching their huge chests and their very thick thighs exposed by their leather-slatted skirts. I just drooled and drooled, more so when they showed men with moustaches and beards.

Even in church I drooled over Jesus. To the side was a statue of Mary, who was a virgin and a very clean woman. I saw nothing in that. I just kept drooling over Jesus.

My teachers emphasized that I had good speech while growing up. But when I found that other people couldn't understand me, I felt really put off. It really affected my own self-esteem — if people couldn't understand me, my self-esteem went down, and if they did understand me, my pride went up.

ASL is a neat language.

I was twelve and he was seventeen. He was Puerto Rican, and his dark skin always made my heart flutter. I just drooled over him. One day I said, "What is a fuck?"

Somehow he said, "Let's fuck."

I said, "No, you're joking."

He said, "Sure."

I wasn't sure whether I should go ahead. Remember, I was going to this deaf Catholic school and I was still thinking about sin. I also came from an Irish family.

---

*This interview was conducted by the editor on April 10, 1992.

But I went ahead anyway.

He exposed his hard-on.

I thought, "Wow, what a monster." I couldn't believe it. He jerked off for me and came in huge spurts. I felt shocked. I couldn't believe what I'd seen. Remember, I was twelve.

Later, when I turned fifteen, I fucked him. I realized that his cock was really okay, of average size. See, I was twelve before, and I was short; at fifteen, I realized that he had a regular cock.

✦

Once, my friend took me aside and told me that all the men I'd been attracted to wore glasses. I didn't realize that of myself, that I was really attracted to intelligent-looking men. (Of course I still have a weakness for dark skin and dark eyes.)

Hearing men try to learn signs from me, and then they talk with their voices without really remembering their signs. Also, I'm rather tired of them talking about sign language with me. To me it's a boring topic.

✦

I was fourteen years old when I came out. That summer — August '64 — I'd looked at the word "homosexual." I thought, "Beautiful and sexy word." I looked it up, and then I decided to go down to Greenwich Village where I'd heard they were. I was really curious.

My friend joined me for company on the long subway ride south from the Bronx down to Greenwich Village. I got off and looked around a little. I saw a cop and wrote down on a pad, "Where is fairys?" [*sic*]

The cop pointed toward Sheridan Square.

I said, "Really, really?"

I walked over that way and looked for a long time for homosexuals. That time it was a beatnik neighborhood, but I found none.

So I went home.

✦

In my research on deaf gay men, I've asked this question of them: Suppose there are two candidates running for president, the first one for rights of the handicapped and the second one for gay rights. All said they would much rather vote for the one supporting the rights of the handicapped than for the one for gay rights. Which means, the deaf gay person is more concerned with deaf rights than with gay rights.

This is also true of us in the deaf community. We think of ourselves as gay first, then deaf second; but in the hearing world we think of our deafness first, our gayness second.

We switch back and forth depending on where we are.

I've also noticed that we deaf gay people have our own language, our secret words. When we are introduced to a new person, we look at each other out of the corners of our eyes to make sure that he is indeed one of us, and that he isn't close-minded. Once agreed upon, we really relax with that person. We all have this special feeling, and we do this all the time without even discussing it. We have this sense of inner support among each other.

✦

My first gay bar was the Blue Bunny in the Times Square area, on Forty-third or Forty-fourth Street, I think. It was in 1966, and I was sixteen. I just went in there, and I was shocked to see two boys dancing all over the place.

I thought, "WOW wow WOW."

There is a big need for role models. Back when I was young in the sixties and the seventies, the older deaf gay men were my role models. They were often emotionally negative and unstable, and I thought, "Oh, that's what I have to do."

No, that has to change.

I have no respect for anyone who stays and stays and stays in the closet. That's his problem, and that's sad.

I think that those gay men who become sign language interpreters are often the ones who always liked to keep their hands busy all over the place. (Wink.)

I've just about seen it all: I saw the pre-Stonewall gay lifestyle in 1966, and Central Park I thought was truly heaven, getting touched every which way. Older deaf men warned me to look out for cops, and then later for VD. They kept saying, "VD, VD, VD. Watch out!"

Sure enough, I got VD. But so what.

Then my deaf friends and I would compete to see how many men we had, and I almost made a career out of that. (Of course we all can't compete for AIDS the same way these days.)

I also remember the Mafia-owned bars. They'd look into the peephole and let me in if they knew I was gay. And if there was a cop at the door, all the lights would go on to warn everyone of the fact.

I also went to the truck stops. At first I was disgusted by how they treated sex as dirty, shameful, and something to be hidden. But I got into it after a while: "When in Rome, do as the Romans do."

I used to go to the Stonewall Inn, but I missed the riots there that famous night.

In 1970 I joined the first gay march in New York. At that time everyone shouted, "Gay Power! Gay Power! Gay Power!" Later the word "power" was changed to "pride." We were mostly long-haired hippies, smoking pot and dropping acid.

Then in the late seventies, leather become popular. I tried fistfucking at the Mine Shaft and all those places, and picking up all kinds of men.

Then AIDS cropped up, and we were all so afraid...

Now people are paying attention to relationships and they are more sensitive that way. Before they didn't care, but now they do.

I've seen all those changes, and now perhaps in the future we will have men in pink spacesuits, shiny and glossy all over.

I'm looking forward to that.

DRAGONSANI RENTERIA

REJECTION

SOCIETY REJECTS ME for being Deaf.
The Deaf community reject me for being a Lesbian.
The Lesbian community reject me for not being able to hear them.
The Deaf-Lesbian community reject me for being into S&M.
The S&M community reject me for being Deaf.
Society rejects me for being Chicana.
The Hispanic community reject me for being a Lesbian.
The Gay Hispanic community reject me for being Deaf.
Patriarchal society rejects me for being a woman.
I am rejected and oppressed,
Even by those who cry out readily
Against rejection, oppression, and discrimination.
When will it end?

"PABLO"*

BLACK, DEAF, AND GAY: TRUE IDENTITIES

HOW WELL CAN YOU HEAR and how do you communicate with the hearing world?

I can hear any noise but I have a difficult time identifying where the noise is coming from and what kind of noise it is. For example, I can hear fire-engine sirens and police-car sirens, but I can't tell the difference between them. I communicate with the hearing world by having hearing friends who know basic sign language. Of course, I do talk good and lipread pretty good — at least average.

Do you see yourself as a black deaf gay man, or a deaf gay man, or just a deaf person? Which one do you see yourself as first?

I'd see myself as a black person first, then as a deaf person, and then as a gay person.

Any particular reason why you feel that way?

Well, since my skin color is visible, they can identify me as black. Then they find out I'm deaf. As for being gay, it's a sticky situation. I'm not really in the closet, but I just have to use my best judgment to trust people to accept me as a gay person. That is the last thing, yet the main concern of all my identities is my gayness.

You mean to say that above all you are most concerned with your gayness?

Yes, because I see that I have my own rights as a black person already. Then again I have my own rights as a deaf person. As for my rights as a gay person, they are not quite established.

---

*This interview was conducted via TDD by the editor.

When did you first tell a friend about yourself?

I was in high school, and I knew I was gay, but no one knew about it until one of my friends came out to me when she was in her first year of college. Then I came out to her, and we've been good friends ever since. (That person was white.)

From your own viewpoint, how do you think the black community as a whole view gay people? Do they accept gay people better than white people accepting gay people?

Well, unfortunately for the black community, homosexuality does not exist in their belief system, because religion plays such a big role in their lives. Many black gays fear that if their families ever found out, they'd be thrown out of the house. Now AIDS is coming to the black community. To them it's still a "white gay disease," and there is still a lack of education there. The black community ignored the warnings all along, but now they're regretting it a lot. I feel that the black community should wake up and try to educate its people to accept homosexuality in spite of their religious beliefs.

Have you ever been involved with other black men? Any serious relationships there?

To be honest, I only *attempted* to have some sexual experiences with other black men, but it didn't work for me because I feel they are my brothers, as part of my family, so I never had a real relationship with any black man. Of course, I do have black gay friends. I happen to be much more interested in interracial relationships.

You mean if you sleep with a black man, you feel it's almost like incest?

Yes, you could say it that way. I may feel uncomfortable doing it, but I'd rather *be* a friend with him than go to bed with him.

Because you are interested in getting involved with white men, do you feel that makes you a so-called Oreo? Or do you prefer to maintain your black identity?

First of all, I happen to be proud of being a Jamaican-American, which is my true identity. I'm glad that the gay community has finally accepted interracial relationships, because I remember about ten years ago there were none. But now there are more everywhere. I see them wherever I go, especially in the big cities in the Northeast. Gay bookstores feature literature such as "African-American Literature" and "Latin Literature"; I am glad that I don't have to feel inferior. I also know that white men are attracted to me more than black men.

I believe in the quote "Opposites attract." And I'd like to have an interracial relationship. I know there are many eyes staring at me behind my back whenever I'm with any white person, but I don't give a damn about them as long as they give us respect.

Do you feel discriminated against by other white deaf people, straight or gay?

Ummm, not really. We deafies tend to care about our deafness more than race. Yeah, I feel discriminated against by straighties, but who can argue with that issue after so many years? But overall, I don't feel any discrimination placed on me at all. I'm thankful that I was born in the right year — if I were any older, I would've been beaten up by white people. Or I would've been sent to a deaf residential school due to my deafness. Or I would've been beaten to death because of my gayness. But I am here now. I don't feel much discrimination, so I'm glad in that way.

A white deaf friend of mine has suggested to me that a lot of deaf gay black men are effeminate. Do you agree with that assessment?

Boy, aren't we stuck with stereotypes!?!? I don't think so. Not all are like that. Maybe some are, some not.

That's what I thought. Your signing seems so-called effeminate. Did you ever suffer being called "fag" or "queer" in high school because of that?

Well, not really. I come from a large city that provides many gay resources, so I don't recall being called nasty names. If you are very strong and stand on your own feet, people won't call you names. If you don't do that, then they will do that. It's only logical.

Do you find it difficult to form relationships with white men?

Really, I don't think that way. I'm more concerned about the communication barrier between deaf and hearing people, because it requires a lot of attention and work within the relationship. If I thought only of racial issues, guys would call me a racist and they wouldn't have a relationship with me. I'd have a more difficult time as a result.

How do you meet other men?

One of my friends calls me a "social butterfly." I meet men through a network of friends, at gay organization events, in bars, or at gay-resort beaches like Rehoboth Beach or Fire Island.

What do you seek in an ideal lover?

My ideal lover should have a hairy chest. He should know the basics of sign language (either fingerspelling or ASL) and the basics of deaf culture. He should be willing to spend more time with me and give me respect as a whole person. He should be willing to work on our relationship. I don't want to be the only person who does all the work in the relationship. And I wouldn't depend on the horoscope too much, because that can devastate your hopes of getting involved in the first place. And of course, he must understand interracial issues.

What about the age factor? Does it matter?

As long as it's much closer to my age, up to his forties. I wouldn't dream of having a sugar daddy, though. I'd rather die!

What makes you so proud to be a deaf gay black man?

I'm glad that I am the right age in the right year in the right century. If it were otherwise, I would've lost my rights and privileges.

Meaning that because you were born at the right time, you feel very proud and lucky to be what you are now?

Yes, that's correct. I tend to think positive. Of course, I'll always struggle to prove that I can do it as a black person by being educated, as a deaf person by being successful, and as a gay person by preserving my rights. If I were living in a different time in another world, I wouldn't have all those privileges. I wouldn't be here and you wouldn't be able to interview me like this. You have to think positive and be glad that you are here.

Yes, you are absolutely right. Is there anything else you'd like to add?

I'd like to tell every black deaf gay person: "You are not alone in this country. Be glad that you have friends around to give you support. If you don't have any friends, then go find a gay organization that interests you. You will be able to form a new group of friends. As for relationships, be glad if you have an opportunity to have a man by your side. If you are not happy, then move somewhere else that can provide you with a list of gay resources. That way you can get all the support you need. It's also important not to lose your true identities. They make you a whole person."

JACK FENNELL*

THE OTHER HALF OF HIS DOLLAR

A DEAF WOMAN I KNEW made a point of introducing me to many other deaf people at special events and festivals at St. Rita's School of the Deaf, a residential school near my hometown in Dayton, Ohio. (I had speech therapy while attending a public school.)

One time she pointed out two boys and said, "You know they slept together?"

I said, "No. No. Impossible." I had never heard of such a thing.

At that time I must've been fifteen, sixteen, or seventeen years old. I didn't really feel anything. I'm just not the type to gossip and spread rumors. I knew nothing about gay sex. Well, I did learn the signs for "homosexual" and "queer" from St. Rita's. But at Gallaudet, I learned what the word "gay" meant.

I never thought of sex, really, until I was nineteen years old at Gallaudet. Up until that time, I was always popular with girls, but I did nothing with them. I was just fun to be with. I just never thought of sex until at Gallaudet, where I met all kinds of gay people.

Even then I wasn't really that wild about sex, even when I lived in D.C. Sometimes I'd sneak a run at the local bathhouse, depending on the time available in my class schedule, and come right back to my next class. I enjoyed the baths, because they were comfortable.

I never had problems in the dark room at the baths. Even if someone tried to communicate with me, I never heard him. He probably took a look at me and figured that I was deaf, because many deaf people went there.

*This narrative was created from two interviews conducted by the editor on April 4, 1992, and August 23, 1992.

✦

I graduated from Gallaudet in 1972 with a major in art and a minor in drama. I could've had two majors — I had only six more credits to go for drama, but at the time I didn't think about it. I should have, but I don't really care now. Later, in 1986, when Gallaudet College became Gallaudet University, I got two diplomas — one from the college in 1972, and again from the university.

After graduating, I worked on illustration and color separation work on children's books for the Signed English Project (*not* Signing Exact English) under Gallaudet's Department of Psychology. I worked with three other deaf girls. But I soon got tired of it, and I wanted to go somewhere else.

After a while, I decided on New York City because of its theaters, art, and everything. I moved there and found that New York was not for deaf people. It was such a hard task to get in. It was so hard.

So with one of my deaf friends, we went out to work at a Fire Island beach resort, washing dishes, mopping the floors, and cleaning up. The money I saved would pay my rent over the winter months while at the same time I could look for a winter job. I got drawn into doing restaurant work from ten p.m. to six or seven a.m. with the doors closed. This place was an ice cream parlor. I had a grand time eating and munching.

Of course it had nothing to do with art, but I was so *busy.* I enjoyed most of it anyway. Later I was laid off from my restaurant job, went back to my old job at Fire Island, and then I was offered a job to help set up a new restaurant at Key West, Florida, for six months during wintertime, and I had a good time. I was invited to stay on, but I said no. So many of my friends were here in New York.

I moved back here and worked again at that Fire Island beach resort. Then I was fired.

It turned out that the bartender there who insisted that I take free drinks from him, even though I didn't think it was right, had tattled to my boss about me. He was jealous of me because everyone liked me. Also, one of my hearing friends there found out for me that my boss's mother had passed away and his money had just been stolen. He thought I took the money.

After a while, a friend pulled me into a group of caterers where I could have some fun and earn some money at the same time. I really needed the money — I was really struggling at the time.

As it turned out, I had a fabulous time.

When my boss decided to move back to New York, he brought me along. I worked out of his apartment on Christopher Street, helping out with all kinds of dishes and packing the huge van. I was good at that, and I became a chef's assistant. It was quite successful, but so many caterers in New York were competing against each other. Eventually my catering career folded.

So one day my boss was walking along Christopher Street and noticed the old people working in Lilac Chocolates, a small specialty chocolate shop. They were slow, and it looked like their business was in a slump.

My boss went right in and asked for a job sweeping the floors. He learned quickly enough the details of the business, and he wanted to buy it as long as they shared their experience and recipes. Of course, when that happened, I became the first employee of Lilac Chocolates. I worked there for eleven years, and it was great.

Finally, due to my illness two years ago, I had to quit. I was depressed over that, but I had so many little things to do, so it was all right.

✦

My first roommate at Gallaudet was my first love. I was a preparatory student, and we had just moved from College Hall to Fowler Hall — which was supposed to be a girls' dorm, but that year they had too many boys. I soon found out that my French-Canadian roommate was bisexual, and he was having a lot of problems with me because I knew nothing about gay people. (He spoke very well, but he could also sign.)

Finally, one oral student — a real expert on gay life — took me aside to explain in detail what being gay meant and everything. But it didn't make any difference to me. All I knew was that l-o-v-e was there: Wow. I didn't understand that it was "puppy love," but anyway, my roommate and I had sex. He taught me many different things, and I learned from him...

For the next five years I didn't have a problem on campus. It's funny, because many people had done all kinds of things to hurt other gay students — like writing dirty words above their names on the bathroom stalls. Remember, this was 1970. But I was never mentioned or hurt in any way. I was puzzled, so I decided to check every bathroom stall on campus to see if anyone had written my name anywhere. I was surprised to find that my name wasn't there.

I couldn't understand why my gay friends had problems and I didn't. I later found out why — I was much too nice to everyone, and they liked me a lot.

✦

After moving to New York, I met this guy in a bar. We were really attracted to each other, and he knew some signs. I felt very comfortable with him, and so did he with me. I thought, Perfect match.

So we slept together, taking turns at my house and his.

He was a chef, and I was in the catering business, I think, at the time. After a while he wanted to introduce me to his best friends. One of them was also a gourmet chef who traveled to Europe a lot, and his lover was an artist. They were really "classical" people, and they were very choosy, very selective.

Later he tried to say something to me, but instead he wrote a full two-page letter to me. I read it, but I didn't understand what he said. "What do you mean by your writing?" I asked.

"I'm trying to tell you that I can't continue with you."

It turned out that his friends didn't accept me as his lover, and that he had to choose between me or them. Well, he picked his friends.

That hit me so hard.

I got so tired of it, trying to find the right lover. I've never had a long-term love relationship; they were always short, and the longest one I had lasted only one year.

At that time I couldn't be lovers with anyone. My life was so different then, and I had no time for it. Besides, all my life I grew up lonely, and I love being alone. I'm used to it. Most people can't live with it, and have to have some hearing lover who can help out with the phone or whatever.

I like to look and look, and then when it feels right, I let it happen.

✦

The first time I heard about the "strange gay sickness" was back in 1980. I didn't think much of it at the time.

Joey Hines was the first deaf man I knew who died from this sickness. But because he was a rather old man, I didn't think too much of it. I mean, Kaposi's sarcoma (KS) was supposed to affect old men only.

Then Bruce Taylor was next. He was very young, and he got KS. He lived out in New Jersey, and so many of us tried to pull him out of his sickness. He had gotten CMV (cytomegalovirus) in his eyes, and he went blind and had to resort to feeling our signs with his hands.

He was so young. Cute and sweet, really. He died fast, so fast.

That really affected all of us.

One time, a bunch of us went over to his house to give him some company. That night as we went to bed down, Bruce chose to stay downstairs instead of upstairs in his room, which had been recently renovated. I thought that was strange, but downstairs as we lay next to each other, he said, "Please hold me."

I held him. I held him all night long. And while I held him, I thought of many things. So many things.

And I wouldn't let him go.

The morning after he said, "Thank you so much. I feel safe now. Thanks so much."

✦

Once, when I trimmed Sam Edwards's hair and moustache — he was so thin, worse than me — he pointed to the KS lesions on his face and said, "Look at my beautiful makeup."

I don't have KS, but I already look so much like so many people I know who've died.

It's odd that when Sam had those nightmares as he was dying, he wouldn't describe what scared him so. I tried and tried to get him to talk about it, but now ... I understand what he means.

ASL is not practiced enough. There are so few opportunities for deaf socializing. Sure, there are deaf theater gatherings, but not frequent enough. It's not even like before, when deaf gay people would get together all the time. Most of my friends have passed away, a few of them are left, and some have moved out of New York City.

The hardest thing about being a deaf gay person is losing friends like Sam Edwards and Bruce Taylor.

I took the HIV-antibody test because my doctor was trying to find out what was wrong with me: I had this buzzing noise in my head that just wouldn't go away, and I had been tested every which way.

Finally, I took the test. I tested positive. This was done only once.

✦

A few years later, I had been getting together frequently with this deaf friend of mine — he lived only a few blocks from me — for brunch and things like that. I had been telling him about my medical progress from one prescription drug to another, and finally, one day at brunch, he stopped me. "If you could write a list of all the drugs you've taken since testing HIV-positive, and if I could show it to my lover who's very familiar with drug treatments for AIDS, he might be able to give you a better sense of what's going on." Keep in mind that I'd never mentioned my doctor's name to my friend; only that she treated a lot of deaf clients with AIDS.

I said, "Okay."

Later that night I went over to meet his hearing lover. He took one look at my list and asked if I was seeing that doctor.

I said, "Yes."

My friend was shocked that his lover had named the doctor just by looking at my list alone. It turned out that she had quite a reputation for giving her clients all kinds of drugs, and he did not like that. "You can't do that to anyone's immune system — it's too fragile to withstand that."

That was when his lover started to explain the importance of questioning everything.

He was even more appalled to learn that I had taken AZT for my diarrhea, which lasted for five weeks. There was really nothing else wrong with me. The diarrhea could have been due to — anything. My friend's lover felt that my doctor should've known that one of AZT's many side effects was diarrhea: why did she have to make my problem worse? She was definitely not thinking, and I had accepted everything she said. After all, she'd been my doctor for fifteen years. But when it came to AIDS, she was not doing things right.

From that point on, I became much more assertive. I questioned every doctor and specialist about the medication I was taking, why I'd have to take this or that drug, and so on. Some of them were pissed that I'd bother to ask. Anyway, I began to get better once I cut down on the number of drugs I was taking.

Eventually I gave up on that doctor and switched to a different one.

✦

After many tests, my original doctor found that I had CMV of the colon, which I meant I had to start with IV (intravenous) medication for the CMV. I thought, Okay.

So I had this operation in which a Medi-Port — a small metal plate — was put under the skin of my right pectoral so I could self-insert an IV tube through the skin, clean the skin, and so on.

That helped for a while.

But the Medi-Port got infected.

I went back to the hospital. They took the Medi-Port out and cleaned it, and then they put the same kind of metal plate near the crook of my right elbow. They called it the Pass-Port. (The next one, near my heart, was called the Life-Port.) I think they just created names to make it sound like it was a different solution, but really they were all the same thing.

I suspect that they were looking for something that I wasn't allergic to. I should add that the same Asian surgeon did all three operations. I thought, Hm.

Anyway, my Medi-Port got infected and was taken out. I had to keep cleaning this big hole in my chest; otherwise, bacteria could come in and infect it. Then I'd be really sick. With the help of antibiotics, the hole was healed.

They said, "Good job."

I thought, Hm.

Then I got the Pass-Port. That was the hardest one for me. It meant that I had only one hand to insert the IV tube into my arm; before it was so easy to use both of my hands to take care of the Medi-Port. It was so frustrating. The doctors didn't tell me anything. That was the problem.

The Pass-Port got infected in a very short time.

So they took out the Pass-Port and put in the Life-Port near my heart. It was okay taking care of it, but I got another infection.

I had these three operations in one year.

I thought, Come on. I looked at my doctor and asked, "What's the matter?"

But I let that go.

Then that Asian surgeon came in to talk about having a Hickman put in my chest. I asked him, "Why didn't you do that in the first place?"

He said, "It'll be easy for you to take care of, instead of having to deal with tubes and getting them tangled in your hands."

It turned out that my original doctor wanted the Hickman — this was before I left her. That was when I wondered if I was an experiment, a guinea pig, for them. But no one would say anything. I noticed that many other people with AIDS got their Hickmans first. They never got Pass-Ports or anything like them; in fact, I was the only one I knew who got them. So why did I get the Medi-Port, the Pass-Port, and the Life-Port? I'm the only one I know who went through all that.

I suspect that it's because I'm deaf. They thought because I look like I know nothing, I wouldn't know how to speak out. I just have this feeling, and after much analysis of this situation, I still wonder: maybe so, maybe not.

Okay: the Life-Port was taken out. That time I didn't have a diarrhea problem, so I decided not to have the Hickman.

My doctor got furious.

And then the Asian surgeon came in and said, "Ready for tomorrow's surgery?"

I said, "I don't want to. I don't want you. I got infected three times from your operations. Something's wrong with *you.*"

He just looked at me and said nothing.

My doctor said, "He's the best surgeon. He is really the best."

I sort of laughed. "Look at me. You want my body to get cut up even more?" I said, *"No."*

She said, "You must listen to me! I'm your doctor!"

Her insistence turned me off. What the hell was going on? What was the matter with her? Why is she talking like that to me? That made a real impression on me.

I still said, "No."

"Okay, let him go." She said, "Let him go." Then she added that I should die within two months.

I said, "Fine."

Then I became very excited with my plans for a two-week vacation: I'd visit for five days with my parents in Ohio, visit for six and a half days with my friend in Chicago, and then spend the rest of the week with a friend in Michigan.

I made a big mistake. I did so much flying around — guess I was a peabrain right there. I wasn't feeling very well when I arrived back in New York on June something, and then the following Tuesday I was supposed to see my doctor. It was to be my last appointment. It turned out to be the last time I saw her face.

I walked into the reception area, and everything seemed to stop. Everyone, including the receptionist, gave me this frozen stare. Their eyes wouldn't blink at all. Their stares were so penetrating.

I said, "I'm here for my doctor's appointment."

They kept staring at me.

They'd thought I'd died already. (Chuckle.)

My doctor said, "Still alive?" She was very impressed. I wish I knew what was going on — maybe she was trying to get rid of me because I had been with her for too long.

They just kept staring at me. They were so shocked.

I went in and sat down in her office. I thought that she was ready for our routine checkup. She always checked my blood pressure, took tests, and looked at the results from the lab.

She hadn't even bothered to order the results. So there were no results. Nothing. *Nothing.*

She was dumbfounded and just kept staring at me. "Still alive?" Then she asked me if she should prescribe Bactrim to prevent bacterial infection of my lungs.

I said, "Seems that I need more."

So she wrote out the prescription for me.

I said, "See you next month." I had refused to tell her about what happened to me during my recent trip, even though I'd felt funny inside. I felt so sick.

But they didn't make an appointment for me.

She just didn't want to see me again.

Later that week on Friday afternoon, my deaf friend and I went to see this other doctor recommended by his lover. He said, "Come on into my office. Show me your hands."

He took one look at them and said, "You've got pneumonia. You've got to go to the hospital *now.* Which hospital do you want to go to?"

I said, "Lenox Hill Hospital." (I would've gone to St. Vincent's Hospital, which is very close to my home, but I wanted to stay away from my doctor. She would've controlled everything related to me at St. Vincent's. Otherwise the services at both hospitals were about the same.)

So my friend and I took off in a cab.

At the hospital they discovered that I had PCP (pneumocystis carinii pneumonia) and CMV all at the same time. I stayed in the hospital for two months. (Lenox Hill learned a lot through me about the needs and the rights of deaf patients. They'd never heard of sign language interpreters, closed-caption decoders, and TDDs. My deaf friend who'd come with me through the emergency room had to make sure they were aware of my needs. That was so awful.)

I was still druggy when I arrived home on August third. It took me four months to recover fully. I felt almost normal by that time, although a little weak.

✦

Living with AIDS is frustrating. I've watched friends when they visit me choose not to use my glasses to drink water. They just bend their heads over to drink water from the faucet. And when they kiss me on the cheek, they wash their hands immediately.

Services for deaf people with AIDS in New York City have been lousy. Once, when I came back from a two-month stay at the hospital, I had a male nurse who was supposed to stay with me for eight hours or something. You know, to help keep up this place and help me out whenever needed. Then a few days later he told me — rather suddenly — that he was going on a vacation in Florida.

It turned out that he'd used my credit cards and took advantage of them for his vacation. (I didn't find out about it until I got my credit card statements.) That's the problem with home nursing services — they're strangers and you don't know if you can ever trust them. Worse yet, I'm deaf, and they don't know one damn thing about deafness. They don't even use the voice-relay service to call me; it's as if they expect by some miracle a hearing person will answer. There seems to be a high turnover among personnel in home nursing services, so the service is never consistent. I'm tired of it.

Also, I can't get out all the time. I can't do anything. I have to think about what I'm doing in order to do it.

And if being deaf is expensive, living with AIDS is even more expensive. I'm not rich, and worse yet every agency you can think of keeps screwing up my paperwork for the checks that I need in order to survive. I sometimes don't have the energy to fight all of them all the time.

A few times my landlord has threatened to evict me because I was late with my rent. By law in New York City, they can't evict me until after three months of nonpayment, and by that time I'd have to pay for those three months if I wanted to stay on in my apartment. That took some straightening out. And even then they still want me out, not because I'm deaf but because they know I'm sick and because my rent is very low. (I've lived here on Christopher Street for twelve years; the rent for this apartment — once it's renovated after I go — would be at least a thousand dollars per month.)

✦

The meaning of life for me now? I'm just fighting for my life. Fighting for my life!

What else am I supposed to do? I have to fight for my life. I'm on medication. I'm on everything. I'm near death. I feel myself near death. I'm approaching that time: when?

Sure, I think about death, but then again, sometimes I just forget about it completely and think positive. It's hard because I find myself getting weaker all the time.

And I feel so stupid in having a fourth-floor walk-up apartment. I can't walk up the stairs — it takes so much energy — and what do I do about this place? I have to give up, give up, give up all my things.

And I am so stupid. I wanted to spend on something, so I spent over $2,000 on that 75-gallon fishtank. I feel so stupid.

✦

My ideal lover wouldn't smoke or drink, and his ASL skills should be ready-made. If he can't pick up signs, then trying to teach him would be worthless, even if he still wants the relationship very much. I've tried to teach many times, and I find that teaching them ASL doesn't work. He just has to take courses in ASL and see if he can withstand it.

My ideal lover would have to have dark hair, blue or brown eyes, and be around my height. He should be about my age — I learned before that old men weren't my type. It was too easy to get roped in when they could give me everything. It's not what I want — I don't want an easy life. I like the hard life — that's me — because that way I learn a lot about myself. If you get the easy life, what happens to you? What if the older man dies? You'd be at a loss what to do. I don't want that kind of life.

He should be sexy, outgoing, and comfortable with himself. If he enjoys cooking too, driving around, and camping — though I haven't done that in a long time — it would be great. If he was a country person and had experiences with raising horses, I'd like to learn more about that, too.

I prefer that in the beginning we live separately and have an open relationship, taking turns between our homes. After a while, we'd have to look at whether moving in together would be a good or bad idea by looking at our budgets. We have to look at our jobs and how they can help our household budgets. I know I don't want a joint checking account because it's just impossible. It always screws up the relationship.

✦

One of the most memorable nights of my life started at the Saint. The occasion, I believe, was a White Party in which everyone had to wear white. The reason was that it was wintertime.

Anyway, Sam Edwards and I went; we had gone out together for years to all kinds of discos.

It was very late. Most people came in at around ten, but they were nothing. Once they were out of the way, *our* people came in between twelve and two.

The Saint was *the* big disco at the time. It had a *huge* dome inside above the dance floor. It used to be a theater, I think, and then the dome was built to keep in the sound so neighbors couldn't hear anything. It didn't make much of a noise, not outside.

Later, after dancing for a while, I sat down quietly and looked at the crowd.

Then this man in leather came up to me. He looked English *and* Italian with his moustache, dark skin, and very blue eyes. He was about my height, slender and nice with a leather vest.

He tried to talk to me.

He realized that I was deaf, but he was still interested in me. I could lipread him well, so we started to talk a bit. His name was John.

Then we parted after a while.

We met again, and parted again, about three times.

Finally, the dancing had to end soon. It was nearly two that afternoon, so he asked me to leave with him. I had been in there for so long, I couldn't tell if it was night or day outside. I knew I had been in there for more than twenty-four hours.

I said, "Sure, no problem. I have no plans or anything." This happened on a Sunday, I believe.

He wanted me to meet his friend who lived on Fifth Avenue and Twenty-first Street or something. The building was tall and you couldn't tell if there were apartments inside; the only way you could get in was around the corner through a special entrance.

Anyway, there was a blizzard on when we got out of the Saint. It was hard to get a cab, but we caught one.

The cabdriver went very slowly, trying to move ahead in all the snowing. Cabs were still around; I was so surprised that any were around.

We arrived at last. The man told the driver to wait for one hour and a half or whatever.

We went up in the elevator. I felt so nervous, thinking I'd misunderstood, thinking it must be his home, but it turned out not to be.

When we got into the loft, I looked around. It was so huge and so beautiful. It had the largest kitchen, with rows of lights all over. I thought it had to belong to some famous chef on TV or something, or a set for TV, it was so big.

There was a woman sitting to the side in the living room. I didn't know who she was.

He guided me around.

After a while I saw a room. It was a special doctor's office. For what, I didn't know, but it had these stirrups over a table. Everything was black leather all over.

Then I saw the bedroom. It was so beautiful and elegant. The bathroom was huge. It even had a sauna and foot massage sink. It was really nice. There was also another bedroom that was just ... unbelievable.

We returned to the living room. He introduced me to the woman sitting, who was really a transsexual. She'd been a man before her sex-change operation. She was so beautiful and so friendly. As I shook her hand, I thought, "I'm meeting a transsexual for the first time." She was even better than women you see on the street; they sometimes don't know how to hold their heavy breasts, they keep trying different clothes, and they make mistakes. This woman was very fashionable and self-confident.

I sat while they talked. They were best friends.

Finally he said, "Let's go."

I said, "Bye-bye."

As we went down in the elevator, I was so relieved because I was afraid that they'd change me into a woman.

We got out to find the blizzard still roaring at full force.

Even the snowplows had broken down and had to be carried away.

I thought to myself as I looked at the cab: How could the driver keep himself warm?

We got in, and I sat in back with the man.

The cabdriver drove us over the bridges from Manhattan to Brooklyn to Staten Island.

The snow was so high on the bridges, and I kept looking at it.

There was no traffic and nobody was around. It was just the three of us.

The city lights shimmered through the blizzard, and it was so beautiful at the same time.

The man and I made out in the cab, which was pretty nice.

We finally arrived in Staten Island and went around the island to his house.

I got out and turned around to look at his house.

It was such a beautiful home set in the middle of an acre. It was so gorgeous with the woods and a fence all around, and it had three sets of bay windows all around.

We said bye-bye to the cabdriver.

When he left, we threw snowballs at each other and got into a snow fight.

We laughed and laughed so hard.

The minute I walked into his house, I was paralyzed with amazement. Antiques were all over the place. There was a very long dining-room table with twelve chairs, and there was a cabinet just as long with glass doors. This one had pink plates, and each plate was designed for a particular function. There was a turkey plate, cream pitcher, and two gravy bowls...

The plates were like squares with corners cut off. There were many different dishes: the entree dish, the salad bowl, the cups and saucers. There were two cups for coffee; one was for espresso, the other a regular size. Then there were three different kinds of glasses: one for water, one for wine, and one for whatever else you wanted to drink. Then there was silverware spread in a long row. There were four kinds of forks, four kinds of spoons, and two kinds of knives — one was for butter. And the silverware was set on the most beautiful cloth that matched the cabinet.

Wow.

Later I found out that he was an antique dealer. Such a beautiful home, and the carpet was so thick!

Then when I entered the kitchen, I got a big surprise. A big brown Great Dane came at me, licked my face, and jumped all over me.

The man was surprised. The dog usually growled whenever his friends came over, and it was the first time he'd ever gotten friendly with anyone.

I said, "He's so *heavy.*"

The man said quietly, "Stop. Stop. Stop."

Finally the dog stopped.

I had to rest a little.

The man said, "He just needed some exercise."

This was a very young dog, so keep that in mind.

The kitchen had a huge fireplace with a huge kettle with a hook on top. There were pictures above the fireplace. The kitchen cabinets had really thick wooden doors — they were no thin and cheap wooden doors. There was a short kitchen table that was ideal for a couple if they didn't want to eat in the dining room. I thought only the man lived there in that house.

Anyway, I was so tired.

So I went with him up this long and wide circular staircase. It felt like forever walking up there; the two stories in the house were so tall. The steps were made of beautiful wood.

We got to the top floor.

When I entered the bedroom, I got another surprise. There were six bay windows all around the room and it was very circular. What was even more awesome was the snow still falling down. It was so — wow.

Then I looked at the bed. It was bigger than king-size, and it had to be handmade because it was such a big square. It had brass poles at each corner.

We took off our clothes.

I sat down.

He showed me an old, long, and heavy key. He said, "You must never lose it."

I thought, Okay.

He gave me the key. "You want me to hold the key? How do I hold it if I'm naked?"

He said nothing and showed me a huge closet filled with all kinds of leather things. "Do you want anything?"

I said, "No. I don't like playing with those toys."

He said, "Fine," and closed the door.

Then we made love all night.

I don't know how I did it, but I held on to that key all night. I knew that if I put it somewhere, he'd take it away. He even told me to put it beside the bed, but I wouldn't.

After we had sex, he was stupefied to find that I hadn't let the key go. I didn't know what the key was for, but he seemed very impressed.

I could tell the key was a very expensive one. He told me that it was made of gold. I was amazed. I said, "Made of gold? Don't tell me!" I finally put it down, and he put it away.

I woke up to find a thick blanket of snow outside the bedroom windows.

It was morning. The man asked me, "Want breakfast?"

I nodded. "I'm very hungry."

So after we got dressed, down the stairs we went into the living room.

I was shocked to find an old lady sitting there. Her hair was pulled back like an Englishwoman's. She wore handmade clothes with ruffles around her neck and a very long dress. Her boots were the kind that had long laces going up to her knees. Her heels were strong but pointed. She had a very small face.

She smiled and said, "Good morning."

As I shook her hand, I saw how fragile and smooth her skin was.

I found out later that it was his mother. That rattled me because I'd thought it was his grandmother.

Then he told me that she'd slept in the room next to us.

I felt so embarrassed.

She gave a tiny smile and laughed quietly.

Next to her was the Great Dane, sitting bored.

I learned that whenever she got up, the dog was not allowed to touch her in any way; he couldn't jump on her or her thin bones would be crushed. The only contact between them was a pat or two on the dog's forehead, and that's all. I was very impressed with that dog. Usually when a puppy is that big and that young, they play and play and play until they learn to calm down. Well, that dog was a fast learner.

The man said, "We'll go in the kitchen and have our breakfast."

He cooked me such a delicious breakfast that I kept eating and eating until I was stuffed.

Finished, I said, "It was so nice to meet you all."

Then the man showed me around the rest of the house. I was so impressed with the different rooms — each one was so beautiful. He had an office, a den, and so on.

Finally I was ready to go home.

I looked at him and thought, Wow.

He couldn't take me home by car because of the snow, so he showed me how I could take the train back to Manhattan. When I got home, I just sat all day and thought about it all.

It was so wonderful.

Later I saw him again. I never knew that he went to Lilac Chocolates to buy chocolate for his mother, and he never knew I worked there.

So we met frequently.

Then one time he ripped a dollar bill in half, and he said, "Here's your half of our dollar. One for me, and one for you. You must not lose it. When we meet again, and if you have it, we'll stay together."

I looked at him and nodded, "Okay."

I made a big mistake. I put it in my pocket, and it stuck out, and someone must've stolen it thinking it was a whole dollar.

When I realized it was gone, I felt so lost.

Then he came into the store for some candy and looked at me.

I said, "I lost my half."

He looked at me and said nothing. He bowed his head and left.

I think about him sometimes.

✦

Editor's note: Jack Fennell died on December 18, 1992.

KEITH R. MITCHELL

MARK & KEVIN

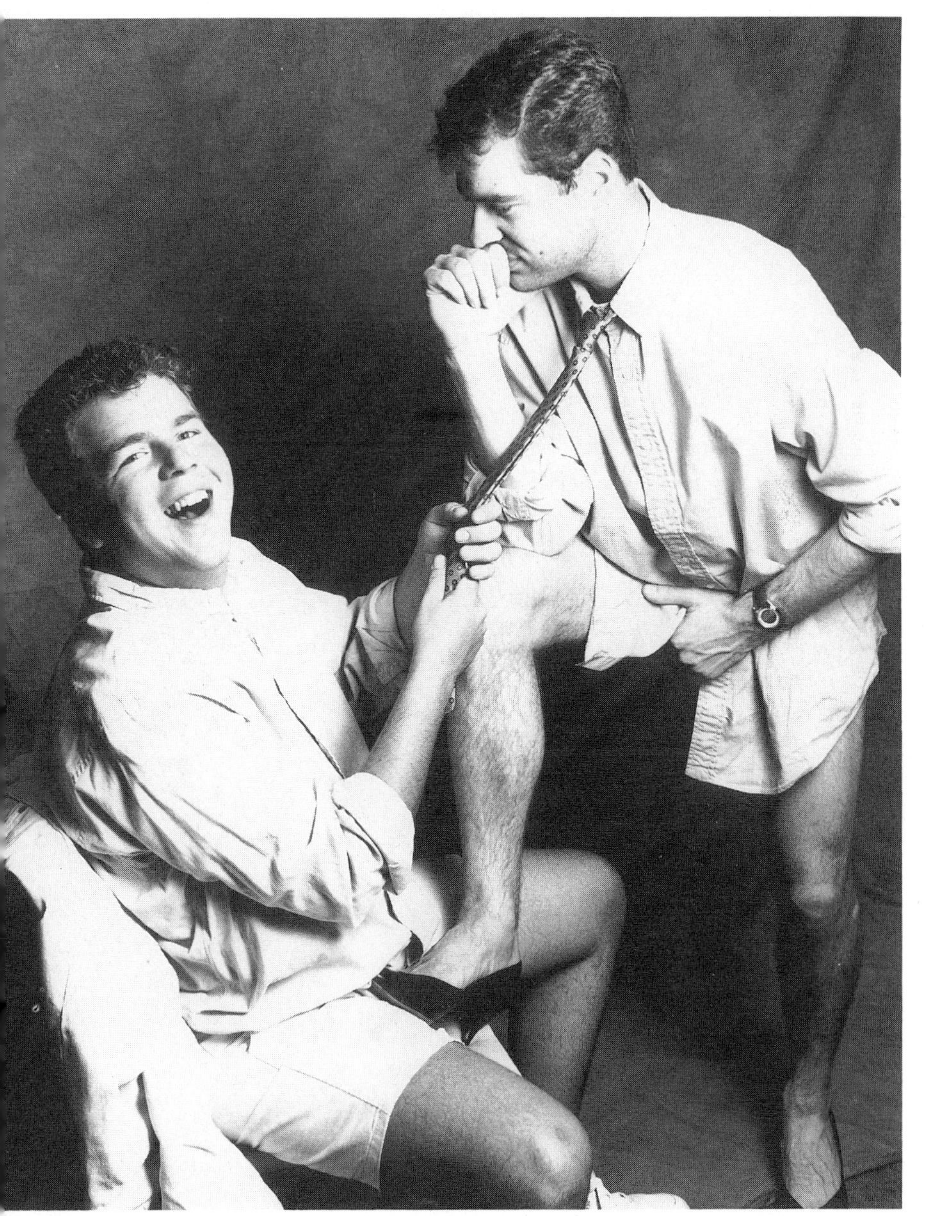

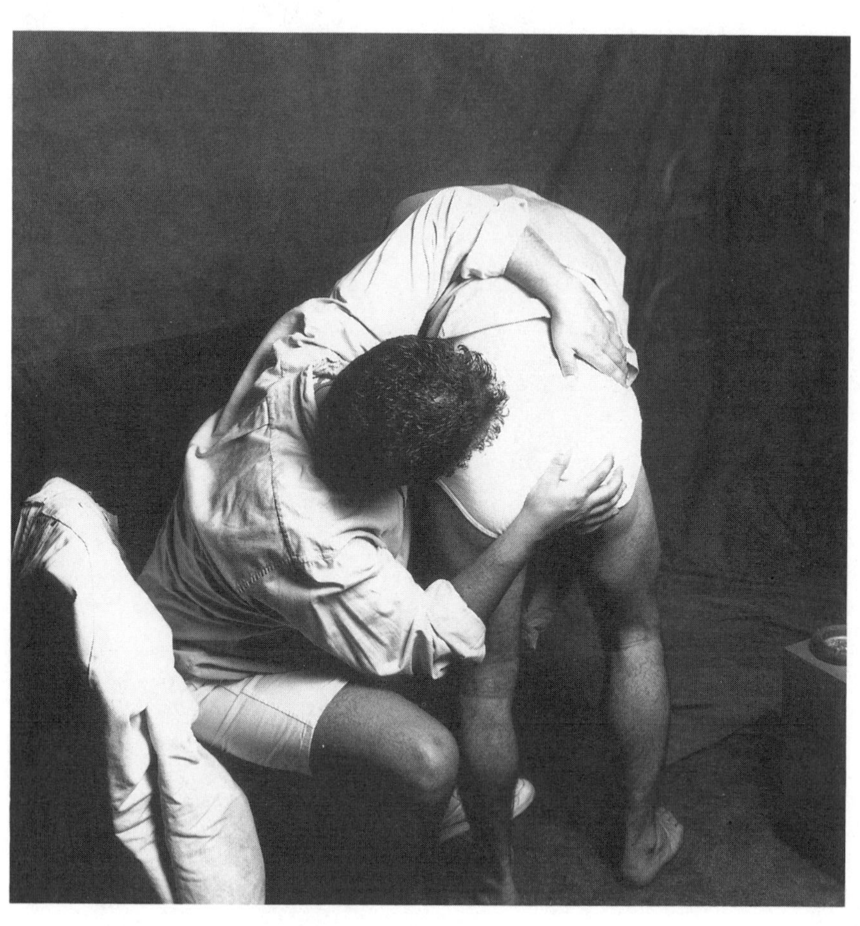

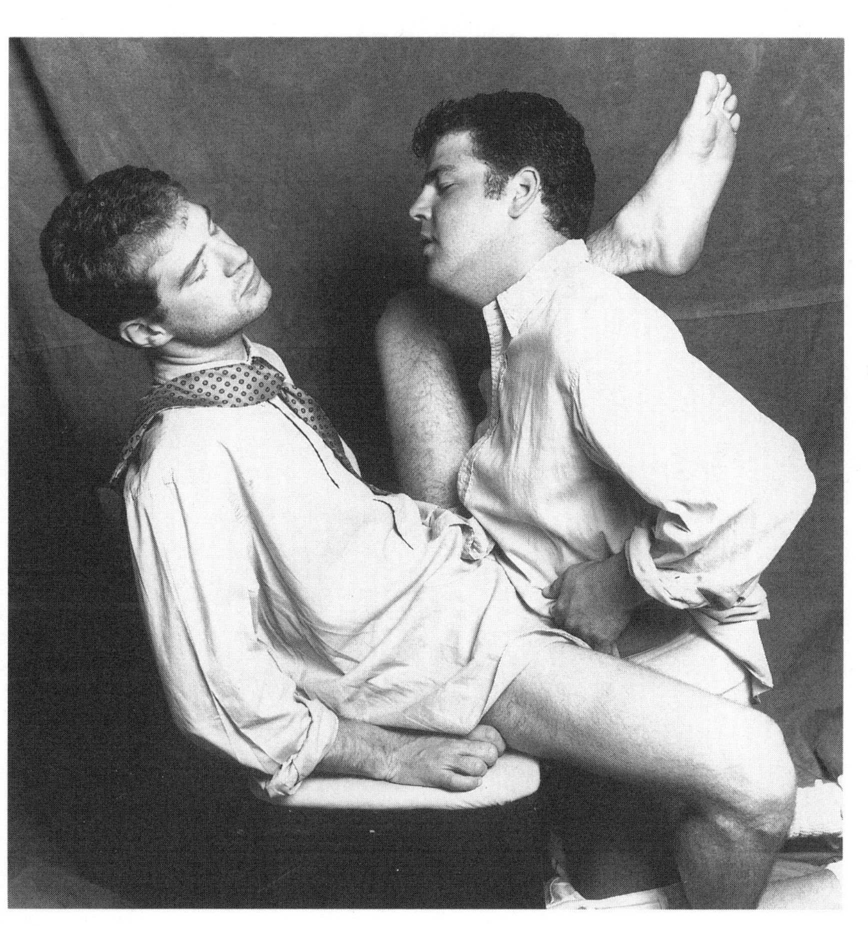

TWO

TANIS

WHO ARE YOU?

WHO ARE YOU? What do you mean? My name? **Okay. What's your name?** Tanis. **Well, who are you?** What kind of information are you looking for? **Age, job, purpose in life?** Why do you need to know? **It's just what I ask everyone.** Well, I'm not everyone. I'm Tanis. **Okay, okay. I just asked a question.** You asked several questions. I'm Tanis. **Why are you so defensive?** Because you want to judge. You will if you get the information you're looking for. **Why? What do you have to hide?** You see, that's the point — how do you know who I am is negative. I really meant things like, "Wow, you've done a lot for your age," or "You are so brave." That kind of judging. **What's so bad about that?** Lots, particularly when it leads to other judging, and that's what happens. **For crying out loud, you are paranoid.** Yep, that's been one of my labels. **Forget it.** I don't. I won't. I can't — who am I? I am a mother. I am a daughter. I am a sister. I am an aunt. I am the only deaf daughter of a hearing mother who has three other daughters. I am a deaf mother of a deaf daughter who is adopted. **So what's bad about all that?** It brings up more WHOs. I am also a deaf adoptive mother, a lesbian, and a single person. **I know lots of lesbians, and a few mothers. Big deal.** Let me give you some information here. I am a deaf, adoptive, single, lesbian mother of a deaf child. But my deaf child is ten years old, adopted at age five, and she is black and born in Jamaica. This makes her a landed immigrant and a racial minority in my community. I am a nonblack lesbian mother raising a black (not sure of her sexual orientation yet) deaf daughter. I will wait till she is older before I ask her about her sexual orientation, but I am sure it won't be a problem anyway. **So she is black and you aren't; she might be straight and you aren't.** She is going to learn a lot about a male-dominated, hearing, white, and straight world when she grows up and I want to make her as comfortable as possible. This means she has been exposed to deaf, black, feminist, and lesbian communities up to this point. I have to add here that I have also been heavily involved in disability issues. So my daughter is exposed to not just deafness but different forms of disability. I use a crutch and a scooter when necessary. **You have a disability *and* you are deaf?** To complicate the WHO, I am not only deaf, but really deafened — which means that I was not born deaf but lost my hearing after I'd already acquired two languages. So, yes, I can speak. **So?** I can also sign fluently in several languages. **Good.** I can lipread quite well, mmm, sort of. **What do you mean, sort of?** Well, I could lipread very well until I became visually impaired, so now I squint a lot. I also have photosensitivity which means I get severe eye pain from bright lights. **All right. So you wear sunglasses.** I also have a reduced ability to see the lower peripheral and upper-right-hand field which makes the total picture a bit lopsided. My visual acuity is restricted and I use bifocal tinted glasses inside, so the way I look has also changed. **Changed?** From before, when I had no glasses. **Before when?** Oh, the visual problems. They were caused by a respiratory arrest from anaphylaxis, which is a severe allergic reaction. I have multiple and severe allergies and sensitivities to chemicals. All of this was unexpected and caused severe limitations in all my activities. **What kind of activities? Who were you "before"?** Another WHO? I was me. I have always been me, but I was a doctoral student in university, finishing my dissertation. I was also a teacher and a trainer who spent considerable time traveling and giving lectures and workshops. I also taught in a local school program and in homes with severely disabled children, and deaf children as well, at colleges and universities. **But WHO were you?** I was also a community leader giving many hours to networking and representing the deaf community in the greater disability movement and I did consultant work for the goverment until the illness struck. **Then what happened?** I don't think it happened, but other people thought I became a cripple, an invalid, sick, weak, helpless, or disabled. I was not the "before" Tanis anymore. **What did you do?** I cried a lot. I got depressed — no kidding. I lost my lover at the time, I lost my pride (which was considerable), I lost my temper and my mind. Psychiatric difficulties go hand in hand with severe and chronic illness, I am told, but I would like to opt out, thanks. If not for interpreters — I mean the *interpreters,* not the deaf community — I would be *dead*. Only by the sheer skill of having a hearing person with me in the hospital to sign and speak for me was I able to communicate enough to reduce the risk of death and to become finally stable enough to leave the hospital. Now I live cautiously. (I suppose otherwise I'd lived dangerously.) I am very grateful for my sign-language interpreters, but I am very angry that I had to fight so hard for them. Some people call it defensive driving when people learn to avoid accidents. I call it "preventative living" when I live my life avoiding the potential triggers of my reactions. So. I avoid, I meditate, I treat if necessary, I educate others, and I resuscitate only if I stop breathing, which still happens far too often for my liking. **What causes you to be sick?** Oh no, don't ask. Sulphites — they are in everything — drugs, food, drinks, also propane gas, perfumes, bleaches, dust, pollen, cats, antibiotics, etc. **Oh! Sorry I asked. That's who you are — a sick deaf person.** No, no. I am a disabled deaf dyke with a deaf daughter and I am also a student and a leader and a person too! **You are getting more and more complicated.** Yes, I am complicated. **So what part of you is the most important?** To me? It's not me that matters. **Of course you matter. What you feel matters.** No, I have all these identities and I live them every day, but what matters to everyone *else* is what affects me. **What are you talking about?** I'm talking more about how other people exclude or include me that makes a difference in my life. Store clerks do not care that I am gay. I just want to buy something, but they see how I walk and talk funny. They treat me weird because of that. Deaf people do not care that I am deaf, but I have to ask them to stop smoking or wearing perfume, and I wear clothes that tell them I am a dyke. That matters. "Don't bother coming to our parties, Tanis, if smoke and perfume bothers you. Besides, you don't like men anyway, so why bother?" That matters. Lesbians could care less that I have a crystal earring and purple pants with a button showing a triangle, but they can't or don't sign, and most of them still wear perfume or cologne. Both the dances and bars are usually inaccessible because of the stairs. That matters. I can't be a person in their world. Parents' groups don't mind that I am single or that I am an adoptive mother but ... "Your daughter is so loud, can't you tell her she is noisy? Can't she learn to be quiet?" Oh, and — "Wouldn't it be better for her to have some male role models?" She is deaf, and yes, we tried having men around, but she got molested. Thanks for the advice. BYE! Lesbian mothers don't seem to have a problem with me being gay or her being black, but they still find the deafness a bit too much to deal with. Because she can't speak and because she screams (not from anger, but from laughter) and bangs around, hearing people find it difficult to have her around. That matters. No matter where I go, or what I do, who I am matters to other people. At the welfare office I am told, "You are too well educated to be on social assistance. Get a job — go to the employment center." And at the employment center I am told, "You are too sick to work. Go apply for disability benefits at the rehab office." At the deaf rehab office (where I can sign and understand the worker), I am told, "Your needs aren't related to your deafness, so you really need visual and occupational rehabilitation. You should go to that other office." Since the deaf rehab office was not accessible and I couldn't use my scooter, I hobble along to the other office. I arrive at the rehab office, which is accessible, and I ask for an appointment in writing (I don't expect them to sign). "Oh no, we don't deal with deaf people here, dear. You have to go to the rehab assocation of the deaf. We don't have anyone who signs." **Never heard of an interpreter, eh?** Ahhhhhh. At the university: "You are too young to be in the Ph.D. program, and you are too young to be a mother." Why am I not too young to get sick then? At the women's studies department: "You are so *courageous* and *brave* in trying to study and learn at this level with all your difficulties." Nothing about how good my research or my writing is, but how wonderful it is that I am there at all. At the disability conferences or events: "You are so obvious about being gay, Tanis. Why don't you try to tone down a bit?" Oh, sure. Why don't you try to hide your wheelchair or camouflage that white cane? When I try to be more moderate or more mainstream, I am accused by fellow lesbians and gay men of being "in": "Why aren't you out at these events? You should be proud to identify with us more. Where is your feminist support of our struggle?" I left it at the door when I had to climb steps to get into your club! Do I have an attitude problem? I can't please everyone all the time. At the deaf-lesbian-single-mothers-with-black-adopted-children support group, I can finally be myself. But I am the only member. However, I do have a community! **Who?** Really — I do. Lots of friends. The survivors. People who have survived sexual and physical abuse. That kind of experience transcends race and disability, and unites people. I have support from them. Most of my friends in that group are gay or lesbian, but some are straight. They accept me, and they seem to accept my daughter too. Both of us. Deaf professionals — I'm not being classist here, I mean deaf people who work with deaf issues for a living — have also been open-minded in their attitudes. I think most overlook my "failings" and accept the whole person that I am. Some of the immigrant and mixed families living in our area have also welcomed us, even though my daughter is "loud" and deaf and I am deaf and "gay." We have explored our options, and we have found community where we can go. We have friends — good friends — and I know they will support us. But they cannot guarantee access to other communities and services out there in the world. **How do you get by, then?** Interpreters are my main allies. Gay or gay-positive and lesbian interpreters have made me comfortable with a great number of conferences and even helped me meet a few new friends. Not only have they helped in emergencies and at hospitals, but they also have been socially supportive and offered their friendship outside their professional roles. This is rare. I have been able to maintain some of these friendships despite great distances between us. I appreciate them far more than most can understand because they are my link to the world. I am single. **Don't you want a lover?** I am single now by choice. I have had two deaf lovers and a few short relationships with deaf women, but I am not with anyone now. By choice. I even tried unsuccessfully to have relationships with nondeaf women. One was a young Haitian immigrant who had never been with a woman before — let alone with a deaf dyke with a kid. Another was a more experienced dyke with a disability and a long history of activism in the lesbian and disability communities. Neither relationship lasted, but I did love both of them. I was becoming sicker and sicker — less and less able, and less and less the old Tanis all the time. I moved to be with my last lover, and my illness was just too much, or the relationship not strong enough. Finally I was on my own, with my daughter; I was sick, sad, and seriously considering moving again. But I had to stop running and find my own community. I needed support. I built up support where I was, where I am now. This is where I am now: I am alone, with my daughter, although she is away during the week at a residential school. We are trying to lead our lives with the least amount of toxic chemicals and medications and doctors and bigots. It's not easy. **It doesn't seem easy at all.** I am giving this description of WHO I am to explain what it's like to be a "multiple minority" member (not to be confused with multiple personality, but that's another story).

I have membership in so many groups and categories that no one can list them all in one sentence. It is not easy, but it does matter: it matters to me and it matters to other people that I am me. I cannot be out in all the communities, and not all the labels I have are overlapping or mutually exclusive. However, it is only possible to be honest some of the time. It is not the worst thing in the world. After all, I survived. I did it. I'm here. I'm Tanis. I'm me. That's who.

"ALEX"*

A LESBIAN MAN AT EASE

EVEN WHEN I WAS BORN DEAF, I knew deep inside that ASL was a part of me, though I never realized it until later. I had depended on sight so much that when I learned ASL years later, I discovered a strong affinity for it.

When I was younger, my hearing parents wanted me to learn how to talk. It was not long, though, before I learned to sign ASL from other people at the Lexington School of the Deaf.

I was very lucky that all my hearing teachers at that time had deaf parents. The policy then was speech only, even if the teachers knew how to sign. But it was okay, because when they spoke, they used lots of facial expressions and body language to convey what they needed to say without signing.

I think that when people talk about deaf issues, they should remove the word "deaf." When I tell hearing people that I'm deaf, the word inspires pity in them.

I don't want pity.

On the other hand, if I tell them that I'm "seeing," they feel equal to me. I find that saying "I'm seeing" is much more effective than saying "I'm deaf."

In the summer of '69, New York Society of the Deaf — when their building was on East Fourteenth Street — provided "Deaf Youth" with events like bowling and swimming every Saturday.

---

*This narrative was shared with the editor on May 27, 1992.

One day, when we were done at four o'clock, we wondered what to do next. A group of us boys was curious about Greenwich Village, so we went. This was right before the Stonewall Riots, remember, and we saw two boys kissing on the streets. They didn't care what the passers-by thought, and I thought, "Wow, that's perfect for me!"

But my friends were straight.

I felt so *good* inside, but I had to be very careful. A few weeks later I read about the riots in the paper. It didn't seem to make sense, because I wasn't sure if that was me.

Then, as a sophomore in high school, I bought a book called *What Is Homosexuality?* I read it and realized that I was one also. The book was rather murky on the issue, describing how homosexuals would make eye contact and have sex with each other, and how sad they couldn't have families because they didn't marry and have children.

I hadn't had sex with a man yet, even after I arrived at Gallaudet. At that time Gallaudet was notorious for spreading rumors about certain deaf gay people, and they'd be beaten up.

So when I came out, it was here in New York, when I was a sophomore at Gallaudet. A friend of mine came up here for Christmas and New Year's Eve parties, which were wonderful; then three of my friends simply announced, "I'm gay."

"I'm gay."

"I'm gay."

They obviously had had sex with men before. I was so shocked — my mind was paralyzed. I was still a virgin.

Let me tell you about my first sexual experience at Gallaudet. During lunchtime at the Ely Center — this was before the cafeteria was moved to the back of the campus — one boy came up and asked me, "What are you doing for lunch?" He was the president of a fraternity there, and very much a gay man. I knew that he slept around, but I didn't know that he liked fat boys.

"I'll be in my dorm room," I said. I wasn't even thinking at all.

Later that afternoon I had a truly horrible, horrible fight with a friend. Oh, it was so awful. That left me feeling depressed and upset. My roommate was sleeping on his bed when the doorlight in my dorm room blinked.

It was the boy from the fraternity. "Can I come in here?"

"Sure." I was feeling lousy, so I felt, "So what."

He stood there, and touched his crotch. Then he said, "I want to fuck you."

"What?" My mind was confused. "You want sex with me? You're the president of your fraternity. You have to be careful."

I should say here that my roommate was really flaky. He couldn't make up his mind about anything. He slept with both men and women and did all kinds of things, and he had a big mouth.

So I was nervous, of course.

But we had sex, and my roommate slept the whole time. He didn't even know what happened right there in our room.

Three days later the boy came back. "I'm horny, and I want sex with you again."

I was so tempted, but my roommate was there.

What I didn't know was that he and my roommate had had sex before. He told my roommate that they needed to talk in private. So they went out, and I sat in my room doing my homework.

My roommate returned with a cigarette in his hand. He sat down with his legs open, stared at me for a while, and then said, "I'm so pissed off at you. *I* want to fuck you!" He was so angry at me because he had been wanting to have sex with me for the longest time. He drummed his fingers and continued smoking.

Then the other guy came in.

He and I had sex.

But my roommate insisted on joining us. I didn't enjoy myself one bit, because I never wanted to have sex with my roommate in the first place. We all had a fight in the nude, and it was truly an awful experience!

My roommate kept smoking heavily the whole time, and stared at me afterwards for three hours while I did my homework.

It was such a mess.

Actually, I never had sex again until after I graduated from Gallaudet and moved back to New York.

✦

That fraternity president turned out to be my first love. It really struck me how powerful love truly was. The taste of love was — wow — I just forgot the world and everything. Love. I just went wild. It was like medicine.

Three or four weeks later I told him, "I love you, and I want a relationship with you."

"Well," he said, "I don't love you. Fuck you."

I was so shocked, and so hurt. And I got the understanding why so many people often feel so hurt by love.

✦

In my experience I find that most hearing men who want relationships with deaf men prefer deaf men to be stupid. They want control. They won't form relationships with smart deaf men because they want control. They want deaf men to be human dolls. If they wanted a blow job, or the house cleaned, the deaf lover should do it on command.

Let me tell you about a disgusting experience. It was so *disgusting*...

I was on vacation in San Francisco. One of my friends told me about this engagement party for a deaf man planning to marry his hearing lover the following week, when I'd be back in New York. The party was at the Twin Peaks, a famous apartment building with beautiful views of the city.

I watched all the men celebrate.

The couple were both into leather.

Watching them, I felt so shocked and disgusted. The deaf man wasn't very smart; it was also clear that he wasn't very educated. He was from Michigan, and I looked at him and rolled my eyes.

He was just like a machine, cleaning up after them, and none of them tried to communicate with him. They just took advantage of him.

That really disgusted me.

✦

My ideal lover would be well-off, responsible, and older. He doesn't have to be an *International Male* type, but he should be attractive, smart, open-minded, down-to-earth, cool, and easy to communicate with. He should enjoy having sex with me, living together, and having fun. I'd like to share in his work, and he should like to share in my work as well.

He has to have friends of his own. That way he can enjoy his life and I can enjoy mine. I don't want a relationship with a hearing lover who has no friends. Forget it. *Forget* it. He'd end up depending on me for company.

✦

Three groups of deaf gay men live here in New York. The first is the lower-educated deaf gay men. The second is the deaf gay loners. And the third is the better-educated deaf gay men who went to Gallaudet and also tend to interact with the deaf theater community.

The deaf gay loners don't fit in anywhere in either group. They spend a lot of time by themselves and stay at home a lot. There are quite a few of them.

The lower-educated deaf gay men tend to associate with each other. They tend to go out to the piers, and they are heavily involved with the Hispanic gay world at their dances and all that.

The third group — the better-educated deaf gay men — used to be really large, but due to the epidemic, so many have died. They used to hang out at Ty's Bar, but I don't know about them now.

✦

One time I went into Bogart's on Eightieth Street and First Avenue. I sat there with my drink, and a cute hearing boy came up to me and started a conversation. It turned out that he had been involved recently with a deaf Puerto Rican boy — I knew who he was — and had had a very bad experience.

The Puerto Rican boy had taken advantage of him and then robbed his apartment. The hearing boy wanted to know why was I different from that boy. "Why?"

I felt so embarrassed and tried to explain that it was just his way, and not mine. My background was different.

And he had wanted to know where that Puerto Rican boy had gone.

Once in a while when I'm in a bar, certain people there know that I'm deaf, so they give me free drinks without saying anything more. They don't try to communicate with me, or even show any interest in me at all.

I always felt insulted because the only reason they'd give me free drinks was because they felt sorry about my deafness.

Charisse Heine would have to be my heroine from the deaf gay community. She went through a lot at Gallaudet in order to set up the Gallaudet Lambda Society of the Deaf. [It's now called Lambda Society of Gallaudet University.]

Wow ... She went ahead and set up the club even with everyone on campus staring at her. Wow!

✦

As for being deaf and gay, I must add that I love women's culture. Women are different. Now I don't mean that I'm interested in their bodies. It's that I love their souls, and the way they have strong feelings of pride. It's not like in the "macho" culture, where they don't understand women.

Yet I am proud to be a man, and I prefer a woman's soul at the same time.

That's why I consider myself a "lesbian man."

"NICKOLAS"*

MY MOTHER KNEW ABOUT ME BEFORE I DID

IN 1988, I entered the National Technical Institute of the Deaf in Rochester, New York. By that time I'd had a girlfriend for three and a half years. I'd been switching between her and hearing men in the gym where I worked out (just jerking each other off, and nothing more). And one reason I went away to college was to avoid my family and my girlfriend, and to focus on my inner life.

So at NTID I met some gay men and I soon got involved. I made some good friends from Ohio who've taught me a lot. With them I got involved in the bar scene and everything else.

Through my business class I met David, a deaf man who's now my ex-lover. At Christmastime I talked of nothing else — how wonderful he was, and what a great "best friend" he was. He was my first love. I was so in love. Looking back on it, he was my puppy love.

He lived with his parents in Chicago. I asked my family if it was okay to have him over for the first week in May, as I had a co-op interview. My deaf family said that it shouldn't be any problem, and then David would call me on the TTY. (Oh, I was so in love with him!) And if I wasn't there, my sister would take the message. Naturally she became very suspicious about my "best friend." He'd call again, and I kept talking about him in this very positive way to my family...

Then on one Sunday when I wasn't there, my mother pounded on the dinner table at home and asked my family: "If Nickolas were gay, what would you do?"

*This interview was conducted by the editor on July 19, 1992.

My sister said, "Nickolas has been able to go to college, and he's done so many things. I'd still cherish my brother. He's truly wonderful."

My mother thought, Okay, okay. It turns out that my mother had this feeling about me ever since I was a baby in her arms. She just knew I'd be gay way back then.

Anyway, the following week I was very excited. David was coming. When he met my family, they took to him, chatting away and teasing him, and then at one point near my bedroom, my mother said, "You two can sleep together over there."

I said, "Don't be silly."

David, embarrassed, gave a nervous laugh.

Then, the next morning, my sister from New Jersey brought him a mug of coffee with printing on it. When she gave it to him, he read the words "You are the best..." then turned it around to find "lover." He was so shocked and embarrassed!

Then my mother asked me to tease David with a dildo. She wanted me to show my fake dick to David.

I said, "No, no, mother, no. I don't feel comfortable."

Finally I gave in for her sake, put the dildo into my fly, and let it hang out. I was so uncomfortable.

I walked into the kitchen where David was eating.

He was very shocked, and my mother was hee-heeing so hard. I took it out finally and threw it out. I was so embarrassed. I felt something was very wrong.

The next day we went to visit my grandmother, and my aunt came to visit and to say good-bye. The following day David and I went in my girlfriend's car for the drive up to Rochester. I was thinking about all this when my lover said, "Your family's really neat. They seem to know you're gay."

Then in the last week of June, I was very depressed because he had to go back to Chicago and I had to go back to New York.

My mother came over. "What's wrong?"

"I miss school."

"No. You miss your boyfriend."

"Wait a minute."

"David."

"Do you love me?"

"Of course I love you. You're my last baby."

"You understand me?"

"Of course."

"I'm gay."

So that's how I came out. My mother cried and we hugged. Then she asked, "What about your girlfriend?"

"Oh. We broke up last December, and we didn't want to tell our families because we knew how much our family cherished her, and how much her family cherished me..."

She said, "I don't care about her. I care about you."

Then my sister came in the room. "What's wrong?"

My mother said, "He's gay."

"Oh, I understand and respect that."

Then my brother came along and asked, "What's wrong?"

My sister said, "He's gay."

He said, "Oh, be careful of AIDS."

"Of course," I said. "I know how to protect myself."

And so they knew all about me.

Back when I was single for three years, I didn't mind bars being badly lit or filled with smoke. I thought it was sexy. I was just wild then — I was taking some drugs as well — and so I didn't mind it, even with hearing men. But after I met my current lover, I started to complain a little about the lighting because I needed to sign with him, and because I have never liked to wear glasses in the bars.

Many hearing men in my experience found it hard to learn ASL because its syntax is so different from English. So with these one-night stands we'd write back and forth.

When I met my hearing lover, we wrote back and forth the first day, too.

But then by the second day he had learned the manual alphabet.

And on the third day he was already learning signs.

That made me feel so impressed with him.

Most hearing men I've met have surprised me with their knowledge of fingerspelling. They don't know ASL, right, but they sure know the alphabet. I'm really impressed with that.

I wish more hearing people could understand body language and feel more comfortable with that. It'd be nice if they could fingerspell, gesture, and sign too.

The best thing about being a deaf gay person is that I have guts. I have the guts to trust myself.

✦

My straight brother always says, "It's the nineties. Being gay is no big deal — just get on with it." I like that.

"YVETTE"*

CAUGHT IN THE ACT

When I went home for vacation in Puerto Rico, my mother said, "I plan to take a sign language course." I was shocked because while I was growing up, she forbade signing in the house.

I asked her, "Are you taking this course because of me?"

She said, "No, because I'm working in a travel agency and I want to help deaf travelers for their vacations and to guide them around."

That still bothered me. It was as if these deaf travelers were more important than me.

"Look," I told my mother. "Why can't you take a sign language course because of me?"

She said, "You can talk very well, so why should I sign to you?"

That pissed me off. I couldn't understand her.

Because of our differing philosophies, we don't really have a close relationship. But I do have a close relationship with my father.

Before my family knew about me, my sister caught me kissing another woman. I forced her not to tell my mother about it. I gave her some money, and she never told my mother at all. Instead, my mother caught me later sleeping with someone else in my room. At first she was very upset, but she accepted it because she had a few gay and lesbian friends.

I was planning to tell my family that I was gay, but I was forcibly brought out by someone else.

---

*This interview was conducted by the editor on July 23, 1992.

At the time, I was going to college. My mother called me one day to ask me about coming to my brother's wedding in Puerto Rico. But that weekend was a bad one because it was the same time as my finals. I was very concerned about my grades. Both my father and mother thought, "Well, okay."

But my sister here in New York went to the wedding.

At the reception many people asked my mother where I was and when I would be getting married. (I'm the oldest child in my family, and my brother's second in line.)

Initially, she said, "Well, she doesn't feel like getting married." But somehow that night she felt tired of saying that over and over again.

So she decided to announce the fact that I was gay right there at my brother's wedding reception. Everyone in my family got very upset because it was announced at the wrong place and the wrong time.

The guests there talked about nothing else, and my brother was very, very upset because it was *his* wedding.

I didn't know about this at all, not even when I flew home two weeks later for my spring break. Nothing seemed different. No one talked about the word gay, so I didn't know anything had happened. I went back to college, and then went back to New York to stay the summer at my mother's house.

Then one day my sister said, "You should ask mother about what happened at the wedding."

"What do you mean?"

"Just ask her."

So I went over to her and asked, "Can you tell me what happened at the wedding?"

She looked about awkwardly, and worse yet, my sister sat there, listening. She knew that I'd get very angry.

Finally, after going back and forth, she said, "Well, I announced to everyone at the wedding that you were gay."

I was so angry. "Why couldn't you let my brother enjoy his wedding?" I wanted to tell my family myself, "By the way, I'm gay," but no, it was too late. I was so shocked.

Yet the fact that my family was still very proud of me as a deaf lesbian woman really made me cry and we all hugged.

I'm really lucky to have a family like that.

✦

I was sixteen when I had my first lesbian experience. When I first moved to New York, my mother knew I needed some new friends, so she introduced me to the daughter of one of her woman friends. We looked at each other, and I could tell that she was a lesbian.

We were both attracted to each other, and we fell in love. The relationship lasted only a few weeks. When my mother found out about it, she was very upset and forbade me to see her.

But since that time, I've always been an active lesbian.

✦

During my high school years one girl from my class came up to me and pointed out a certain girl. "She's a lesbian — watch out."

"What do you mean by the word 'lesbian'?"

"It means two women having sex."

She didn't know that I was a lesbian, so later I went up to that girl. "Are you a lesbian?"

She said, "Yes."

I said, "I am, too."

So we became friends — and had a short relationship also.

✦

I was involved with a hearing woman recently. She learned to sign and communicate pretty well — I taught her — and in the beginning she had lots of patience. But later on she lost patience.

I suspect that she had other problems with her own family that made her lose interest in sign language. That's my feeling.

"Why?" I tried to ask her. "What's the reason?"

Because I was her first deaf woman, she was having a hard time with the relationship. "You don't know how to communicate with me."

I said, "Simple. Learn sign language. Simple. I learn to lipread your speech. That's the only way communication can work between us. It's no big deal."

She said, "Oh, communication's such a big deal because you're deaf."

I said, "No, I'm starting to lipread you, and you're starting to sign. Communication goes both ways. It's not a big deal."

✦

It doesn't matter what my ideal woman looks like, but I like dark hair, like black or brown. It doesn't matter what a woman's skin color is, but when it comes to blond hair, it affects me. I don't know why, but I think it has to do with the fact that my mother's hair is dirty blond and my father's hair is black.

I like going out with a woman who considers herself feminine. (I consider myself feminine.) Any woman acting in some role — butch or otherwise — turns me off.

She should have had education and a career, and should enjoy artistic things. And she should be challenging, because that's my way, too.

It doesn't matter to me whether she's hearing or deaf — as long as we are able to communicate with each other in signs.

✦

Sometimes, when I like a certain woman in a bar, I go up and ask her to dance with me.

Sometimes, they say, "Well ... I have someone."

And I say, "Okay," and back off.

I feel embarrassed when they turn me down because they realize that I am deaf.

✦

Deaf people are not interested in pity.

And I'm not just deaf, but a human being. Period.

ERNEST HOFFMANN*

LEAVING SOUTH DAKOTA

I WAS BORN WITH MY HEARING LOSS in Faith, South Dakota. I attended a public elementary school for the first four years before transferring to the South Dakota School for the Deaf. Then I graduated at the top of the class from SDSD in 1962, went to Gallaudet, majored in history, and graduated with a B.A. in 1966. Then I stayed on in D.C. to work for the FBI from 1966 to 1969.

I moved to Denver, Colorado, for ten years, from 1969 to 1979. Then I attended the National Leadership Training Program (NLTP) at the California State University at Northridge (CSUN) in 1980, where I earned my M.A. in administration, education, and supervision. After a year working in a group home, I went back to D.C. as a fundraiser for Gallaudet University's Development Office before transferring to its Alumni Association Office.

ASL is a beautiful language, very colorful, and it's easier for us to express our feelings with it than when we use straight English. In straight English we lose a lot of "deaf" meanings, whereas in ASL one sign can mean fifty things.

Within the deaf community ASL has been taken seriously; now the hearing community has started to take ASL more seriously when they study deaf culture and linguistics. The hearing community's view of ASL as a legitimate foreign language is improving; it's not moving fast enough, but...

✦

*This interview was conducted by the editor on April 10, 1992.

I knew I was attracted to boys and men at the age of five or six, but I didn't understand it until I was in my twenties. I had some gay experiences at my residential school, but I didn't really understand them. I didn't meet any gay people until *after* I graduated from Gallaudet. It was then I finally understood the words "gay" and "homosexual" — partly because I met gay people in Denver and then when I came back to work later for Gallaudet ... If I had known that some of those people were gay during my college days, who knows what would've happened? (Sigh.)

Because I played wild all along, my first real love didn't happen until my late thirties. I met this deaf kid. We had a lot of similar interests, but unfortunately he was too young. He was eighteen, and I was in my thirties — that was too much of a gap.

It didn't work out, and I had no one for a while.

I had a brief relationship with another deaf lover, but it didn't work out because we were just too different from each other.

Then I met this hearing guy who's my partner now, and Bill and I have been together going on five years.

In the past, the hearing gay community didn't have that much interest in sign language, nor a lot of patience for writing back and forth with a deaf gay person. Many of them, when they discover that the deaf person can't speak, will write back and forth — "Hi, nice to meet you, see you around" — and leave. This still happens to many deaf people today. But many people are now more interested in sign language. Yes, there's been a change in the hearing gay community's attitudes toward the deaf gays, all for the better.

Before meeting Bill, I thought my ideal lover had to be tall. And if he happened to be hearing, he'd have to understand that deaf culture is different and that compromises must be made. If he's deaf, it's not a problem, of course. I always wanted a deaf lover, but it was hard to find one who was compatible enough with me. If my ideal lover was deaf, it'd be easy to delete a lot of things communication-wise off my list (smile). But it's hard to find a deaf lover who shares my interests. My ideal lover would like going out to the theater, going out for the evening, having home entertainment and quiet dinners at home — things we'd enjoy doing together as well as apart.

✦

The number of deaf gay people in the Washington metro area must be at least 5,000. It sounds crazy, but remember that some people know other deaf gay people that I don't know, and so the number of people spreads out. I think that 5,000 would be a small number, really. It'd be nice if we could have a complete list of all the deaf gay people here, but we don't.

✦

I strongly oppose outing of deaf gay people in the deaf straight community because some people aren't ready to come out of the closet. I feel that if they want to announce that they're out, they should say so themselves, not me. I've had many people come up to me and ask, "I've heard So-and-So is gay. Is it true?" I usually say, "I don't know, I don't know." I may know, but if they want to ask, they should ask the person themselves. Other deaf gay people may just say, "Yes, yes," but it's wrong to "out" them. Each gay person has to be ready to come out.

To be happy as a gay person, one must love oneself first and be very comfortable with the life one chooses. I don't believe that gays are "molested" into becoming gay — it is only an inner feeling that one develops for the same sex. I also believe that we are born with these feelings.

Deaf people's knowledge of the world is limited compared to hearing people's, who can pick up what's new by listening to the radio. So deaf people's understanding of gay people is limited. Of course, there are always some anti-gay hearing people, but the straight deaf community is worse than the hearing straight community in their treatment of deaf gays. Many people may disagree with me, but if you watch the straight deaf community carefully, you'll notice that they are rougher on deaf gays.

I'd estimate about ninety percent of the male sign language interpreters are gay, while forty percent of the female interpreters are lesbian. Come to think of it, those numbers are high. I don't know why that field should have such a high percentage.

✦

The one thing I'd like to encourage in the hearing gay community is "communication and understanding." By that I mean, they should make every effort to communicate in whichever way is best. It can be done by writing back and forth, gesturing with hands, speaking, or learning sign language.

By "understanding," I mean that they should understand that deaf people have a culture that is very different from hearing culture. That was where my partner Bill had such a hard time at first. Because he's black, I insulted him once. I said, "Is that black culture?" But I didn't mean anything negative. In fact, there are many parallels between deaf and black cultures, and we have to make room for all kinds of cultures all over the place. That is so important.

"JAMES MACKINTOSH"*

DANCING WITHOUT MUSIC: MOMENTS WITH DEAF GAY MEN

ONE HOT SUMMER EVENING, I went into a popular West Village bar for a drink and some company. In the brightest corner of the bar was the company I was seeking. One of the men there, Sam, broke off from telling the others something so he could greet me. The others followed with similar greetings, and Sam then resumed his story: "...and I told him that I thought hearing people looked pretty silly using only their mouths to talk. It looks rude — like chewing gum — the way their mouths work up and down..."

He grimaced and pantomimed to make his point, and we all laughed because we knew exactly what he meant. Often while we were talking, people would point to us because we were using sign language. We were a bunch of gay men having a good time, and it didn't bother *us* that we were deaf.

I was interested in the reactions of the others in the group. Some were more flexible with hearing people, others not. So I decided to find out from some of them what the gay world is to them. I was already familiar with the stereotypical deaf gay man, a creation of many a hearing man. This fantasy figure is someone who can't talk, can't communicate except by writing (and poorly at that), can't enjoy music and dancing, is only good for a one-night stand, and is a terrific fuck.

*This piece first appeared in the December 5–18, 1983, issue of the *New York Native*. Mackintosh's comments, shared with the editor nine years later, in September 1992, follow.

The following afternoon I called Leon, one of the group at the bar, and asked to have a conversation with him. He was overjoyed that a gay deaf writer was going to do a story. I could understand this reaction, for many deaf people, both gay and straight, have seen so much distortion from writers who happen not really to comprehend the world they live in. In so many articles of this sort, too much is filtered out — the sensitivities and the hard-nosed realities of what it is like to be deaf. (By the way, not once during any of my conversations did I detect a sign of disappointment from any of these people over the fact that they are deaf.)

Leon is thirty, tall, and a little chubby. Employed as a teacher's aide at a small, exclusive school for deaf youngsters, he enjoys his work. He interacts with many hearing people during the course of his daily duties, and he has found no problem at all in communicating.

"Actually, I could say it's because of everyone being aware that I'm deaf," he said. "On the other hand, I'll get angry if they start patronizing me. There's no need to patronize me if I didn't ask for it."

When queried as to whether he feels more comfortable with deaf or with hearing people, either straight or gay, he responded that hearing people were more his type. "They do mind their own business," he chuckled. "Many of the deaf people I know tend to interfere in whatever I do — they think since they're deaf and I'm deaf, we're related, like a mother and daughter. No, no — make that a mother and a daughter-in-law!"

In the deaf world — especially in the gay deaf world — people do tend to look out for one another. That world is so small that news of any importance (and sometimes of no importance) makes the rounds so fast that everyone else knows all the details before the subject of the gossip is aware that anything has happened. Many times deaf men I've never met before will come over and ask me if I'm deaf. And when I reply in the affirmative, they make themselves at home and start talking away as if they've known me for years. (I find it an intrusion on my privacy and sometimes have to be rude to get rid of the man.)

I commented on this to Leon, and he agreed with me. "Being deaf yourself doesn't mean you're obligated to leap joyfully into the arms of every other deaf person you meet. Do black people jump with joy when they meet other black people? That depends on the situation.

"I came out at the age of nineteen, and boy, were those the years I went wild," Leon continued. "The first week of my coming out, I made the rounds so many times I lost count. It's taken me a long time to come to the point where I can just stay home and enjoy my own company. New York has changed during all these years. And with those changes, attitudes toward deaf people have changed, too. Some things are still the same, such as the one-night stands and the 'drop-dead' attitude of many gay men. I've often noticed that the more prestigious and rich a gay man is, the more 'attitude' he has. The same thing applies to many deaf gays. There is even an 'A' group and a 'B' group. All that attitude!"

The A group is made up of college-educated and successful men who tend to live in Manhattan. To many deaf people, living in Manhattan, in itself, is an impressive feat. Partly because they are prevented from holding jobs that require hearing ability, many deaf people earn less money than the average hearing gay man. But for some, such as Leon and other gay men I know, the types of jobs they hold have nothing to do with their ability to enjoy to the fullest what the city has to offer.

The term "B group" applies to those who have a maximum of a high-school education and, more to the point, live in places outside the city. Oftentimes, when an urban deaf gay man is approached by another deaf gay man, he is likely to ignore the less "cultured" one. As Leon put it, "To be honest, I haven't worked hard to become an information booth for those who don't live here."

The deaf gay man in the city is exposed to visual delights, as well as disappointments, and he develops an instinct for what goes over and what doesn't when it comes to the latest in everything. It is not easy to stay current when one cannot overhear gossip or good conversation, which is when new facts are often learned. Much to my embarrassment, I didn't find out about the Saint [a legendary place quickly acclaimed as such] until two months after it had opened. (And I thought I was doing fine by myself with what I knew!)

I suggested to Leon that we end our conversation, because I was due at a dinner party to be given by a close friend, Ed. And I thought it a good opportunity to talk to Ed, and whoever else might be there, about themselves.

✦

Ed answered the door a little too fast. He laughed and said the doorbell light flasher wasn't working, so he'd been keeping an eye out for everyone coming to dinner. His easy laughter made me feel good — he is the sort of man who is easy to get along with, despite the fact that he has never verbally spoken a single word all his life.

Ed is a 34-year-old free-lance designer and carpenter. He's done some admirable design work, and it shows in the apartment he lives in: it's totally white with black floors and built-in banquettes, and everything gleams with a sheen of warm luxury. The man himself isn't bad-looking, either — tall with blue eyes and a face that exemplifies the word handsome.

In a few minutes another friend, Charlie — a tall, rugged teddy bear of a man — came by. Ed told me his third guest had had to cancel in order to "lover-sit" his sick lover.

With a white ceiling fan whirling above us, the smoke from Ed's cigarette weaving lazily upward, and the food on the table indescribably delicious, we talked for a long time. Ed punctuated his conversation with gestures of his hands — when he wasn't talking, he'd make emphasized repetitions of the signs he had used. His style of signing was beautiful — soft, rich, and flowing — and I was held in rapt attention for a long while, pausing to take down a note or two.

"I remember when I came to New York ten years ago — no, eleven years, now — and I'm telling you, it's been quite a journey. And the only thing I still haven't been able to deal with is not being able to use the phone freely. I'm an interior designer, and you know, interior designers have to use the phone for their work! Orders, foremen, contractors, and the like — all have to be reached every day if I'm to be doing a job for someone. Can you imagine running from place to place every day? I'd be dead before I knew it!"

Some clients, he said, are put off by the idea of working with a deaf person. "I've known many major designers over the years, through doing small jobs for them — free-lance, you know — and they have yet to hire me as a full-time designer. One big department store knows me well, but every time I ask them about work, they always find a way to avoid giving me a job. That hurts, especially when I hear that they just gave jobs to two of my designer friends who happen to be younger and hearing, and have never worked for them before."

Ed shifted in his seat and, looking at me, said, "Deaf straight people hire me because they know I'm good — and deaf! They'd rather work with another deaf person — there's no communication problem there. I can't say the same for deaf gay men — most of them already have wonderful apartments!"

I asked Ed whether he finds it frustrating to go out to parties or bars.

"Not really. I'd rather have parties at home — with a good mix of deaf and hearing people. I enjoy the contrast, and it's nice to see hearing people signing along with everyone else. I've been to quite a few hearing parties, and let me tell you, I'm totally bored! Parties are fun when everyone's *sharing* a good time. The hearing parties I've been to didn't give you the same feeling. Everyone's so reserved, and they're trying too hard to have a good time and not thinking about other people in the space they're in. I mean, parties are where you meet new people, and it's fun to learn new things — often in surprising ways." With a mischievous grin, he added, "And sometimes the surprise goes home with you!

"I think I have plenty of patience for the rest of the world. A while ago, someone I was seeing broke up with me. He told me I had no patience in communicating because I'd been trying to teach him sign language, and he wasn't taking it all in easily. And when he said that, I looked at him and asked if he realized how hard it was for me — *me* — to read his lips, and I wasn't complaining yet. He was speechless. I knew that because his mouth didn't open again for a while!" We all laughed.

Ed looked at both of us and said, "I'm pleased with what I have — some good friends, a nice home, work to do, a family like the both of you. Of course, I have a real family, but you both are part of my New York family. We check each other out, support each other." He sighed and looked at the wall, his eyes rolling heavenward, as he continued signing: "Now, if the rest of the world learned sign language, they wouldn't feel so handicapped with us."

✦

After dinner, walking with Charlie to his apartment for coffee, I learned that he is a teacher of deaf children; he also teaches sign language in New York, as well as courses in deaf culture and community relations.

Deaf people have a rich culture based on sign language, with components in theater and communication methods. They will not hesitate to go to the theater if a show features a deaf character or if the show is interpreted for the deaf. Community meetings and cultural events are popular among deaf people if they're told that sign language will be used as a means of communication. The influence of this popularity is even reflected by the New York City Gay Men's Chorus, which provides a signer for its concerts — a good indication that deaf gays are as visible in the smaller gay world as straight deaf people in the larger world.

"You know," Charlie said, "if I didn't know you and you were walking on the street, I wouldn't know the difference. That's where the problem comes in with deaf-hearing relations. It makes some things a little more important — such as signing with someone to let other people watching know that I'm deaf. It helps when I'm out cruising: I can immediately gauge the reactions of someone I'm interested in. If they get upset and walk away when they see me signing, I say to myself that it's their problem. Of course, I do get disappointed sometimes, but there's always this knowledge that so many other men are around and more open to communication.

"I remember a time when I was with someone and he was telling a story about Cornelia Guest — you know, that vacuous girl with money to throw away — and after he finished I started talking with him about what he'd talked about. I'd had some difficulty understanding a part of what he said, and he told me to shut up. That made me angry. I mean, a half hour of talking about Cornelia is more important than five minutes talking with someone real next to you!

"However, I have found gay hearing men to be more sensitive to deaf gay men — they know the feeling of being part of a small group, a minority. Sometimes I think the minority groups are more realistic in their views of the world, that the rest of the world is just an illusion of exaggeration. For years I'd tried to fit myself into a mold, trying to make myself acceptable to the world. I got married, and found it didn't solve anything. I always continued thinking about my own feelings toward other men, and that had nothing to do with my being deaf. At the same time, I was trying to be a good role model of what a deaf person was supposed to be: a copy of a hearing person, what with taking speech lessons and curtailing my signing. I reached the point where the closet I'd created by listening to other people was too small." We were now at the front door of his building, and we went upstairs to his apartment.

His apartment was nice and homey, a reflection of Charlie himself, with personal pictures and objects everywhere; it was obvious that no designer had laid hands anywhere.

He led the way to the kitchen, set the coffeepot on the stove, sat down, and impulsively asked me if I'd heard the latest deaf riddle. "Why do deaf people make great lovers?"

I couldn't think of an answer.

"Because they can't hear a 'No!' in the dark!"

We laughed over that one. Recalling the popular myth among many hearing gay men I knew that deaf gay men are terrific in bed, I asked Charlie if he agreed with that view.

"I haven't heard anything negative yet!" he replied.

Again we laughed. Deaf people are often perceived as being sexually adventurous and very sensitive in bed with their partners. Perhaps this is because deaf people grow up more tactile, in order to make up for their loss of hearing.

I asked Charlie if he would change if he suddenly could hear. He looked at me a long time and then said, "I don't know. I have a deaf soul, a feeling that binds me with other deaf people, because we all know what it's like to be in a hearing world. I'm happy being me. People tell me I miss a lot by not being able to hear — but how can I miss what I've never known before? I cannot negate myself by wishing for the impossible. I'm perfectly satisfied with not being able to hear, and I think I have a wonderful life. If I have problems it's because they're human problems, not because I'm deaf."

✦

It was well past midnight when I got home. Charlie and I had talked of many things that concerned us: our friends, the movies, AIDS — we were amazed that, to our knowledge, not one deaf gay person had died from it yet — as well as our families, and our mutual interest in the theater. But mainly we dished.

Knowing that my friend Sam would be up, preparing to go out, I called him. He's a wiry man who works as a storyteller, actor, sign language teacher, and advocate of dancing. He is a veteran of the original dance places of gay liberation New York — from the Fire House to the Tenth Floor to the Saint and the dance palaces of 1983. When he answered the phone, we agreed to meet at West Nineteenth Street at one-thirty.

Impatient and excited, he jumped his way to the entrance of the dance place, his sneakered feet making a tattoo of shadows on the pavement. The moment we were inside, he got on the dance floor and started dancing. I joined him, and it was pleasurable feeling the music work its way up my legs and into my chest. We started talking. In a booming disco or noisy bar, it is the hearing who become deaf. They end up shouting at each other, while all we have to do is sign.

As we danced, I let Sam talk to me in freeform, all to the beat of the music. I'd make some comment now and then, but mostly I just watched.

"Hearing people should learn how to sign. It exercises their faces, keeps them looking young and beautiful! Unfortunately for many, they're embarrassed to look beautiful, so they'd rather sit on their hands and wear masks!" He laughed as the lights changed from purple to gold and the music became softer to the beat.

"I really identify myself as a gay man first, and as a deaf man second. I've a strong minority identification — my mom was upset I was deaf, gay, and a dancer to boot! I mean, all those are minorities! She wanted me to be like everyone else. But who's everybody else? If I want to be a macho man in the eyes of society, fine — I'll go along with it. But I think it's more fun to listen to my feelings and be human. I'm a sissy — that's what I am — and a human being!"

He twirled around and came to a stop as some of the other dancers came around to him. I watched in silence, seeing him interact with the other men with no problems at all. He laughed and gestured most of the time. From my previous socializing with him, I knew he couldn't read lips very well, but now, he didn't seem to be bothered by that. The men crowded around him were beautiful; some were his friends from the early seventies.

Sam broke away from the group, waving at them to get back to the dance floor. I commented on his lack of skill in lipreading and reminded him of what he'd said the night before at our bar gatherings, about hearing people looking like they were chewing gum.

"I grew up with so many people making fun of me signing. They'd mimic me, and the signs they threw around were meaningless. One day I noticed how so many people really have their mouths going full speed, without ever remembering what they said. And I thought talking was only about as important as chewing gum — if they're going to make fun of my way of communication, I can say the same for their way of communication.

"Often I wonder why so many people don't realize that we're basically all the same, with all our fears, needs, loving, and hatred. We all do have a need to be acknowledged. We all tend to overplay those characteristics that we don't understand in other people, to make ourselves superior. It's more like hiding from our own fears. So what if I cannot hear? I've often danced with men who've enjoyed themselves dancing with me, and then when they find out I'm deaf, you should see how they react. Some have even fled the place. It freaks them out that they were dancing with someone who can't hear the music."

Sam leaned closer to me. "I have this sense of inner rhythm that makes up for what people think I'm missing — whatever it is — 'sound.' It's not words but *sound*. I think sound means so many things, and one of the things it means is feeling good, deep inside. There's music for those who love it, there are voices for those who listen. There's rhythm for dancers like me. Even after the music — after I see other people stop dancing — I still keep on dancing. People can listen to music without dancing. What about dancing without music?"

✦

As I walked home, the sun making its welcome entrance through the alleys between the buildings, I caught myself dancing a little. The streets were quiet, and the blue haze that accompanies every sunny morning was everywhere. At home, looking from my bed out of the window to the morning sky, I caught sight of the last night star, and it seemed to twinkle.

What's the sound of a star twinkling?

I didn't really want to think about it, and I went to sleep.

✦

On September 15, 1992, James Mackintosh commented:

Although the preceding piece had nothing to do with AIDS, it should be pointed out that when I wrote it in 1983 AIDS was beginning to take its toll on gay people. At that time, the deaf gay community in New York was much stronger and more cohesive, and I felt that something should be said about that. But right after the piece appeared, the deaf gay community began falling apart due to the epidemic. (Half of the people mentioned in the article have since died.)

✦

The A group is gone here in New York, but the B group still exists. Yes, there are members who could've been part of the A group, but they're "floaters" now. I mean, they're much more adaptable; they can plug into different groups when they need to.

Look at the B group now. They haven't changed, and they still hang around at the end of Christopher Street. The only difference is, they're not white anymore. They're black and Hispanic.

I've noticed one other big difference. Members of the A group back then were proud to be deaf. Some of their partners and dates may have been hearing, yes, but were never included in their deaf gay activities. The A group was very much a clique. Now they're so busy trying to include their hearing partners, dragging them into the deaf culture, that they've mutually created a kind of a cultural gridlock.

As a matter of self-preservation, this concerns me, because the very nature of two deaf people communicating changes instantly whenever a hearing person gets involved in the picture. This is just like the idea of a woman going out with "the girls" to play cards with her friends while her husband stays home and watches football on TV. The minute the husband joins in the card game, the atmosphere changes because the group dynamics change.

That's a big reason I make a point of spending some time with my deaf friends. I don't want to have to be an interpreter all the time. With them I can relax and just be myself. That was what the A group was like. My hearing partner has begun to say, "You go on ahead now." It's no longer an issue with him.

✦

Hearing partners are in a Catch-22 position: They can never expect their deaf partners to be part of their world, because the hearing world is more intolerant of deaf people than deaf people are of hearing people. I mean, deaf people live in a hearing world.

Deaf people need a break every day from the hearing world, not just once or twice a week. Choosing how to get that break is their right. Hearing people with deaf partners have to respect that right. They can't force a deaf person to become hearing by learning English or speech.

But, on the other hand, hearing partners of deaf people have to learn sign language. The balance is unfair, yes, but deaf people will always be in the hearing world. The hearing partner gives a little back from the hearing world by learning sign language, because it's not easy for a deaf person to grow up in a hearing world. Hearing people never give it a second thought: "So what?"

So the hearing person has to work a little hard. I'm not saying that learning sign language is necessarily the answer, but the important thing is that the hearing partner must love that deaf person for what he is.

The bottom line is that when two people relate, it's because of the things they had in common before they *ever* met. Just because some hearing people learn sign language, they want a deaf partner. No, that's not a good bond. The relationship must have to do with things other than being deaf and being hearing.

My advice for deaf gay people is that they should put their sexuality on the bottom of the list — I mean, the very bottom of the list. They should think for themselves, and they should realize that they don't need to prove themselves to anyone. And more importantly, they shouldn't waste their time on other people — straight or gay — who don't care for them in the first place.

DAVE SCOTTON*

BACK IN L.A.

ABOUT A MONTH AND A HALF after entering Gallaudet University as a freshman, I decided to tell my parents about myself. Some of my friends had already told their parents, and I felt as if my parents didn't really know about me. Plus I knew that during my Christmas vacation in L.A. I'd want to go out to bars and places, and I knew I couldn't lie about where I was going.

So I wrote a letter to my mother and sent it off. I waited one, two weeks, and heard nothing. I became a little paranoid so I copied down the address for P-FLAG [Parents and Friends of Lesbians and Gays], and sent that off to her as well.

About a week later she wrote back saying that she was — um, surprised that I told her. But she was still glad that I told her and that I chose to tell the truth, and she said she'd love me no matter what. She accepted it pretty well.

She even told my stepfather about me. (My parents had divorced before I was born.) He then wrote a letter to me, which felt odd: was that how he writes? In the letter he said that he hoped I'd do well in school, blah blah blah, and then he said, "Your mother told me about you, and I hope you're handling it well," blah blah blah.

My older sister even wrote a letter to me. She was pretty supportive as well. After that everything was fine.

I was twelve years old when I realized that I was gay. My best friend, from my oral deaf school, was one class below me; we had sex occasionally at his house. (He first joined my school when I was seven years old and he was eight. I fell in love with him

*This interview was conducted by the editor on April 10, 1992.

because he was cute; I became his best friend.)

He showed me his penis, and so I pulled down my pants to show mine. We sort of touched each other, and then got into sex, especially when we slept over at each other's house. I had sex with him for seven years.

In my last year at the oral deaf school (I'd transfer later to a public school with a deaf program), my friend teased his cousin by writing the word "homosexual" on a sheet of paper. I watched them argue back and forth. I knew it was a bad word, but I didn't really understand it. I just kept staring at the word and memorized it.

I came home and looked it up in the dictionary: "homosexual." I read the definition and I said, "Argghhhhhh, that's me!" I got so paranoid and confused about it. I struggled with it and tried to be straight until I read in the newspaper about the gay pride parade, and that's when I learned the word "gay" meant the same thing as "homosexual."

I felt a lot better after that, but I stayed in the closet until my senior year in high school.

✦

My first love was a deaf guy at GLAD (Greater Los Angeles Council on Deafness, Inc.), a deaf services organization near my high school. He brought me out of the closet and helped me a lot. The GLAD office was so nearby that I visited it every afternoon after school. He and I almost had a relationship, but it didn't work because I was nineteen years old and just out of the closet, and he was a lot older, about forty-three. He explained that he wanted to give me the chance to experience the world more and have more opportunities to meet other people.

I was hurt at first, but later when I entered Gallaudet, I realized that he was right.

✦

I hated speech therapy. I wasn't warned that not everyone could understand my speech. Some could, some couldn't understand me. It was really frustrating and confusing, and I felt lied to. After that, I just refused to have anything more to do with speech therapy.

I sometimes find anonymous sex a problem because I may be caught without a pad and pen. The hearing guy will be talking, and I'll be trying to figure out where he wants us to go — his home? mine? — and it's frustrating. On the other hand, setting up a relationship is easier. Then there's time to write notes back and forth if needed, or learn to sign.

I wish that the hearing gay community would understand that not all deaf people can speak. They've assumed too much about us. Some of my hearing dates found ASL hard to learn; some would fingerspell over and over again. But, yeah, most do try to learn, because I don't speak very well. The few who wouldn't learn ASL — well, they were gone pretty quick.

I'd describe my ideal lover as deaf and taller than me. He'd have red hair, a nice moustache and beard, and a nice body (of course). He must be very flexible and easygoing. He'd have to enjoy going out with me to bars and parties, and the beach and the mountains. We'd travel and share things together.

✦

One time I was standing in a bar, holding my drink, when it slipped out of my hand and I had felt nothing until it shattered on the floor and everyone was staring at me. I was so embarrassed. Later that evening it happened again — I must've had butter fingers — so when I had my next drink, the bartender gave me a drink with a mug and said, "Hold the handle."

✦

When I lived in D.C., my lover and I had this understanding that when I went to L.A., I could play around for a little bit on the side. So when I was home for Christmas, I met this really cute guy in a country-and-western bar. We kept looking at each other until he finally came up to me. I discovered that he was really hard to lipread because he was from the South — Mississippi — and so his accent was very different.

We tried to exchange names, but it was too frustrating. I sort of gave up on him and went to talk with my deaf friends for a while. Then I ran into him again, and he asked me to dance.

After one song he followed me and then I took out my pad and pen.

"Hello Gavin," he wrote.

I thought at first that was his name, and I said, "I'm David."

It turned out that he'd thought my name was Gavin, and I thought his name was Doug when his name was Duncan. Misunderstanding names is a big problem for me, but from that point on, Duncan and I had a good conversation writing back and forth.

"FINNEGAN"*

DAVID VERSUS GOLIATH: A DEAF GAY PRISONER SPEAKS

DAVID MEANS "BELOVED ONE." He is a friend of mine. He is frail and kind. He has a bad heart. He isn't frail because he has a bad heart. It's because he is frail by nature. He likes to sit with me in the yard, gossip, and absorb the warmth of the sun. We gossip a lot, but it's a very harmless sort of pastime. The gossip never gets past our meetings. We talk of what we might do to each other if ... David is well tanned and very slim. On the other hand, I occupy twice the space, and three times the density that he does. And he still likes to keep company with me. That pleases me to no end.

We don't show too much affection toward each other in the prison yard, for very obvious reasons — we've seen the way those certain few who do are punished for their openness. We are not so bold. That is to our shame, of course, but I am here for violence while I was drinking, and I am not soberly violent. I prefer to fight only when left with no alternatives. I think David has never had a fight, and he is not ashamed to admit this fact. That is one more reason why I love him.

David comes from a well-off family. He doesn't play that against anyone or try to strut about it. In prison a person in his situation is very vulnerable, and a prized catch for some of the hardened-criminal types. These are the same mental-unfortunates who go gaybashing around the state until they are placed where they will do the least harm. David was recognized by one of these people a few weeks ago. He didn't realize the danger of associating with them. They asked him to use his family to send in reference letters

*This originally appeared in *Coming Together News* (April–May 1992).

to them saying they had jobs waiting for them on the outside, in case they made parole. This sort of thing is common, but David didn't know how to handle it. He didn't tell me about it until it was too late. He told the fellow who approached him that he'd try to get his father to help them out.

Unfortunately, David's father said no. David relayed the news to the mental-unfortunates' representative, and David promptly forgot about it. A few weeks later, David was called off his worksite by this mental-unfortunate fellow who had befriended David. David trustfully went out to see what he wanted, and he was beaten about the face and body for a few minutes. He was then told to pay for the right to live on the same yard as the mental-unfortunates. A few days later, news of a waiting tank was relayed to David, and he had an attack related to his heart condition. He lay on the ground for ten minutes or more waiting to be taken to the clinic, which was two hundred feet away. He was given CPR by a friend while he lay on the ground. His face had turned pale with lips blue. This coloration coupled with the black eyes and swollen features made David the butt of everyone's joke. David appeared to be a dead man — but what was funny?

David is gone now, having been spirited off by the California Department of Corrections (CDC). I know that he's going to be okay, but I don't know if I'll ever see him again.

I stand corrected. I stand in this cesspool called CDC. I stand and watch.

"JADE"

LOST

DOWN AS I FELT of sorrow
Lost beyond the river,
As if there is no tomorrow,
Left my soul to shiver...

I watch her leave.

"JADE"

4 IN THE MORNING

SHE CALLED ME at 3
In the morning,
Longing for me...
She cried out my name.
But no answer yet...

Then again at 3:15
In the morning, she calls...
Half-awake, I listen.
She begs me for mercy,
Wanting me in her arms.

So at 4
In the morning, I take
My pillow and on my bike,
Riding down feeling ill
And coughing to go to her open arms.

"JADE"

MELODY HEARTBEAT OF A BLACK DEAF WOMAN

I AM A BLACK DEAF WOMAN
With a character of harmony
The music of my songs
Silent to my hearing
But visual to my world
Listen to my melodies
Beneath my flapping wings...
I hear no tunes...
I put my hand on my chest
Just to feel my heart beating...

I am a proud black deaf woman
The music of my song
Who plays the tune
By singing with my hands
Moving, animated in the air
To your dear heart

So powerful is the name of my song,
I can be seen signing hummings
Through the night breeze
I hear no tunes
Just feeling my heart beating...

"JADE"

WRITING

THERE.
She wrote out of commitment to herself.
Her pen scribbled and scribbled.
Acknowledging her own writing,
She kept on.

Yes...
She wrote of love and peace.
She wrote of life's mysteries.
Everything was a story to her beliefs.
She kept on writing.

Yes...
She was born with a pen.

"JADE"

LOCKOUT

WEEPING HER HEART OUT,
Feeling anger, depression, and fear,
There are five walls around her,
No way to any opening,
Somewhere lost in soul, hoping
One day someone will guide her out
From the ordeal of walls around her.

Struggling to push down walls...
        She fails.
Screaming her lungs out for help,
        No one hears.
Pounding on the walls...
        No one opens.

Weakening ... can't push anymore ... ready to die...

The key ... to the opening
Will lead her out of rages.
There's got to be a clue
To her being alive...
Until one day she found the key

        and

Reached out in touch with herself.

        Free...

At last ... she lives.

DESTINY

THE PAIN
    (welts my fragile heart)
The rain
    (pours on my soul)
The gain
    (bound to love you more)
The chains
    (I carry around me)

You tell me.

Destiny will reveal itself when it's right...
Why waste any more of my time?

Only time will tell if it's too late.

SHE SMILES

LIE STILL. Face the moon.
Observe.
See her face there?
Look how she smiles
In the dusk of the low tide.

Lie still.
Observe the ocean bed.
The full moon shimmers.
See the aura around her?
She's telling us something.

Imagine her lustrous lips
Embedded in mine, caressing
My soul, giving full body
And strength of my own
Vibrancy and sunshine...

(Oh she smiles so dearly!
How can anyone forget her face?)

Look how she glows in the breeze.
Face the moon. Observe.
You can see the shape of her face
In the waves of the night sea...
She smiles.

"DEAN"*

INTERVIEW WITH A DEAF LEATHERMAN

HOW DEAF ARE YOU? Can your speech be understood by hearing strangers? And how do you communicate with them?

I am profoundly deaf. My speech can be understood by hearing people exposed to deaf people. Otherwise I use paper and pen to communicate.

At what age did you realize you were attracted to men?

At the age of fourteen.

What happened? Was it your first sexual experience?

I was attracted to this guy who worked at my residential school. I always felt warm and close to him, and I realized that he was gay. But I never had the opportunity to have sex with him. I had my first sexual experience with an older guy. It wasn't too pleasant. It was more about force, but at the same time I was willing. I wanted to experience it. I later had sex with the first guy I was attracted to, which gave me a very different, and positive, feeling. Then I dated a girl and had sex with her. That first time with her I broke her virginity, which made me feel good. And then the second time I dated a girl it was a very different experience. I didn't really enjoy it that much, and I realized I was sexually more attracted to men.

Are you saying that before you got involved with leather, your sexual experiences were rather unsatisfactory?

I always felt something was missing from the sex I had. The guys I dated were "vanillas," but then I met this deaf leatherman. He

*This TDD interview was conducted by the editor on September 3, 1992.

informed me about the culture and the lifestyle of a leatherman. I became interested and started to explore, but I didn't come out as a leatherman until two years ago.

What happened then?

There was an orgy where guys practiced safe sex, fistfucking, golden showers, nipple torture, and so forth. I found the scene erotic and I started to meet more men of my kind. Spanking ass really excites me.

Do you mean that you like to be spanked? Or do you like to spank? What is it about spanking that excites you so?

I like to spank leathermen. It's so erotic and I fantasize...

So when you are spanking, what do you like to fantasize about?

I like to fantasize about masculine men like ex-construction workers, gas station attendants, soldiers, Marines, and so forth. You know how fantasies change every time you have sex.

It seems that you are attracted to uniforms. Do you think it's because of your deafness — that you are a visual person and these men in leather/uniforms are easy to identify?

I have always been attracted to men in leather/uniforms, even when I was a young boy. But I never realized that until I got into the leather scene. I do have a leather outfit — chaps, harness, vest, hat, motorcycle boots, and gloves. I am starting to collect police uniforms.

But don't you have any explanations of why you are so attracted to uniforms? Is it the implication of authority that turns you on?

Yes, it turns me on. Wearing uniforms and seeing other guys in their uniforms makes me feel masculine. I mean, nothing like those who wear makeup and pink clothes.

So you got involved with leather only two years ago. Did you undergo a period of initiation or an apprenticeship of some kind? To a master or as a slave?

I never got training as a master or slave. I am actually into both top and bottom, but I prefer being top. I didn't come out until two years ago due to pressures from my deaf family and my family's friends. I have learned to appreciate myself and that was when I came out. When I came out, it was very easy for me, because I had the right motive. Although I am still learning every day about roles and fetishes.

Sexually you are a top, and you've mentioned liking spanking. Are there other specialized sexual activities you enjoy?

Sure. I do like seeing men get their hair and body hair shaved. I went to a uniform party called "Clippers" last weekend. Clippers is a group of men who are into uniforms and getting their hair shaved. While they get their hair shaved, a group of us men masturbate in front of the guy in the barber's chair. I am also attracted to a boy who wears an earring in his nose, or in his nipples, or in his penis. And I do like giving golden showers to a boy.

Did you feel funny when you pissed on a boy for the first time? What was it like?

It was a very awkward experience, because when I was growing up I was taught that I must go to the bathroom all by myself with the door closed. It was against my beliefs, and I have analyzed this and changed this value to meet my sexual needs. Yes, when I first pissed on the guy, it took me a while before I could pee on the guy. It is becoming better every time. I was once peed on by a guy, and I came.

How did it feel to be peed upon? Yes, you ejaculated but didn't you feel dirty? I don't mean in the hygienic sense, but in the societal sense?

I didn't feel dirty, because I felt the warmth from the pee and it aroused me sexually. I know it's not socially acceptable. But it really makes me feel good, so I ignore the norms of society.

In other words, when you express your sexual self beyond the "vanilla" variety, you are rebelling against the oppressiveness of your deaf family? Yes, your family must love you but at the same time you feel you can't be yourself totally. Am I right in that assumption or not?

Yes, you're right. I was oppressed growing up. My mom told me at the age of twelve that it was sinful to masturbate. That really got me blocked mentally and emotionally. My parents don't feel very comfortable talking about sex because they don't feel comfortable with their own sexual selves. They believe that sex is for marriage, not for pleasure. I have come a long way overcoming that idea. Sex for me is now beautiful and enjoyable, and I accept myself as a gay person into leather.

It's so wonderful that you have found yourself as a sexual being. Now aren't you interested in training to become a master?

In fact, I plan to get into training soon. I should inform you that there are not too many good masters or slaves. Often they do not practice what is called safe, sane, and consensual sex. Often the master gets into too much alcohol or drug;, they lose their proper judgment and end up hurting their partner during their rituals. I am very cautious about this, and I support the safe, sane, and consensual philosophy when it comes to sex.

In your sexual relationships with others, just how important is trust to you?

Trust is a very important issue for me. I do not develop fast relationships. I take it one day at a time. I was dating a guy for four months with no commitment involved. We stopped dating each other when we realized that we were both too different, and that also involved trust. Trust comes from feeling assertive, not passive or aggressive.

It just now occurs to me that if your parents were oppressed and if they affected you in that manner, do you think their religion had any impact on you so that sense of religious ritual has carried over into your sexual life?

Yes. My parents would be affected by the idea of me being into leather. They'd interpret it as "heavy sex." I went home a month ago for the first time in one year. I have two rings on my nipples, so when my parents saw the rings, they called me an African and said that moving three thousand miles away had changed me. I said, "I'm basically the same, but my interests in life have changed." They didn't seem to accept the fact that my religious values have changed.

In your sexual relationships, just how important is physical pain to you? Do you find that you have to build up a higher tolerance of pain in order to induce true pleasure?

Often people think that when a person is into leather, he is into physical pain/torture. It all comes down to the agreement between the partners about what excites the person. I do know what makes me feel good. I like nipple torture and I like having my dick slapped. That gives me pleasure.

What would be your ideal lover, physically?

I prefer a straight-looking guy with a military haircut, and he should be muscular with an average-sized thick dick.

Does it matter what race or nationality?

I prefer white men, as well as light-skinned Italians and Mexicans with a white background.

Aside from these physical attributes, do you think you'd want a long-term relationship? Do you believe in open or closed relationships? How do you think it would affect your sexual life?

I believe in closed relationships. When my partner and I share the fantasy of having a third guy for sex, we would have to agree on who we pick. It just has to be safe, sane, and consensual.

Yes, of course. Do you think that you are jealous at heart?

No. I enjoy giving and receiving from other people.

I mean, what if he expresses to you that he thinks this or that guy is really cute? Would you tell him to go take him home or share him with you?

I think it's very healthy to discuss how a person thinks about other people.

For this long-term relationship, what qualities must your partner have in order to maintain it?

He should be intelligent, committed, sensitive, and knowledgeable about deaf culture, which means he'd have to know signs. I'd love to have a deaf lover.

Do you have a partner now?

My partner and I decided to call it off two weeks ago, and I'm looking for another partner, although I already have two partners outside of town.

So you have fun with them when you can and when they can. Is age of any importance to you? Are you attracted to older men or men your age?

It'd all depend on how this person carries himself. I prefer men my age, but older men are fine.

Do you have any particular recurring fantasies you'd like to share? And if you are with a hearing partner, is it hard to convey that kind of fantasy? How do you do it? Or don't you even try at all?

I do share my fantasies with my partners, and when the time is ripe, it will happen. I do have fantasies of being naked in the desert and meeting some hot guys. The fun would begin around the water and the mountains nearby. I also fantasize about having sex with a Harley-Davidson man while riding his motorcycle.

In those fantasies, what is it that turns you on the most? Being put in a position over which you have no control? For example, being bound in such a way that any man can choose to penetrate you?

It'd have to be discussed before that happened. It'd turn me off if he decided to go against my request.

Have you had other deaf people express repulsion or horror at the idea of you in leather, and at the fact that you're getting more and more involved in that scene?

I have faced a lot of comments from friends whom I went to Gallaudet with. But I am a completely different person from when I was a student there. I have discovered a lot about myself, and I feel good about that. When my friends make a comment, I simply ignore their judgments of me. I believe that if this is what makes me happy, I should have the respect of others who have faith in me; I am not into labeling or stereotyping. I find it difficult to bring up leather issues within the deaf gay and lesbian community because they haven't been educated about the leather scene, and they are limited by what they've learned in their lives. I guess it has a lot to do with the oppression of growing up, of being limited by what a person has had.

I was wondering: Why leather? What is it that turns you on? What kind of leather? And what is it exactly that makes you want to dress up in chaps? I mean, is it just the smell?

I find many leathermen down-to-earth, hardly like those guys who are into materialism. I am more interested in the guy who thinks about life and makes something out of it. I love the smell of leather because it turns me on. When I'm wearing it, it feels good and it brings out the masculinity in me. I happen to have a straight look, but I'm gay as well. I'm easily attracted to both sexes, but of course I'm into men. I'm easygoing. That's what I am.

One last question. What do you think makes leatherfolk different from other "vanilla" gay people? What makes them so special?

People involved in the leather scene are true individuals. They were able to explore their own sexuality and come out in leather. I do know that there are so many deaf "vanillas" struggling with the idea of leather, and they are afraid to come out because of the pressures from the deaf gay and lesbian community. I do believe that leathermen and leatherwomen are very creative people.

Thank you for telling so much about yourself.

"DWAYNE"

A LETTER
11 MAY 1992

OK, ME AGE 42 have experiment in my life at deaf school. I first had sexual experiment by 13 or 14 years. Male babysitter when I age 4 at farm when my parents go out. He exposed himself to me near outhouse. I was not really know what is up to him for; but I can't believe in my eyes to see like that in my age; and I started feeling orgasm (play with my cock on my bike). I can remember clear: loves to look at ladies' dress, shoes, purse, etc. in Sears Catalogue, play and wear lady dress and high heel shoes. My mom was aware and wonder why I do that; but seem leave me alone. I have pictures of me with dress. I clear remember that.

I came to Alberta School for Deaf in Edmonton in 1956 and was frightened at first, then fantastic later. I remember in shower and bath with boys that I see all boys' penis in different size and shape. One night I slept with one deaf in bed in my primary wing at 6 years old, and had several boys with me until I was 17 years old.

So I first experiment to masturbate at age 10, then first anal intercourse (fucking) at 12, and first got fucked at 12 in deaf school. (In my puberty time I had few with girl during my teenage years; but not comfortable.)

So I have been come out since I was 20. In these days they allowed that age at 21 so I was 1 year early, and is very experiment for me what is feel like to be in gay club at my age. I felt it open into a new atmosphere for that kind of social for me because I gay. I did not think I'm the only 1 who is gay. I wrong. Many of us (deaf people) are! It delight me keep social and activities.

I now understand and be social with all gays and lesbians here problem also. It is fair, I think. And now AIDS is here on world, so

I understand and still educate in that event. I have new responsible in this for few years now. I became less sexual activities, but still social with them.

I work janitor midnight at hotel nightclub for 3 years; and I got used to that shift, but little hard because I have dog, Pekingese (her name is Li). I have to take her outside everyday that I sometime sleep little everyday, but happy to have a dog, my own home and myself what I am now.

I glad to tell you about myself, because I find it wonderful experiment in my life, but I not often go to deaf community very often because I work night. Keep me busy at home and my dog, so I still is happy.

"VICTOR"*

MORE LIGHTS, PLEASE

WHEN I WAS TWENTY-FIVE YEARS OLD, I had a good deaf friend at this school near Philadelphia, which I was attending at the time. He told me that he had Usher's syndrome [a condition that causes deafness and degenerative blindness]. He felt that I might have that, too, because I was deaf, and my sight was going.

I said, "I don't know what you mean by Usher's syndrome." I had seen blind people with canes and all that. I didn't want any part of that.

Much later, he kept saying, "You should see a doctor and see if he can do something about your eye problem."

So I went. A doctor at a university clinic analyzed my situation very carefully and said that I was legally blind and also that my test results indicated that I had Usher's syndrome. (The cause of my Usher's syndrome is unknown. Sometimes it happens genetically, sometimes not.)

I didn't know what to say.

I called my mother. "Do you know what Usher's syndrome means?"

"Yes. I know. Why?"

"My doctor told me that I have it."

"Yes, I know. It's not true. Don't worry."

"It's real." I was so angry that she had said, "Don't worry." It was really awful that I had Usher's syndrome. I was really angry, because I had gone to college to major in accounting. Everyone told me that it was not right for me, but I ignored them.

I got very depressed.

*This interview was conducted by the editor on September 10, 1992.

I left Philadelphia and moved to Boston, where I'd heard they had a better program called Mobility Orientation and I could receive computer training.

Someone from M.O. even came down to Philadelphia to see me, which was really nice. He said, "Come on up. Vocational Rehabilitation will help you. Don't worry."

I felt good. I had been to Boston, and I'd heard it was a pretty city. I was fed up with Philadelphia anyway. Boston was a much better gay city, of course. And so I went to school and work, and I played a lot. (Smile.)

✦

When I was a kid at my deaf residential school, many people made fun of me over and over again. They said: "Stop looking up above our heads. Look at me." I couldn't help it. They told me: "Stop thinking about women." "Stop dreaming about girls. Look at me now."

They made me so mad because I was frustrated with the whole thing. Everyone else was frustrated, too. Oh, I suffered so much at that school. Some made fun of me, others didn't; but I couldn't stand that school.

People also knew I had a balance problem. "You look like you're drunk. Stop it."

I said, "I'm not."

That made me so mad, too.

I asked my mother about my balance problem. She said it was sort of related to my deafness. At that time I didn't know anything about Usher's syndrome.

In college in Houston, I met my first lover. Max was a beautiful, black, hearing man, and he really fell in love with me. At that time I could still see fine at night. He knew about my vision and balance problems, but you know what he said? "Don't worry. I can take care of you."

That scared me a little. I was nineteen years old, and he understood my problems, even if he was in his mid-twenties with a good job. He said, "I will always respect you no matter what."

He really changed my life.

He infused me with confidence. He said, "Don't worry."

I decided to go steady with him. He knew sign language, and I loved him so much that it scared me.

I finished college, and he wanted me to stay on in Houston and find a job in accounting. I said, "Okay," but at the time I wasn't thinking in terms of anything permanent. I was so young and confused over my vision problem. But he kept saying, "Don't worry."

A year later I decided to move back to Chicago. I needed better schooling and Chicago had better public transportation.

He said, "Oh, don't go. I can support you here."

I didn't feel that was proper. I was then twenty years old, and my mother and family didn't know that I was gay. Both my gayness and my vision problem was in the closet.

I just didn't feel comfortable.

He kept saying, "Don't worry."

I quit my job anyway.

That got him so upset. He cried and he was so mad at me. He kept saying, "I can be your lover for life."

But I felt it was the wrong time. I said, "Wait."

Before I left, he cried so hard.

I felt so guilty about the whole thing, but I went to a university near my home for my B.S. in accounting.

I kept in close contact with Max, writing back and forth. He kept pleading with me to move back to Houston and be with him.

I still didn't feel ready, but I decided to visit him.

What happened was that my mother called him. You have to understand that in the early seventies I didn't know anything much about TDDs, and what's more, the TDDs were really old-fashioned — very bulky and noisy at that time.

When she called Max, she was put off by his voice. She could tell it was a gay person, and that made her mad.

She asked me, "Is your friend gay?"

I knew what she meant by the word, but I didn't say anything. I was so embarrassed. "How do you know?"

"He has a high-pitched voice. You should not be going way out to Houston to see your friend, because he isn't right for you."

"But he's my old friend."

Remember that my mother was paying for my flight, and so she cancelled the trip.

I felt so bad.

When I informed Max of the change in plans, he was upset and shocked.

My mother had said, "He says he misses you." That was when my mother began to suspect about me, but that didn't matter.

My relationship with him was over, and I never saw him again. Last I heard, he'd moved back to his hometown Milwaukee.

Partly because of him, my goal is to have a black or Puerto Rican lover. That first night I spent with Max was so beautiful. We'd met in the elevator at the YMCA where we were both living at the time. I can still remember every little thing we did in bed that night. This was back in 1972.

I miss the old days.

✦

Before, when I was attending a deaf school near Chicago, I was on the train home after school; I was thirteen or fourteen years old. I really, really had to go to the bathroom. So I went to one of the subway bathrooms where you had to drop in a nickel or something so I could use one of the stalls.

After I finished, I noticed men standing around. I thought that was odd. As I washed my hands, I noticed two men playing around with each other over near the toilet.

That made me so curious.

Watching them made me crazy, and I got so horny. Wow.

The next day I went back and I never stopped going ever since.

They gave me a blow job every day, and I loved it. If I was horny after school, and if my deaf friends whom I'd been jerking off with didn't want to jerk off, I went to the toilets. It was so easy, and it was more secretive. Eventually I got to know a lot of other subway toilets. It was 1965, or around there.

I loved it in those places.

And later on, in the Houston YMCA where I was staying, a lot of cruising went on in the bathrooms on each floor. I went all over them every night. I was afraid that Max would catch me, but this was before we had committed ourselves to each other. I was just looking for a hot time.

When Max said that he wanted a serious relationship with me, I was shocked. But I said, "Okay." He explained what a serious relationship meant, and so I cut down on my time in the toilets.

I went to the toilets because they almost always had good light. Bars were always dark, and what's more, I was not yet twenty-one. At that time, you had to be twenty-one to get into bars. It was either the toilets with bright lights or in some park when it'd be too dark for me to see.

My favorite toilets are still those Houston YMCA bathrooms.

✦

Just before I go into the toilets, I fold up my cane and tuck it inside my knapsack. I've found that I get better luck without the cane, so that's why I do it. Sometimes that doesn't work at all, but then sometimes I get lucky.

✦

I met my next lover in Chicago. A deaf friend of mine knew that I wanted a black or Puerto Rican lover, but he kept postponing on his promise to help me.

Finally he called me over for dinner.

I said, "Okay." I didn't know what he wanted. I thought the dinner was for fun.

When I arrived, I saw this cute boy. Wow. He was Spanish-looking. Wowowow ... I didn't expect to meet someone so good-looking.

At the dinner table we kept looking at each other.

After my host introduced us, we wrote back and forth. He was a hearing man from the Dominican Republic. He was so cute, and his name was Willy.

Then it was time for a movie. My host had a 16mm movie projector and had a captioned movie. There was a group of people, but Willy sat next to me, and that scared me a little.

Sure enough, in the dark, he caressed my leg. That made me so horny that I didn't pay any attention to the movie.

We started to make love. I didn't even look at anyone, because I couldn't see them in the dark. I didn't know that other people were watching us instead of the movie. That made me feel so embarrassed, and they were all laughing at us.

With a big smile, my host said, "You two go to bed. In the bedroom over there."

"Really?" It didn't feel proper to use a host's bedroom for sex.

But we went in there and made wonderful love.

After that night he gave me his address and phone number. TDDs were still not that prevalent yet, and it was so frustrating. My host and other friends helped me all over the city when I needed to call him. That was so hard, and *so* old-fashioned.

We met frequently, and became lovers for one year, which was wonderful.

But he had one problem: He kept looking at my body because he liked my penis. I was circumcised, and he wasn't. He wanted to have surgery so he could make his penis look the same as mine.

I said, "No, you don't have to copy my penis."

He still wanted circumcision.

I said, "No, you're silly."

He decided to have the surgical operation anyway.

I shrugged. "It's up to you."

He went to the hospital. After that our relationship turned sour. He was in constant pain, and he had to take drugs to lessen the pain. Worse yet, if he had an erection it was even more painful. I was frustrated with not having sex with him. That scared me, because I saw he was becoming a drug addict. That made me very nervous, and we got into a lot of fights. At one point he didn't even recognize me.

What's more, he knew where I was living with my mother. Once, I even invited Willy over to her house when she was off on vacation. I shouldn't have, but I did anyway to have sex. Now that he had become a drug addict, I didn't want him to show up at my mother's house.

I left him and Chicago for Philadelphia, where I became a college student.

One day he showed up at the front door of my house, waiting for me when I arrived home. "How did you get here? How did you know where I was living?" It turned out that my host had given him my address; he shouldn't have, but he did.

Anyway, he wanted us to get back together. He was sorry for what he'd done.

I said, "No. I don't feel it's right that you beat me in our fights."

He still wanted me back.

We got into this awful fight. I ended it finally with,

"O-U-T."

I never saw him again after that.

✦

I've met a lot of deaf gay men, and I've asked them out for a date. But they've always made excuses not to go out with me. I know why, and they don't even say it: they are not comfortable with my Usher's syndrome.

I can understand that, and I am not angry or upset over that.

Yet when I ask hearing dates out, they accept my vision problem. They always say, "What's more important is your heart."

So I see a very big difference of attitude toward deaf-blind gay men between deaf gay men and hearing gay men.

But something that frustrates me even more is that deaf people know how to communicate in sign language, and that hearing people don't know how to communicate. We have to write back and forth, and that means he has to be patient with me, and I have to be patient with him too. I just prefer a deaf lover or a hearing lover who knows how to sign.

But I should say that the recent National Rainbow Alliance of the Deaf (RAD) Conference in Dallas surprised me. I thought they wouldn't provide interpreters for the deaf-blind. [These interpreters sign in the deaf-blind person's hands what the deaf speakers are saying onstage.] But they did — finally. I was really impressed, and I hope to see that continued at future RAD conventions.

✦

I should add that I'm sometimes, still, angry with myself for having Usher's syndrome. If I didn't have it, my life would've been very different. I wish I could throw out my Usher's syndrome. I can accept being deaf, but my eyes — well, people are always looking at me. They look so uncomfortable when they see my cane. It used to bother me too, but so what.

Sometimes I look at a cute man, and then he gives me a look of shock. Then I feel put off by his look.

It's just not fair.

I hate using my cane, but it's better than getting hit in an accident.

✦

One time I wanted to go to a sex club, and I'd heard about this "JO Club." It was supposed to be good, clean, and very safe, so I asked my ex-lover to take me there. I knew it'd be dark as such places tend to be, and I didn't want to fall down the steps and hit my forehead. He agreed to show me around once so I could memorize my way around, and so then if I wanted to come back alone, I could.

One thing I found out right away was that it had too many steps all over the place. I thought if it had one floor instead of platforms here and there, I'd be all right. I didn't want to fall down the steps by mistake and have everyone look at me.

He left me finally, and I was alone. I tried to walk in the dark alongside the walls, but that made people there uncomfortable and they left that room.

Then I tried to join a jerk-off circle, but they all gave me the same expressions of discomfort. They left too.

It was so frustrating because I was just wasting my time.

Then I tried a gay porn movie theater. It was too dark.

All that was only once. I've asked my friends to help guide me around, but they all said no. They're too shy or too embarrassed, and they'd rather do those things privately.

Even personal ads haven't helped me much. I got many hearing dates, but that meant the same old thing over communication, writing back and forth. It's just so frustrating.

But I still hope I'll find the right person.

Last March I paid for an SSP [Special Support Provider] to come with me to Thailand. I had dreamed of going there for a long time, and it was finally time. My SSP did a lot of work for me, interpreting and guiding me around; he really did.

I discovered that the Thais — hearing or deaf — were much more open-minded about my Usher's syndrome. It didn't bother them at all. What mattered to them was my heart. That was a big culture shock.

There is one big difference between Thailand and America: Buddhism teaches people how to respect others, even if they are handicapped. They must respond more with love, and to them, a person's heart, personality, and communication are far more important than age or anything else. Americans are much more stuck-up, and they look down on people with Usher's syndrome, blacks, and so on.

Also in Thailand it was very easy to meet both hearing and deaf gay men. My SSP took me to the bars and the baths, and I found the people much more understanding of my Usher's syndrome. Those places were still dark, but at least they were more understanding.

✦

When I went to Boston for the first time, the special event was the Bicentennial in 1976. I loved it, and I fell in love with it. I met many men and tricked with them. I couldn't believe how easy it was to have sex. Wow — I loved it.

When I came back to Chicago, I felt something was wrong. My penis was itching all over, and the rest of my body itched too. I thought it was the result of hot weather here, or a change of weather between Boston and Chicago. The itching made me crazy, and I didn't know what to do.

I went to see the doctor. He analyzed me and said that I had the crabs. I was so embarrassed — I'd heard about them all the time, but I never thought I'd get them.

Worse yet, the doctor told my mother. She had wanted to know what was wrong with me; the itching had gone on for one week.

My mother had suspected that I was gay, of course, because Boston was well known for its gay people. "Did you meet someone there?"

I simply told her that I was bisexual.

She was really upset. "Shame on you!" She got so depressed.

Then she said, "If you're bisexual, it means you met someone dirty."

She went to see a psychiatrist, and then we went together. She wanted to know if it was possible for me to change me. I said, "Impossible."

But she still wasn't happy about me.

I moved to Philadelphia anyway. Then when I moved to Boston, my mother came out to visit me.

She saw that I had so many gay and lesbian friends, and they'd helped me out by picking her up at the airport — things like that. She said, "Your friends are really nice to you." I was also living with a hearing lover at the time, and she was impressed by how he had helped her around the kitchen. It was then she realized we were lovers, and she decided that it was best for me to be happy, period.

✦

A long time ago I met my only deaf lover at a RAD convention in Washington, D.C. He was so good-looking, and he was twenty years old.

We kept eying each other. I didn't mention my Usher's syndrome. He knew there was something different about me, but he was waiting for me to say something.

Then a group of deaf people wanted to go out to a bar.

I said, "I don't want to go to a bar. I prefer a different place."

He said, "I noticed that you seem to have a balance problem, and that you must have Usher's syndrome. Well, there's nothing wrong with that. You are a human being."

Wow. That made my heart warm...

Then he continued, "Let's go out and have a drink. Tell me about your life."

And that happened just on the first day!

DOROTHY MARDER

WOMEN IN ACTION

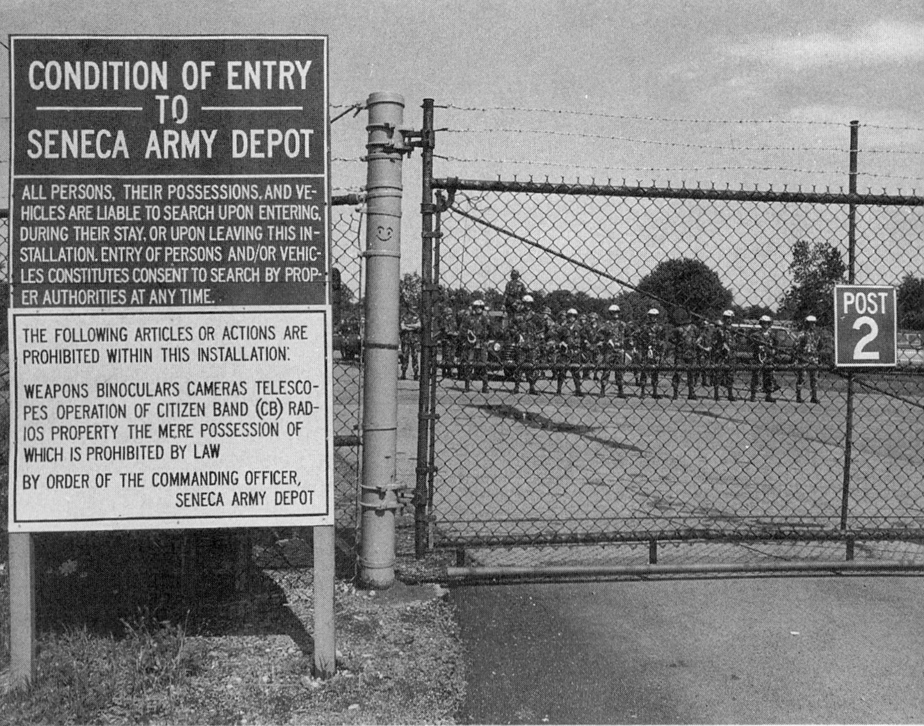

These pictures were taken at the Seneca Women's Encampment (August 1983) and the Pentagon's Women's Action (1980).

IS NO FUTU
CLEAR POW
WOMEN'S ENCAMPMENT

OP

FOR FITNESS
NO

WOMEN'S PENTAGON ACTION
November 16 & 17

WE ARE
DEFIANT

THREE

LAURA L. POST

THOUGHTS ON BEING A LESBIAN SEPARATIST ASL INTERPRETER

An interview with Marilyn Van Veersen

How to communicate with other Lesbians, how to understand each other, how to be inclusive, and how to form coalitions are pre-eminent questions in the feminist cultural network. We continue to educate ourselves and each other about disability and accessibility, race and ethnicity, age, size, socioeconomics, and sexuality. Nonetheless, despite superficial familiarity with sign language, the actual knowledge that hearing Lesbians have remains limited to signing "If It Wasn't for the Women" by Alix Dobkin, recognizing ASL interpreters who work alongside performers onstage, signing "I love you" at pride parades, or fingerspelling our own names.

Professional ASL interpeter Marilyn Van Veersen is one of a number of well-recognized interpreters at Lesbian events all across North America. Through her creative interpreting at women's festivals and concerts, she has introduced the beauty of ASL to hearing Lesbians, and has brought Lesbian music and spoken Lesbian performances to Deaf Lesbians. Through the Lesbian ASL intensive courses that she had planned and generated, Marilyn has helped to advance a mutual cultural understanding between Deaf and hearing Lesbians, seeking to demolish the barriers that so unnecessarily separate Deaf and hearing Lesbians.

How did you learn ASL and about Deaf culture?

I took two years of ASL training, then interpreter training for two more years. After I graduated from all that was offered in school, I continued to take the same classes, part-time and at night, when those classes were taught by different Deaf teachers.

In school, I studied the culture of the Deaf in a class titled, simply, "Deaf Culture." The first time I took the class, it was taught by a hearing person, a Ph.D. who worked with Deaf Media. She brought in a lot of Deaf lecturers because she couldn't represent herself as an authority on Deaf culture. The second time I took the class, it was experimental: half were Deaf professionals, and the other half were hearing students of Deaf culture. The mix was excellent, because the Deaf and the hearing faced each other with questions that were usually never posed. This was like a graduate seminar, but with no teacher; we students sat in a circle, asked each other questions, and deliberated about the possibilities of cultural misunderstandings.

I also took a field study class on cultural conflict. At the time, I was living with a Deaf person and keeping a journal on interchanges between us that were awkward or difficult, or that just didn't seem to work at all. I remember, once, I was at home studying; when my roommate came in from work, I looked up from my books, signed, "Hi," and went back to my reading. My roommate just became furious. She walked over, put her hands on my books, and said, "What's wrong with you? What did you do today?"

I told her briefly what I had done: gone to class, come home, studied. That didn't seem to be okay with her; she went into a description of her day, in minute detail. I thought she was being cranky with me, so I put the incident in my journal and brought it to my professor. She laughed and told me that the misunderstanding between my roommate and me was absolutely cultural, not personal. I learned that in Deaf culture one of the most important values is sharing information. I had broken this rule and been extremely rude by not stopping what I was doing in deference to this higher value.

Did you think that when you first started to study ASL, you'd end up as an ASL interpreter?

No. I have always been fascinated with language, and as a political dyke separatist, I saw long ago that English was a tool of the patriarchy and that I couldn't think of the Lesbian world in this linear, emotionally indirect language. I felt limited by having to describe my experiences in English. I had learned Spanish and a little Italian, and I found more emotional freedom in those Romance languages. I also recognized that English-speaking America is a stubbornly monolingual culture, and that English is the language of the "top dog" mentality. When I saw ASL for the first time, I felt it in my body and felt drawn to it, connected with it.

What was your first experience of ASL?

I first saw ASL at a music festival in 1980; I watched Shirley Childress Johnson, an ASL interpreter interpret for Sweet Honey in the Rock, a performing group.

When did you start studying ASL?

In 1985.

It took you five years between first experiencing ASL, loving it, and embarking on your own program of study?

In the early 1980s, ASL classes just weren't to be found. I did know some people who could teach me signed English, but I knew that wasn't the same.

Your ASL program was two years?

Yes, it was a two-year, full-time program at a community college. During the two years, I was entirely immersed in ASL and didn't do anything else.

How did you learn Lesbian-specific ASL? Was it formally taught to you?

I wasn't taught any specifically Lesbian signs, even though, since I was studying in Berkeley, one of my teachers was an out Lesbian. Because the program was so intense, and because I was a Lesbian separatist, most of my friends were from the Deaf Lesbian community. It was, actually, through my Deaf Lesbian friends that I learned Lesbian-specific ASL because Lesbian-specific signs are never seen in the classroom.

I found that, as soon as I knew enough ASL to communicate, even rudimentarily — this was during the second semester — I was asked to interpret in all kinds of situations, such as conversations, job interviews, doctor's appointments. It was too early in my studies, and I didn't want to do it. I'd ask my Deaf Lesbian friends, "Why don't you get a real interpreter?"

Their response was interesting. They said, "I would rather have a friend, whom I trust, than a stranger." But I think now that I was trusted *because* I was a Lesbian. It was such a complicated procedure for my Deaf friends to deal with the hearing world that the additional burden of having to deal with a straight interpreter was just too much.

All the time, though, in casual situations such as parties, hearing Lesbians would want to chat with the Deaf Lesbians, and they'd ask me to interpret for them. Yet those weren't the situations that proved the most difficult for me. The ethical dilemmas came when I was asked to intepret in specialized ASL, for which I wasn't prepared — for example, when a Deaf Lesbian friend was in the hospital.

How did you make the transition from being a casual interpreter to being a professional interpreter?

The more I learned about ASL, the more it suited me as a Lesbian, and the more I wanted to make it part of my mind's function, and the more I wanted to use it forever. The only way I could see that this would happen was for me to become an interpreter.

I knew by my third semester that I wanted to be an interpreter, and that I wanted to work with Lesbians. The director of the program told me that I would never work as an interpreter professionally because I looked like a Lesbian, and no one would hire me. She also told me that I was too old to learn the language (I was forty). Years after I finished her program (with a 4.0 average), she came to me and asked if she could film me interpreting onstage for a promotional video.

How did you break into the business of professional ASL interpreting?

I was being pulled to interpret before I was done with my training, but I wanted to wait until I was skilled enough not to repeat mistakes. I actually started interpreting professionally in my last semester of training, due to dire financial necessity, by working at another community college.

As for doing ASL interpretation within the feminist cultural network for the first time, I called the ASL coordinator at a women's festival and volunteered to work as a workshop interpreter. Then, I asked her to let me have a shot at interpreting on the Day Stage, and she said yes.

How do you decide what to charge for your ASL interpreting services?

That's difficult, because the fee can't be based on preparation time, since preparation can take a month. The fee also can't be based on onstage time, since the actual service time might be an hour. Usually I negotiate with event producers, but the rates of pay can differ across the United States and from festival to festival. My starting rate is based on a minimum fair exchange, and I always factor in that I love doing this work; it's my life work.

But I have to say that interpreting professionally is so incredibly involved. Neither the Deaf community nor the hearing community knows how technically challenging and time-consuming interpreting onstage can be, and I find it irksome that a performer might get paid $2,000 while I stand next to her and might get paid $200.

What have been some difficulties of being a professional ASL interpreter for Lesbian events?

I still run into producers who believe they can't "afford" to have Lesbian ASL interpeters. I believe that ASL interpretation is absolutely essential for Lesbian culture — we can't afford to leave out the Deaf Lesbians. Other producers assume that I am only a "helper" to be thanked for volunteering, instead of a specially trained professional who should be paid for her services.

What have been some of the benefits, to you, of being a professional ASL interpreter for Lesbian events?

For me, there is joy in interpreting a Lesbian comic, and hearing Deaf Lesbians laugh, or interpreting Lesbian intelligentsia and seeing the understanding ripple among the Deaf Lesbians, or seeing them sign along with a well-loved Lesbian classic song.

So many hearing Lesbians are becoming interested in Deaf Lesbians and in ASL — not to be interpreters or in any way to do what I do — but to be able to communicate with Deaf Lesbian sisters. I think it is vital for our Lesbian culture that we all understand that women who grew up thinking in ASL — this beautiful, body-centered language — have visionary possibilities lacking in hearing Lesbians who grew up thinking in English.

GREGG BROOKS

DOUBLE PLEASURE

HERE ARE TEN REASONS why Deaf-Deaf relationships are better than Deaf-hearing relationships:

1. Communication

There is almost no room for misunderstanding when two lovers communicate in the same language, and in this case, ASL enables the two lovers to become fuller persons.

2. Love

It's much more natural between Deaf lovers, for they know and appreciate what it's like to be different and yet can share the same culture.

3. Trust

It's a very important part of anyone's life, but knowing that they come from the same culture and share the same language helps them develop trust more quickly. With a hearing partner, it's much harder because of the difference in cultural backgrounds.

4. Pride

Knowing that two lovers share the same cultures, such as Deaf culture and gay culture, is a very special gift. I've always claimed that being Deaf and gay is a double pleasure, not a double handicap.

5. Non-Paternalism

There is less of a chance for a paternalistic relationship to develop. When there are two lovers from different cultures, one tends to paternalize the other.

6. Leadership

When two lovers come from the same culture, they tend to be more active in the Deaf community; thus it becomes a plus for the Deaf and gay community.

7. Understanding

We become more appreciative of other cultures by knowing who we are and what we are. In many cases, when a Deaf person has a hearing lover, he ignores the Deaf community or becomes snooty. (This is very true of several relationships I've known here in L.A.)

8. Companionship

When two cultures clash, companionship is no longer there, and negative feelings are often created. A Deaf lover tends to lose out more in terms of friends if he is forced to associate with his hearing lover's friends all the time.

9. Friendship

The Deaf know the other Deaf people for years, whereas hearing friends tend to disappear.

10. Acceptance

When there are two Deaf lovers, Deaf society tends to accept them more fully. (Strangely enough, if two hearing lovers happen to mix with Deaf people, they are more easily accepted into Deaf society than a Deaf and hearing couple would be.)

EDWARD THERIAULT

THE ZEBRA

I ONCE HAD A DREAM about a vast cowfield not far behind my childhood home's backyard. In my dream, instead of cows on the field, there was this lone zebra on a quest for truth. His pain struck me: his pain of being tattooed in black-and-white stripes, and from peering through a fence at the distance between two separate houses of a deaf family signing like devils and a hearing family talking like saints.

Their neighbors grew alarmed when they saw the wandering zebra, but no one dared pet the animal while he roamed the field.

Suddenly, the blue sky thundered, forcing the neighbors to rush back inside their houses. The zebra leapt out of the field and galloped past the lake, finally entering the mountains for solitude. As he shed his tears, he begged the Lord, "Why do I have to live with these stripes?"

After I woke up, I became so obsessed with the zebra that I sat staring out the window of my family's sundeck room to try to catch a glimpse of him in the cowfield. Disappointed to see a barren field, I wanted to run out of the house to find and embrace my new best friend and whisper, "It's okay. Cry, curse, scream, laugh — but you cannot escape the *gift* of your stripes."

For days afterwards, I thought of nothing but the zebra. I gradually realized that in the dream *I* was the zebra, that the zebra represented what I am in my life. That is, I am hard-of-hearing, often torn between the deaf and hearing worlds.

Being hard-of-hearing, I feel like a misfit. Like a zebra, if my hearing aid is turned off, or if I'm talking with a deaf person, the black stripes represent my isolation from the hearing world. Black is dark, and dark is lonely. The white stripes connote the times when my hearing aid is on, for white is clear and bright, standing out in our dark world.

✦

After a nine-year absence from the deaf world, during which I transferred to a public school and graduated in 1984, I went to Northern Essex Community College in Haverhill, Massachusetts. Arriving at Northern Essex, I had long abandoned sign language; then someone told me about a small hearing-impaired program on campus.

My counselor put me in a deaf classroom with a deaf male teacher. When he asked me to read a paragraph from the textbook, I wanted to crawl under the desk at the idea of signing in front of those students who were better signers than me. I politely asked a classmate, who was a hard-of-hearing adept signer, to explain my circumstances to the teacher.

I'll never forget the Nazi evilness on my teacher's face as he signed unapologetically, "Too bad." I was appalled. How would he feel if I used my voice without signing and read that paragraph? He would've pounded his fists on the desk.

Well, too bad.

The memory of my first deaf teacher's cruel remark haunted me more than the humiliation I'd endured in front of my hearing classmates. I refused to have a deaf teacher again.

It was then I discovered that some deaf people dislike hard-of-hearing people because we can talk to hearing people and hear partially. I must have quarrelled with at least twenty-five deaf students during my last three years of college. If a deaf person and I get into a clash, I just talk without signing. It is my way of getting back at my deaf teacher.

But then none of these deaf students were aware of my background. I grew up in a Salingeresque shadow in a hearing public school. J.D. Salinger's *Catcher in the Rye* was my Bible. I understood Holden Caulfield, the hero of that novel. And I was too busy reading all the time, learning new words, and not falling behind in what my hearing peers had already learned. I didn't have the time to lose my virginity, or get smashed over the weekend with my hearing classmates. And I resented deaf students who were able to graduate together from a high school where they had four good years of parties, proms, adventures, and so on, when I had simply lived on books.

✦

What I've learned about being hard-of-hearing is that I always had to be ready to defend myself against hearing or deaf people pressuring me to label myself one way or the other.

The longing I had to be accepted by both worlds has created tremendous difficulties. I found I couldn't allow myself to socialize with either deaf or hearing people one hundred percent. So I learned how to talk for the hearing world, and I learned how to sign for the deaf world. I've tried to split my socializing in half with both worlds. Actually, I find that I hang out more with hard-of-hearing friends because they understand what it's like to be stuck in this tug-of-war.

Why?

Because I am bombarded with hearing — and reading — the word "deaf" in the media, novels, and deaf newsletters. Deaf people have more clout than the hard-of-hearing. At one time, two hard-of-hearing female students quit Northern Essex Community College because they were fed up being in a school-sponsored "deaf club." Should these two girls be angry? Of course. They earned the right to be livid, having to live under the deaf shadow. There were no hard-of-hearing clubs at all.

Can you recall a panel discussion on hard-of-hearing people on Oprah, Phil, Geraldo, Sally Jesse, and other talk shows? What about movies? Novels? Television shows? I don't care if Jane Wyman (of "Falcon Crest"), Lou Ferrigno (of "The Incredible Hulk"), Nanette Fabray (of "One Day at a Time"), Richard Dysart (of "L.A. Law"), Leslie Nielsen (of *The Naked Gun* movies), or Ronald Reagan are hard-of-hearing. What about us, the hard-of-hearing who are grappling with being sandwiched between the deaf and hearing worlds?

✦

Being hard-of-hearing and gay is a double burden. Like the zebra, I am torn between dating a hearing or deaf man. The black stripes represent my struggle with the narrow minds of straight people, both hearing and deaf. The white stripes celebrate my freedom to be openly gay and comfortable with deaf, hard-of-hearing, and hearing gay men.

When it comes to dating, I risk the chance of being seen by deaf gay men as a hearing-thinker if I hang out with hearing gay men. One of my dearest hard-of-hearing gay friends won't date deaf or hard-of-hearing gay men because deaf gossip travels so fast; he dates only hearing gay men.

In a gay bar, I witnessed several gay nonsigning hard-of-hearing men who knew nothing about deaf culture. They were the ones who touched me the most. One of them became baffled when he caught my friend and me talking to a hearing gay man who'd thought we were deaf. And this hard-of-hearing man mumbled to us, "You can talk?" My friend was very critical of this stranger who'd hung out with a coterie of gay friends.

Why?

My friends felt that the stranger should learn sign language and stop imitating a hearing person. I defended the hard-of-hearing man's choice of not signing or even learning sign language, because I was once in his shoes. And who are the deaf or hearing people to determine what is most beneficial to the hard-of-hearing people, be they gay, straight, signer, or nonsigner? Hearing people have one choice: the hearing world. Deaf people have one choice: the deaf world. The hard-of-hearing people are entitled to make their own decisions.

✦

I get a big kick whenever a hearing gay man struggles to talk to me thinking that I'm totally deaf. He is often shocked when I respond to him with my voice just like a hearing person. In a way, it's fun to be hard-of-hearing because hearing gay men have no way of knowing if I'm deaf or hard-of-hearing.

Still, hard-of-hearing gay men have to play a kind of Russian roulette with deaf and hearing gay men. We can fool anyone.

There were times when I pretended I was not hard-of-hearing and gay. I impersonated the hearing, the deaf, and the straight, and I got fed up with it all.

Someday I will take time off from work and visit the zebra at the zoo to see how he is doing. Chances are, he will know what I know: what it takes to stay stalwart and sane.

EDWARD THERIAULT

THE SCARFACED LOVER

AFTER WATERING THE PLANTS in his bedroom, David sat on the bed with his huge water gun to admire the plants. They were ten feet tall, and in between them on the wall was the Richard Avedon picture of Nastassia Kinksi with a snake wrapped around her body. Suddenly the birds in his cage screeched, and he squirted his water gun at them.

"Shuddup, it's Sunday," David said grumpily. He then realized that the birds were responding to the telephone ringing in the living room. He ran, carrying his water gun, to the phone.

"Hello?"

"It's about time you answered the phone. Keep your *goddamn* hearing aid on at all times," Ken replied. Ken was his brother, and only two years older than David.

"My hearing aid's been on since morning," David said defensively. "So what's cooking?"

"I'm coming over tonight at seven. Don't make supper — I'll pick up some Kentucky Fried Chicken."

"Well..." What else could David say?

"Good. See you tonight. Bye." Click.

David slammed the receiver down. He squirted his water gun at the phone. He felt rage rise, then explode into panic. His naked chest steamed with sweat. He squirted at himself — his chest, face, hair — to control his own temper. Then he dropped the water gun, flopped down on the couch, and squeezed a pillow against his stomach.

David and Brad had been living together for two years; David was hard-of-hearing, and Brad was also hard-of-hearing. They'd met each other on the subway. And the strange thing was, both Brad and Ken had scars on their faces. Neither one of them knew about the other — not much, anyway. David rarely mentioned his brother to Brad, or his lover to Ken.

He sighed and began repeating Connie Francis's "Who's Sorry Now" on his way to the kitchen. He opened the refrigerator and took out a dozen eggs. He cracked them, dumped the eggs into the blender, and pressed the button. Then he turned the TV on in the living room, found a channel that had nothing but white static, and left it on. He went to his bedroom and found a space between stations on his radio and turned it up; the crackling sounds of static filled the apartment.

He felt good. He wanted to feel fully this disorientation of noise coming from the blender, the TV he couldn't always understand, and the radio he couldn't always understand. He walked from one room to another, trying to make sense of his situation.

Brad walked into the apartment with bags of groceries. With headphones on his ears, he pushed the door open with his ass and belted out "How Will You Know?" at full volume along with Whitney Houston. David passed by him in the living room heading toward the kitchen, and Brad followed him, still singing all the way.

In the kitchen Brad took off his headphones. He glanced at the ear-numbing noises all around the apartment. He ran to shut off the TV, the radio, and the blender. "David, what were you trying to do?"

"I'm trying to understand why life is so complicated."

"Well, you sure are a complicated person. What's inside the blender?"

"Eggs."

"Eggs! At four-thirty in the afternoon?"

"For breakfast tomorrow morning."

"You must be so excited about tomorrow." Brad looked inside the blender. "I can't eat all that. Too much cholesterol."

"I'll give an invitation to every tenant in this building."

"This is not a shelter for the homeless."

"It's my way of showing that good neighbors do exist."

"David! Something's wrong. What is it?"

"Ken's coming here at seven."

"Wonderful! I've been waiting to meet your brother. He's the only one in your family I haven't met."

"Tonight will be history."

"You don't look too happy."

"I'm fine." David could still hear "Who's Sorry Now" in his mind.

"Is there something I should know about Ken that you haven't told me?"

"You won't need to defend me."

David went into the bathroom and locked himself in. He stood in a daze and urinated on the floor next to the toilet. He flushed the toilet without realizing that the toilet bowl was still clean, put down the top cover, and sat on it.

An ambulance sped by their apartment. David got up and looked out the bathroom window, thinking it was Ken inside the ambulance again. He closed his eyes, kneeling before the bathtub. Ken's scar had happened some fifteen years ago when Ken was ten; David was only eight at the time ... He screamed, "Please! Go away. I don't want this nightmare for the rest of my life. Please, please, Ken, stop crying." David covered his ears in an attempt to block out the sounds from his flashback.

David looked up at the sound of pounding on the door.

It was Brad. "Are you okay, David?"

"Yeah. I'm okay."

"Well, come on out."

David washed his face to look fresh before he stepped out of the bathroom with a fake smile.

"You were in the bathroom for so long I thought you were gonna OD."

David scratched his head, avoiding looking at Brad's scars. "I'll write up the invitations." Ken's scar looked like a flat pink tapeworm; Brad had three scars — on his nose, forehead, and right cheek.

"Hey, let's listen to our favorite songs." They had recorded them on a blank tape when they moved together into this apartment, and ended up listening to it once a month, usually on a Sunday.

"No. You go ahead without me."

Brad frowned and sighed on his way to the bedroom.

In the living room David fell back on the sofa and rubbed his eyes. He opened the side table's drawer and pulled out a pen, some white stationery, and envelopes. The first song to echo from the bedroom was Stephanie Mills singing "I Never Knew Love Like This Before."

A spider crawled out from behind an old picture hanging on the wall of David and Ken taken when they were very young. David watched the spider moving rapidly as David struggled to concentrate on writing the invitations. He tapped his pen on his thigh instead.

He gave up any illusions of writing. Besides, he could feel Brad's jumping around and dancing in the bedroom. He looked up at the clock. It was six o'clock. Only one hour left. David listened carefully to the next song, "Freeway of Love" by Aretha Franklin. Then he listened to Donna Summer's "Bad Girls," Prince's "Kiss," Barbra Streisand's "The Way He Makes Me Feel," and Stevie Wonder's "I Just Called to Say I Love You"...

After half an hour, David heard the sharp buzzer *ennnr.* He leaped up from the couch and ran the three flights downstairs to check who the visitor was. Because he was easy to lipread, Ken was able to mouth clearly, "Open the goddamn door!"

David thought of warning his lover about Ken's arrival, but then Ken would say, *"Goddamn* it, open the door, willya?" He opened the door, and the smell of Kentucky Fried Chicken wafted past him. They shook hands, and on the way upstairs they chatted about the weather and the latest family news.

Inside the bedroom Brad was singing along with Irene Cara's "Oh, What a Feeling," and he was dancing with his eyes closed behind the plants.

David felt slightly embarrassed for Brad as he brought Ken in to introduce them to each other. He leaned over to shut the tape off.

Brad opened his eyes and quickly saw Ken. Blushing, he stepped out from behind the plants.

Ken laughed, but stopped when he saw Brad's scars.

Wiping the sweat off his brow, Brad was more shocked than Ken and did not take his eyes off Ken's scar.

"This is my brother Ken, and Ken, this is my..." David couldn't believe he'd forgotten his own lover's name.

"Hi. I'm Brad. How're you doing?"

"Good. Nice to meet you."

Silence pervaded the bedroom, and David put his hands inside his pockets and looked down at the floor.

"So, you are not deaf. You're hard-of-hearing just like David. You sing real good," Ken said.

"Thanks."

"Well ... are we going to eat?" David mumbled.

They both laughed.

"We can eat in the living room."

Somehow both men found this funny, and they laughed.

As Ken left the bedroom, Brad grabbed David's arm and signed without using his voice, "You're in big trouble with me tonight."

They ate the chicken that Ken had brought.

No one said a word.

Ken got up and turned on the Bruins game on TV. It was odd in a way, because David and Ken used to play local hockey for years, and David had a big crush on Ray Bourque, Number Seventy-seven and captain of the Bruins. Bourque also had a scar on his face, but David couldn't recall where.

With each bite of chicken, Brad gave David a mean Linda Blair's *Exorcist* look.

"Do you have any napkins?" Ken asked.

"On the kitchen counter."

A second later, Ken shouted, "There are no napkins."

David rolled his eyes and got up. He pulled more napkins out of the kitchen cabinet.

On his way out Ken whispered, "I'm surprised."

"What?"

"You know what." Ken nodded in disgust, turned off the TV, and sat down in his chair.

Alone in the kitchen, David signed, "Who's sorry now? Oh, Connie, please forgive me." Out of the corner of his eye he watched both Brad and Ken.

They simply wiped their faces and they stared coldly at the blank TV screen.

David cupped his hands below his nose and thought, "Connie, give me the strength to carry on the show." Back in the living room he looked at both Ken and Brad. "Is everything all right?"

"No. I mean ... yes," Brad answered.

"Fine," Ken said.

After a few minutes of silence, David realized he couldn't take the suspense anymore. "Ken, tell me how you found out my address."

"Mom gave me the directions to your apartment."

"I told her not to give it to you!"

"Well," Brad hissed, "that explains everything to me."

"What happened to your face?" Ken looked bluntly at Brad.

"My father and I got into a nasty fight. He called me deaf-and-dumb and other names like that. He was angry because I wasn't a hearing person, even though I could talk and hear pretty well. Well, shit, it wasn't enough for him. I called him, 'You fuckin' father from hell. It's your fault the way I am.' He was real — I mean, *real* pissed off. He pushed me through the sliding window door. My mother filed for divorce the very next day."

"You should've sent him to jail for that," Ken said.

"Well, what about *your* scar?"

"David, why don't you tell him?" Ken looked away.

"I can't. It's your story."

"No, it's not. It's *our* story."

David sighed. "All right. That night, Dr. Seuss was on TV. My sister Janice and our babysitter Beth were busy making brownies. I was watching TV and feeling awful about those goldfish — I remember Dr. Seuss being cruel to them. You see, I had two goldfish in my tank that was the size of a spin top. Ken happened to be in the kitchen. I decided to take the tank out of my bedroom and put it in front of the living room TV set. Ken raced down the hallway as I dashed out of my bedroom. Boom. The tank smashed through his face. His left cheekbone poked through the skin, and Ken was screaming the whole time. I just freaked out when I saw the whole thing happen. I stood there feeling totally helpless and worthless. I didn't care about the goldfish gasping and trying to move around on the floor, or even the blood on the rug."

"It was an accident. You didn't hear me running down the hallway."

"I know that, but if only I could hear..."

"Were you as close as brothers?"

"Never," David said. "We fought like buffalos after the accident."

"David, are we pals now?"

David didn't know what to say.

"How do you feel about the scar?"

"I didn't like it at first. But it became a great way to pick up girls. A great conversation piece," Ken winked at his brother. "Thanks to David."

Brad winced. The whole issue of being scarred so plainly for all the world to see had sickened him to death.

Ken looked at him. "What about you, Brad?"

"I *hate* my scars!"

Dead silence. Again.

David left them to sit down on the floor and began darkening the white letters inside the red box on the cover of *TV Guide.* He felt both their stares as he filled in the letters neatly. Done, he decided to draw a moustache and a Groucho Marx cigar on Roseanne Arnold's face.

Ken suddenly pulled the pen out of his brother's hand. "Don't hide your feelings from us."

"What?"

"You know what I'm talking about."

"No, I don't."

"All right. Did you fall for Brad because of his scars?"

"Yes."

"Why?"

"I've always been attracted to scarfaces. I find them sexy, erotic, and dangerous."

"Would you still have fallen for Brad if he didn't have a scar?"

"I don't know. Probably not, I guess."

"David. Why scarfaces?"

"I don't know. Maybe it's my guilt telling me that I must care for and love scarfaces after what I'd done to you."

"Well, that's news to me," Brad hissed again. "You're criminally insane. I can't believe you hid this from me for two years." He picked up the *TV Guide* and threw it at David. "Am I the first scarface you've slept with?"

"You expect me to answer that question in front of my brother?"

"Yeah."

"No. The first one was a bisexual scarface, but I was more lucky to have found you."

"Did you tell that bisexual guy about Ken?"

David shook his head no.

"Anything else that I don't know about you?" Brad's voice rose to a high pitch.

"You know I had this huge crush on Tom Berenger, who had this scar on his face in the movie *Platoon*. Well, I must've watched that movie at least thirty times and I've always watched it when you're not home. I guess he was my secret fantasy hero."

"Him?" Ken burst into laughter.

"Where did you hide the videotape?" Brad was bristling.

"Hold it. I'm outta here." Ken headed for the door. "I don't want to get trapped between the two of you."

"Okay. See you at Cousin Marie's wedding."

"Yeah. Bring Brad with you. I hope we all can sit together and talk about something else."

The second Ken closed the door, Brad turned to David. "David."

"What?"

"If my scar really turns you on, okay. But I want you to know that I'm not one big scar. There's more than that here, you know?"

"Yes, you're right. For a long time I was ashamed of my obsession with scars. I thought I was the only one with that kind of thing, but I realize that I'm just like anybody else. There's absolutely nothing wrong with my little preference."

"David. Tell me the truth. If Ken wasn't your brother, would you go after him?"

"Brad!" David hurled the *TV Guide* at him.

"It's only a question."

"Ask me when I'm forty."

"David."

"Yeah?"

"Let's watch Tom Berenger and make love," Brad said with a wink. "I think it's time I got acquainted with the naughty little scarface in you."

"NANCY"*

CURIOSITY FOUND THE CAT

I WAS STRAIGHT, very straight, even with my secret lesbian attractions, until I was twenty-one years old.

Sure, I had many gay male friends. Even my ex-boyfriend, back in my deaf residential high school, was bisexual. A lot of people tried to warn me about his gayness, so I asked him about it.

"I don't want to talk about it," he said.

Two years later, after we broke up, I found out that he had been having sex with other men during our relationship. That made me feel so heartbroken.

Later on, I happened to date a lot of bisexual boys, and I became curious what it'd be like to sleep with another woman. I was just curious.

So after I broke up with one boyfriend, my gay friend said, "Come on, let's go out to a gay bar." He knew I was very depressed.

"Sure," I said. I wanted to do something that would make me forget about my ex-boyfriend.

He took me out there to the bar, and I found it all so interesting. I watched a few lesbians make out, and I was *so* curious.

Three or four months later I asked one of my lesbian friends, "Could you teach me your sexual experiences?"

"Do you mean you want me to teach you sex? No, no."

Yeah, I asked it like that. I was just curious. I said, "It's fine if you don't want to."

Eventually we got involved anyway. When she came on to me, I was scared. But I felt so good at the same time. Whereas with men I felt scared too, but I didn't feel good. My heart was beating so

*This interview was conducted by the editor on July 28, 1992.

hard when I first slept with her. But my body went, "My God, this feels so good."

✦

I'm getting tired of drifting around with one-night stands over the last five years. After my first lover — not the first woman I slept with, but the one I slept casually with six years later — I find myself getting tired of it all.

I mean, sometimes I'm not. Then sometimes I am. I just need someone to *be* there for me, that's all.

Bars bother me sometimes. I mean, many women don't wear bras and they act like they don't care about what the world thinks. At the gay pride march, for instance, some women march topless. I don't want everyone to think that's a stereotype, or get the idea that gay people think about nothing but sex, sex, sex. Gay people have other feelings besides sex, just the same as straight people.

Even sex between gay people is similar to straight people. I even know a straight couple who enjoy anal sex. The woman gives her boyfriend anal sex by using a dildo; he doesn't like having sex with men, but he likes having anal sex with just her.

Once, a long time ago, when my mother did my laundry, she checked my pants and she found this letter. She should've just left it in my room, but she took it out and *read* it.

That day she looked really cranky.

I asked her, "What's wrong? Are you having problems with my father?"

"No." Then she said, "You are sick!"

"What? What do you mean?" She knew I had been a drug addict, so I thought maybe she was upset over drugs.

"You've been with another woman."

In my mind I went "Aikkk!" I suppressed my own reaction.

"I think you should go see a psychiatrist."

"No, I won't. You and I should go see a psychiatrist together."

My mother looked at me and didn't know what to say. This happened four or five years ago, and she hasn't talked about it since then.

That makes me so angry. I want her to accept me for who I am. I've accepted her for who she is, so why can't she accept me?

✦

Sometimes hearing people have come up to me and said that they want to learn sign language. I say, "I'm not going to help you. You go take a course in sign language. I've taken speech therapy, so you should do the same. It's your responsibility, not mine."

They say, "You're so mean."

I say, "I'm tired of teaching all the time and having people forget the signs. It's just a waste of time."

✦

I prefer feminine but sporty women. I think someone like Chris Evert, the tennis star, is so good-looking. I prefer dark hair — black or brown — and race doesn't matter. My ideal woman would have a sense of humor and independence as well. I really want an open relationship in which my partner and I have sex with other women, but at the same time support each other. I tried to find a woman who wouldn't mind that, but it's really hard.

✦

Once, I was with a deaf woman who was a one-night stand, and people had never seen me kiss a woman. I always kissed women in private, but that night in the bar I just kissed her, danced dirty with her, and played around with her. (This was up in Rochester, New York, where I was attending the National Technical Institute of the Deaf.)

The next day my friends said, "I never knew you were that kind of woman. We were looking at you, and we couldn't believe that you were making out like that!"

After that I never acted so wild in public again.

✦

I hate it when people come up to me and say, "Your signs are so beautiful. I'm so sorry. Your signs are so beautiful." And then they try to make all kinds of weird gestures. "I'm so sorry..."

I give them a funny look. "It's no problem. It's no big deal being deaf."

✦

I wish that more deaf gay people would accept the unusual sexual proclivities of other deaf individuals. For example, if a deaf gay person likes S&M and leather, other deaf gay people gossip and give him a bad name. Deaf gay people should not judge others and oppress them.

Deaf people should be more involved in the hearing world. Communication is a two-way street.

"MICHAEL"

SNOWFLAKES

FOR THE FIRST TEN YEARS of my life, being deaf didn't make me feel different. Very early, my parents knew something was "not right" with me and they took me to every big-city doctor in the West. Several said that I was "slow." Others went further, saying I was mentally retarded. Fortunately, my parents weren't convinced. When I was two and a half, a doctor diagnosed my deafness. He recommended a hearing aid, audiological training, and speech therapy — along with lots of love and attention.

At the age of five, my father took me to a big, colonnaded building where I met a group of seven boys and girls playing in a small courtyard. I fit quite nicely into this group since we all had hearing aids and the same speech and language training. We shared many lessons together, developed our own homemade sign language to communicate privately, and had fun challenging our teachers. We also challenged each other and competed for the spotlight in school plays, television interviews, and awards ceremonies.

Sometime at the end of the fourth grade, my mother announced that I would be going to a new school. We went for a visit. For the first time in my life, I realized I was different. I was placed with hearing peers in regular classes. The confidence and pride I had in the school of the deaf were no longer there. They were replaced with anxiety and fear. For the next two years, I couldn't always follow the teachers, nor could I join in many of the student activities. My A's and B's in my old school became C's and D's in the new school. During this time my only comfort was reading, which was no longer a chore but a welcome escape.

I found my high school years less stressful, mainly because I was with the same group of students I'd been with since fourth grade, and I played center for the junior varsity and varsity basketball teams. The dedication of my teachers was extraordinary; they made themselves available for additional assistance when I needed it after school hours. But I still had no contact with other deaf people, so I was less aware of what I was missing.

After graduating from high school, I built upon my ability to function independently in the hearing world. Up until then my parents were always in the background, providing encouragement and tutoring me. Since my college was some 150 miles from home, I was really on my own. My first semester was full of frustrations, including a 1.9 grade point average (GPA), few friends, difficult-to-follow professors, and no social life. But my final semester was full of accomplishment — a 4.0 GPA, many friends, supportive professors, and a full social life.

Even then, two thoughts pestered me throughout my undergraduate years. The first involved my future vocation: What was I going to do with my life? The second involved my sexual orientation: was I a "normal" red-blooded American boy or not?

My future vocation was decided by two experiences. My student teaching in a regular classroom for six weeks near my college was a disaster. Even though my major, English, was a comfortable subject for me to handle, I was not prepared for the numerous hearing students forced to take my class. They didn't follow my class rules (e.g., don't talk until the teacher acknowledges you, and speak clearly without obstructing your face).

On the other hand, my experience as a counselor at a camp for the deaf one summer brought back a wave of good emotions from my early years. Ironically, it was not altogether positive at first because I was an oralist — and all the deaf campers and staff quickly saw to it that I learned their language. That summer reminded me that I did belong after all to a group who fully understood my needs. By summer's end, I wanted to become a teacher of the deaf.

My sexual orientation was not as easily resolved. I had felt myself being pulled to other boys, especially around swimming pools and locker rooms. Occasionally, a classmate and I would size each other up, but nothing came of it. My knowledge of sex was limited — I couldn't lipread whispers behind cupped hands so I was left in the dark. But I dated girls, and did my best to be "one of the guys." I always knew this was a different ball game.

It was not until I went to graduate school in New York City that I began to explore this part of myself. Since I enjoyed dancing, I frequented a gay bar with a dance floor. This allowed me to feel the music, get some exercise, and meet other men; unfortunately, they all wanted just one thing — sex — and I wanted more than that.

Being deaf and being gay didn't mix well. Whether I went to the dance bar or any other meeting place, the environment was always poorly lit. Since I relied heavily on speechreading, I was always close to the best source of light. This still didn't do much good, since guys like to whisper sweet nothings in each other's ears. Whenever a guy approached my ear, I would quickly turn my head to face him only to have a collision of heads. Then I would quickly race through my monologue on why I needed to see their lips. This obviously dampened the initial spark.

I played what I call the "nodding game" several times: a guy would whisper into my ear, and I would nod and smile. You can imagine the horror on my face when one guy pulled me out of a bar and into a waiting cab. When we were outside, I managed to ask what was happening. He smiled and thanked me for agreeing to be his date at a friend's party, which turned out to be an orgy — which I promptly left.

Teaching the deaf became my career, and it was challenging and rewarding. My greatest joy was teaching my students to read not just for information but for pleasure. This required countless hours of practice, as well as exposure to English, especially when their native language was ASL. To keep myself abreast of current trends in teaching, I continued my course study in the evenings. This led to a second master's and completion of coursework toward a Ph.D.

Before I began my dissertation, I started my first long-term relationship. He was a bright and athletic Italian who happened to be hearing, and it was also his first long-term gay relationship. Being involved with me created numerous problems: We fought constantly, usually over deaf-related topics, because he had no understanding of what I could, and couldn't, perceive. We also fought over gay topics because he was having difficulties accepting himself. And it would be a while before I realized that he couldn't handle my having a Ph.D.

Three years into our relationship, and two-thirds of the way through my dissertation, I was faced with his ultimatim: "It's me or the dissertation." Since I didn't answer immediately, he assumed that I opted for the dissertation, and he left. The next few months were spent on completing my work, and switching from teaching to adminstration.

Having been involved with a hearing man, I kept asking myself if I wanted that again. I realized that it didn't matter if he were hearing or deaf; whether we cared for each other was more important. It was not long before I began dating again. I avoided the bar scene, trying out "blind dates," video dating, and social clubs. This resulted in several short-term relationships with both hearing and deaf men, but nothing substantial came of them. That expression "It's better to have loved and lost than never to have loved at all" kept passing through my mind. But moving into my thirties and attaining objectives kept me going, especially with volunteer work in deafness-related fields filling my evenings.

Then it happened.

At a September meeting for deaf gays, I met "Jose," a young, hearing Puerto Rican engineer who was studying ASL. He was tall, dark, and bright, and filled with numerous thought-provoking questions. When a group of us from the meeting went out for dinner, something was definitely starting between us that we weren't fully aware of. He was in an unfulfilling relationship, and I was in a short-term, long-distance relationship with a teacher in Vermont.

One night, a mutual friend, who had planned to take me to see the Broadway musical *Into the Woods*, asked if I would mind going with a friend of his instead because he wasn't feeling well. When I realized that Jose was the same guy I'd met at the meeting, my heart skipped a beat. I had to bite my tongue, because I wanted to tell my friend that I was glad he couldn't go. Our first evening together proved to be full of stimulating conversation and flirtations. My "date" practiced his signs by interpreting parts of the play I couldn't follow. It was quite an evening to remember.

We met again for a round of Scrabble in my apartment. Since we both enjoyed word games it was a great opportunity for us to chat some more and to see how adept we were at Scrabble. We played and talked. Our conversations centered on our relationships and why we found them unfulfilling. It was clear that we were keenly interested in each other, but we weren't sure how to proceed.

On a snowy November night, I was driving back from Washington, D.C. Since I promised to pick up Jose and take him back to my apartment, I was anxious to be on time. The snow had other plans, so I ended up in a snowdrift out in Maryland. After I was towed out, I drove as quickly as possible, only to be two hours late.

But he was not there.

I drove home.

To my surprise, he called me when I got in, to say that he'd just gotten home himself after waiting over an hour and a half. I quickly agreed to pick him up. On the Triborough Bridge, we both asked why we were doing these crazy things. It was then that we realized we were in love. From that moment on, I always associate snowfall with our love.

The weekend before Thanksgiving, my new live-in relationship began. Jose and his longtime lover parted (it was an ugly "divorce" in his view), and my short-term relationship conveniently ended with a "Dear John" letter from Vermont. Our first few months were full of introductions to family and friends, as well as each other's likes and dislikes. He learned the life of the deaf through my apartment: the light flashing systems for my phone and doorbell, my closed-caption decoder on the TV, and the TDD sitting by the telephone. Fortunately, he's adapted quite well.

We repeatedly discussed having a ceremony to formalize our relationship. We shopped around and found a lesbian minister willing to conduct a simple ceremony in a nonsectarian church. This would be followed by a reception in a small restaurant ten blocks from the church.

Details for our special day included our guest list, his-and-his rings, invitations, flowers, tuxedos, best men, ring bearers, poetry readings, and an interpreter for the ceremony. When the big day came, we couldn't have asked for a better one! It was a beautiful, cool fall day. Seventy-five deaf and hearing friends and hearing members gathered to witness our ceremony, which included the march, two poetry readings (one in ASL), a musical solo, the exchange of vows and rings, pictures, pictures, and *more* pictures. We all walked festively through the streets to the restaurant.

Almost a year after our Broadway "date," our honeymoon allowed us to rest up before returning to our regular, day-to-day life together. I believe our relationship is successful because we do understand each other's worlds. We communicate well, and it's not just because Jose can sign. He understands that the things that I don't get the first time when he says them shouldn't be swept under the rug with an "Oh, it wasn't important." He never does that, not even when we argue. He respects my needs as a deaf person; and

I understand that he's hearing. He *does* listen to the radio and occasionally *does* watch an uncaptioned TV show (although he admits to feeling funny when he does so).

It's been a game of give-and-take, and of love, for five years now.

"IVY"*

THE RUMOR ABOUT IVY: A DEAF BISEXUAL WOMAN

A TDD conversation

hello ivy whats your educational background qq ga

OK BORN DEAF UNKNOWN CAUSE AND WENT TO SCHOOL FOR THE DEAF UNTIL THIRD GRADE WENT TO HEARING SCHOOL FOR MAIN-STREAMING UNTIL I WAS A TEENAGER TRANSFERRED TO SCHOOL FOR THE DEAF GRADUATED FROM GALLY WITH BA DEGREE AND ALSO WENT TO HUNTER COLLEGE FOR MASTERS GA

great ok so define the word bisexuality ga

SMILE MANY PEOPLE THINK BISEXUALITY IS CONFUSING BUT I DONT THINK IT IS "BI" TO ME IS SEXUAL PREFERENCE FOR BOTH SEXES EITHER ONE SEX ATTRACTED TO YOU THEN THATS IT FOR EXAMPLE I LIKE BOTH SEXES IF I MEET A WONDERFUL WOMAN WHOM I WANT TO STAY WITH FOREVER THEN SHE IS THE ONE WHO STAYS WITH ME IF I MEET A WONDERFUL MAN THEN I STAY WITH HIM GA

i know i am not bisexual however i know i am emotionally attracted to both men and women but physically i am attracted to men do u make those kinds of distinctions in ur attractions to either sex qq ga

I AM PHYSICALLY AND EMOTIONALLY ATTRACTED TO BOTH SEXES BUT I FIND MYSELF MORE ATTRACTED TO MEN PHYSICALLY AND MORE EMOTIONALLY ATTRACTED TO WOMEN GA

so does this mean u are more attracted to men than women qq becuz it appears that most bisexuals are attracted to their own sex

*This interview conducted by the editor took place in August 1992.

but ur case seems different am i wrong or not qq ga

I MET OTHER BIS WHO ALSO ATTRACTED TO OPPOSITE SEXES FOR SOME REASONS DEPENDS ON WOMEN WHOM I AM REALLLLLY STRONGLY PHYSICALLY ATTRACTED TO DEPENDS ON MEN I AM MORE PHYSICALLY ATTRACTED THERE ARE DIFFERENT INDIVIDUALS I MET IN MY LIFETIME SO FAR IN MY LIFETIME I HAPPEN TO ATTRACT MEN PHYSICALLY GA

so does that mean u go to straight bars or lesbian bars or gay bars qq i mean where do u meet bisexuals qq or does it matter at all qq i dont want to imply that bisexuals are whores meaning they dont care which way they go in terms of sex ga

SMILE I GO TO STRAIGHT BARS WITH STRAIGHT FRIENDS I GO TO LESBIAN BARS WITH MY LESBIAN FRIENDS AND TO GAY BARS WITH MY GAY MALE FRIENDS ON DIFFERENT WEEKENDS BUT WHEN I MENTIONED ABOUT BEING ATTRACTED TO MEN PHYSICALLY ... THAT WAS WHEN I MET MY BOYFRIEND AT CAMP AS COUNSELOR I WAS NOT BI AT THAT TIME (I WAS NOT AWARE THAT I WAS BI WHILE GROWING UP) THEN WENT TO COLLEGE MET A FEW MEN THEN MY SECOND YEAR THERE I MET A NEAT GIRL SHE IS STRAIGHT HERSELF AS I WAS WE HIT IT OFF AND STARTED STEADY AS LESBIAN LOVERS AT THE SAME TIME I WAS REAL CONFUSED THAT TIME BEC I WAS STILL ATTRACTED TO MEN WHENEVER I GO TO STRAIGHT BARS WITH MY STRAIGHT FRIENDS WHO AT THAT TIME DIDNT KNOW THAT I STEADIED WITH MY GIRLFRIEND GA

the idea of going to gay bars with gay male friends then lesbian bars with lesbian friends and straight bars with straight friends now did anyone from these three groups know u were bisexual and how did they handle it qq ga

THAT TIME IN MY SECOND YEAR AT GALLY WITH MY GIRLFRIEND MY ROOMMATE WHO WAS MY BEST FRIEND FOR YEARS SINCE WE WERE LITTLE KIDS SHE FOUND OUT SHE ACCEPTED IT BEC SHE WENT OUT WITH BLACK MEN SHE COMES FROM STRONG JEWISH ORTHODOX FAMILY SO I KEPT THE SECRET FOR HER AND NOW HER TURN TO ACCEPT MY WORLD SMILE SHE HANDLED IT VERY WELL I WAS SURPRISED AND THEN SLOWLY MY OTHER FRIENDS ON MY WING (IN MY DORM) FOUND OUT AND ASKED ME PRIVATELY IF THEY HEARD THE RUMOR RIGHT I SAID WELL YEP HOPE YOU ARE STILL MY FRIEND THEY HUGGED ME AND SAID FINE YES I WAS EVEN SHOCKED TO BE ACCEPTED BY ONE BORN AGAIN CHRISTIAN FRIEND I GUESS THEY ARE MY TRUE FRIENDS

SMILE AND WHEN I GRADUATED FROM GALLY I WENT BACK TO MY HOME TOWN (NYC) I KEPT THE SECRET BUT THAT TIME WHEN I GRADUATED FROM GALLY I WANTED TO GO BACK TO BEING STRAIGHT I LIVE WITH MY FAMILY SO I WENT OUT WITH MY STRAIGHT FRIENDS MANY TIMES INSIDE ME URGING TO GO TO LESBIAN BARS THEN FEW YEARS AFTER GRADUATING FROM GALLY I MET ONE GUY WHO ASKED ME FOR A DATE WE WENT OUT HE ASKED ME IF I HEARD THE RUMOR THAT I WAS A LESBIAN I DROPPED MY FORK I SAID WELL YES IF I WAS THEN ????? HE SAID REALLLY AND LAUGHED HE TOLD ME THAT HE EXPERIMENTED WITH THE SAME SEX I WAS THRILLED WE BOTH SHARED OUR FEELINGS HE IS BI UNTIL NOW GA

he is bi until now qq meaning hes gone back to straight qq ga

OHHH SORRY I DIDNT EXPLAIN CLEARLY HE PLAYED "STRAIGHT" WHEN HE MET ME WE SHARED A LOT OF EMOTIONAL FEELINGS, CONFUSED ABOUT BEING BISEXUAL ONE DAY I TOLD HIM THAT I DONT CARE IF I AM A BI BEC I AM ME! I DONT CARRY A SIGN ON MY CHEST "BISEXUAL" NOOOOO THATS ME MY NAME IS IVY PERIOD I WANT PEOPLE TO LOOK AT ME AS ME NOT "HELLO BISEXUAL" HE AGREED THEN SLOWLY WE BOTH SHOWED MORE "BI" THAN BEFORE WE WERE IN THE CLOSET OF COURSE BEC WE BOTH LIVED WITH OUR FAMILIES BUT LAST SUMMER I FINALLY CAME OUT OF THE CLOSET SMILE GA

u came out of the closet to ur family qq how did that go qq ga

HAHAHA LAST SUMMER I WENT TO FIRE ISLAND I MET THIS GIRL WE TALKED ALLLLL DAY ABOUT EVERYTHING WE HAD A GREAT TIME TOGETHER THEN AT THAT SAME NIGHT WE HIT IT OFF I GAVE HER MY WORK ADDRESS BEC I DONT WANT HER TO MAIL TO MY MOTHERS HOUSE OR OTHERWISE MY MOTHER WILL ASK ME QUESTIONS WHO IS SHE ETC ETC (AS YOU SEE MY MOTHER AND I ARE VERY CLOSE WE TALK OPENLY MY MOTHER KNOWS A LOT OF GAY PEOPLE AT HER JOB BUT I WAS AFRAID TO TELL HER ABOUT MYSELF) SOOOO BACK TO FIRE ISLAND ... OK SOMEHOW THIS GIRL DIDNT WANT TO SEND THE LETTER TO MY WORK ADDRESS SHE FOUND MY HOME ADDRESS FROM OTHER FRIENDS OH BOY!!!!! WHAT LUCK! THEN ONE DAY MY MOTHER OPENED THE DOOR FOR UPS MAN HE GAVE HER A SMALL BROWN PACKAGE MY MOTHER GAVE IT TO ME I OPENED IT UP WITH MY MOTHER LOOKING OVER MY SHOULDERS GUESS WHO IT WAS FROM OF COURSE IT WAS FROM THAT GIRL OH BOY SHE DESCRIBED EVERYTHING HOW SHE ENJOYED BEING WITH ME FONDLED ... RUBBING ... TOUCHING ... SHE IS A GOOD WRITER SHE WROTE EVERYTHING BEAUTIFULLY I WAS EMBAR-

RASSED MY MOTHER ASKED ME, "TELL ME ABT YOU I HAVE A FUNNY FEELING ABT YOU ALLLLL ALONG" I WAS SHOCKED SHE KNEW SOMETHING WAS DIFFERENT ABOUT ME SO I TOLD HER ... FROM THAT DAY ON SHE STILL LOVES ME SHE HANDLED IT VERY WELL I WAS SHOCKED!!!!! GA

oh thats wonderful so how does she feel if u brought someone of either sex home qq any objections there qq ga

YEAH A LITTLE BIT YOU KNOW MY GOOD FRIEND "SAMMY" MY MOTHER LOVES HIM SO FUCKING MUCH I BROUGHT HIM HOME ALL THE TIME BUT MY MOTHER ONCE MENTIONED THAT SHE IS NOT CRAZY ABT THE IDEA OF ME BRINGING HOME A LESBIAN ETC SHE FEELS A LITTLE UNCOMFORTABLE BUT AT THE SAME TIME SHE UNDERSTANDS ME AS A BISEXUAL ... SHE WANTS ME TO GET MARRIED ETC GA

do u want to get married qq or would u prefer an open relationship with the one u love qq ga

HARD HMMMMM I DO WANT TO GET MARRIED AND HAVE KIDS BUT I WANT MY HUSBAND TO UNDERSTAND THAT I AM A BI SO I CAN GO OUT WITH MY DIFFERENT CIRCLE OF FRIENDS GA

so what if ur husband is straight qq would u allow him to see other women if he allows u to see other women qq ga

I DONT KNOW SUPPOSE I GET MARRIED TO A STRAIGHT MAN WHO UNDERSTANDS THAT I AM A BI AND I STILL GO OUT WITH A WOMAN? I DONT KNOW ABOUT THAT BEC I AM ONE LOVER PERSON NOT NYMPHO KNOW WHAT I MEAN QQ IF I MET A WOMAN I COULD MARRY HER GA

and suppose ur lover was bisexual would it bother u if he or she wanted to see other people qq ga

HMMMMM NEVER HAPPENED TO ME HMMMM LET ME THINK AND TRY TO VISUALIZE WHAT IT WOULD BE LIKE IF THIS HAPPENS I WILL APPRECIATE IT IF MY LOVER TELLS ME THAT SHE WENT OUT WITH HER OR THIS OR THAT PERSON NOT HIDING FROM ME I BELIEVE WE SHOULD BE OPEN ABOUT EVERYTHING A LOVER TO ME IS THE SAME AS "BEST FRIENDS" GA

so when did u realize that u were attracted to women qq in that second year in college qq or had it happened before qq ga

WHEN I WAS EIGHT YEARS OLD I HAD A BIG CRUSH ON MY NEXT-DOOR NEIGHBOR A YOUNG TEEN SHE ALWAYS SAT OUTSIDE IN THE SUN

GETTING A TAN SHE HAD A BEAUTIFUL BODY I DREW A LOT OF PICTURES OF HER NAME AND MY NAME WITH A HEART WITH AN ARROW MY MOTHER TOLD ME NO NO SILLY I DIDNT UNDERSTAND BUT STILL I HAD THOUSANDS OF DREAMS ABOUT HER SMILE THEN I GREW TIRED OF HER WHEN I WAS TWELVE IN A HEARING SCHOOL I WAS A BIT LONELY I FELT LIKE I WAS THE ONLY DEAF EVEN THOUGH THERE WERE A FEW DEAF STUDENTS THERE BUT THEY WERE MUCH YOUNGER THAN ME I ALWAYS WANTED A FRIEND THEN ONE DAY BINGO! THIS GIRL HARD OF HEARING TRANSFERRED TO MY HEARING SCHOOL SHE HAD BIGGER BOOBS I HAD NOTHING LIKE THAT AT MY AGE HAHA WE BECAME VERY CLOSE LIKE SISTERS MANY TIMES I TRIED TO TOUCH OR FONDLE HER SHE GOT MAD AT ME WONT TALK TO ME FOR FEW DAYS I DIDNT REALIZE THAT I AM DIFFERENT I THOUGHT IT WAS NORMAL I NEVER KNEW IT WAS A SIN OR ABNORMAL THEN LATER ON WHEN WE WENT TO JR HIGH SCHOOL WE WERE STILL CLOSE THEN AGAIN SHE GOT MAD AT ME FOR TRYING TO TOUCH HER I DIDNT UNDERSTAND WHY THEN IN MY SECOND YEAR AT JR HIGH SCHOOL I TRANSFERRED TO A SCHOOL FOR THE DEAF BEC I WANTED MORE FRIENDS FROM THE DEAF WORLD ... SO WHEN I ENTERED THAT NEW SCHOOL I WENT OUT WITH MANY GUYS NEVER THOUGHT OF GIRLS AGAIN BUT SOMETIMES I DREAMED ABOUT THAT SAME GIRL IN MY HEARING SCHOOL THEN I WENT TO GALLY A FEW WOMEN APPROACHED ME BUT I GOT SCARED REFUSED THEM BEC I DIDNT KNOW THEM WELL THEY CAUGHT ME OFFGUARD ... ONE INTERESTING THING WHEN I WENT TO GALLY I MET A GIRL ON MY FLOOR SHE IS STRAIGHT WE BOTH BECAME FAST FRIENDS READ EACH OTHERS MINDS EVERYTHING SHE REVEALED THE SAME EXPERIENCES AS MINE THAT SHE HAD CRUSHES ON WOMEN WHEN SHE WAS YOUNGER SAME AS ME AND SHE MADE ONE FRIEND MAD SAME THING AS MINE BUT WE NEVER THOUGHT OR DREAMED THAT WE WOULD DO IT TOGETHER WE TALKED ABOUT BOYS ENDLESSLY WHO YOU FUCK LAST NIGHT I FUCKED THAT GUY LAST NIGHT WOWOWOWOW ETC ETC THEN IN OUR SECOND YEAR WE FELL IN LOVE ONE DAY GA

wow what happened qq i mean like that qq ga

OK SECOND YEAR AT GALLY ON FIRST DAY OF CLASS WE WERE SHY TO SEE EACH OTHER IMPORTANT NOTE ... I THOUGHT ABT HER ALOT OVER THE SUMMER AS MUCH AS SHE DID TOO WE NEVER TOLD EACH OTHER UNTIL WE GOT INTO OUR SECOND YEAR WE WENT TO GAY BAR WHERE THEY HAVE MALE STRIPPERS AND WE BOTH TALKED ABOUT MEN ENDLESSLY SO THATS WHY WE WENT TO MALE STRIPPERS BAR WE DIDNT CARE IF THE BAR WAS GAY BUT SOMEHOW MANY TIMES WE WENT TO

SLEEP WITH MALE STRIPPERS WHO HAPPENED TO BE BISEXUALS THAT WAS WHEN THE WORD "BISEXUAL" HIT ME BISEXUAL INTERESTING LIKE A SONG IN MY HEAD BUT MY FRIEND AND I LOVED SLEEPING WITH THEM AND THEN WE SAW TWO WOMEN HUGGING AND KISSING SHE ASKED ME IF I WANTED TO DO THAT TOO I SAID WELL TURNING AWAY I DIDNT WANT TO TALK ABOUT IT BEC I WANTED TO DO THAT WITH HER SO BADLY SHIT ... AND WE WERE STONED SHE WAS THE ONE WHO HAD THE GUTS!!!! SHE KISSED ME BINGO! THAT NIGHT WE HELD HANDS WE FELT SO GOOOD BUT THEN NEXT DAY I WAS CONFUSED BEC OF SOCIETY RULES ABOUT GAYS AS SINFUL AND ABNORMAL ETC PLUS MY FAMILY IS JEWISH SHIT THEN I FLEW HOME THAT WEEKEND TOLD MY MOTHER ABOUT IT SHE LAUGHED AND SAID YOU KNOW COLLEGE YOU ALWAYS EXPERIMENT WITH MANY THINGS DRUGS AND DIFFERENT THINGS SO YOU ARE NOT LESBIAN AT ALL YOU WERE CURIOUS THATS ALL THATS NORMAL I FELT A LOT BETTER WHEN I WENT BACK TO GALLY AND TOLD MY FRIEND SHE SAID REALLY BUT I LOVE YOU SHE IS RIGHT I LOVE HER TOO SO I SAID TO MYSELF FUCK THE COLLEGE EXPERIMENTAL EXPERIENCE THEORY THAT MY MOTHER GAVE ME I STEADIED WITH HER FOR TWO YEARS MY MOTHER DIDNT KNOW NOW SHE DOES SMILE GA

have u ever had a bisexual three way experience qq any communication problems there qq ga

HMMM I HAD THREE WAYS MANY TIMES MY FRIEND AND I WERE STRAIGHTS LOVED TO TALK ABOUT MEN ONE NIGHT WE WENT TO BED WITH ONE GUY WE FOCUSED ON THIS POOR GUY HAHHAHA BUT WE NEVER FOCUSED ON EACH OTHER KNOW WHAT I MEAN QQ I NEVER HAD TRULY BISEXUAL THREESOME EXPERIENCES GA

would u like to try them qq or would that be a bit too much for u qq ga

HMMMMM SOMETIMES IN MY FANTASIES YES BUT IN REAL LIFE I AM AFRAID BEC YOU KNOW AIDS... GA

why do u think bisexuality scares people so much qq ga

BESIDES AIDS IN SOCIETY WHEN THEY THINK OF THE WORD "BI" THEY THINK OF SWINGING OR SWAPPING ... ORGY ... KNOW WHAT I MEAN QQ BUT I MET FEW PEOPLE WHO ARE BI I ASKED THEM ABOUT THEIR FEELINGS THEY SHARED THE EXACT SAME FEELINGS AS ME WHEN SHE MEETS A NICE MAN THATS IT SHE STAYS WITH HIM WHEN SHE MEETS A NICE WOMAN THATS IT SHE STAYS WITH HER NOT THINK OF PLAYING

AROUND WITH ANYONE ELSE SAME IDEA AS STRAIGHT FOR EXAMPLE MY SISTER IS FUCKING STRAIGHT SHE MET A WONDERFUL MAN SHE STAYED WITH HIM THEN GOT MARRIED SHE NEVER THOUGHT OF PLAYING AROUND WITH ANOTHER MAN KNOW WHAT I MEAN QQ IF SHE THOUGHT OF PLAYING AROUND WITH ANOTHER MAN THEN IT MEANS SHE DIDNT LOVE THE MAN SHE STAYED WITH ... UNFORTUNATELY ... MY GIRLFRIEND AND I WENT OUT FOR TWO YEARS I WAS THE ONE WHO BROKE UP WITH HER BEC AT THAT TIME I WAS SCARED AND CONFUSED WANTED TO GO BACK TO BEING STRAIGHT STUPID ME NOW MY FRIEND MARRIED A NICE MAN SHE HAS A BEAUTIFUL BABY GIRL GA

have u had lesbians turn u down becuz they find out u are bisexual qq does that make u angry qq or what qq ga

YES A FEW A FEW WOMEN AT THE BAR OR A DEAF FRIENDS HOUSE PARTY SURE THEY TURN SOUR-FACED AT ME WHY!!!!! YOU BI! MEAN YOU LIKE PLAY AROUND QQ THEY GOT THE WRONG IDEA ABOUT BI PEOPLE THAT MADE ME ANGRY BUT ITS MY RESPONSIBILITY TO EXPLAIN CLEARLY WHATS BI I DONT THINK MANY PEOPLE UNDERSTAND BI BISEXUALITY IS THE SAME IDEA AS HARD OF HEARING PEOPLE WHO ARE BETWEEN TWO WORLDS DEAF WORLD AND HEARING WORLD GA

ive thought abt that idea before have u met many deaf bisexuals or are they hard to find qq ga

HARD TO FIND OH BOY SMILE I WENT TO PROVINCETOWN (MY FAVORITE PLACE) I MET ONE GIRL SHE TOLD ME SHE WAS BI I WAS SURPRISED SHE PREFERS WOMEN BUT IF SHE MET A NICE WONDERFUL MAN THAT SHE HAS A LOT OF FEELINGS FOR THEN THATS IT NO MATTER WHICH SEX IT IS THE MOST IMPORTANT THING IS A PERSON ITSELF A HUMAN BEING ITSELF GA

do u think there are more male bisexuals than female bisexuals qq or is it the other way around qq ga

GOOOOD QUES I DONT KNOW MYSELF THIS GIRL WHO IS BI AT PTOWN AND ALSO MY MALE FRIEND WHO IS BI WE WERE FRUSTRATED A LITTLE TRYING TO FIND MORE BIS SO WE CAN FEEL MORE COMFORTABLE I WISH THERE WERE BARS FOR BIS TOO GA

isnt there one in nyc qq ga

STRANGELY ENUF FOR A BIG FUCKING CITY NOPE I DONT THINK SO SO FAR GA not even anywhere in the united states qq ga

NO MY FRIEND BOUGHT AN INTERNATIONAL GAYELLOW PAGES ALLL GAY BARS ALLL LESBIAN BARS I DIDNT EVEN SEE NOT EVEN ONE BI BAR GA

i think thats it for now anything else u want to add qq ga

NO THANK U SO MUCH FOR WANTING TO ASK QUES ABT BISEXUALITY GREAT HOPE TO HEAR FROM U REAL SOON BYE BYE GA OR SK

thank u for ur time u have a good night then sk

SKSK

"PATRICK"*

FROM THE CITY OF BROTHERLY LOVE

MY AUDITORY NERVES WERE DAMAGED by measles when I was one year old. I am profoundly deaf. My speech isn't really that good, and hearing strangers have a hard time understanding me in noisy environments. If I'm in a quiet environment, they can understand my speech if I speak slowly in a soft voice.

When I was ten, I was sexually molested by my maternal grandfather. I was so young. I thought it was play at first, but later I got involved in it again. The second time I felt guilty. I tried to refuse him, but he threatened me with the loss of my swimming privileges. He often took me out swimming, which I loved so much. So I was forced to have sex with him although I didn't want to. (He was an exhibitionist. Did I give him oral sex as instructed? Perhaps I did at first, but the second time I refused to do so. Instead I used my hand to masturbate him.)

For a long time I didn't have sex of any kind. I started to masturbate at the age of twelve. Then I had masturbatory sex with my cousin when I was sixteen years old. Otherwise, my teenage years were filled with masturbation on my bed.

I finally had my first sexual experience with a man who was a little older than I was. I was twenty-three years old. I had known him for a long time, maybe a year. I didn't fall in love with him, but we were good friends.

I didn't fall in love with any man during my twenties; that happened later, in my thirties.

*This was pieced together from Patrick's remarks during a TDD conversation on September 12, 1992, with the editor.

During my twenties I was shy, and so I didn't even look for anyone to be in love with. I had tried to date girls, even though I was still in the closet. I graduated from college, and I still didn't go out on dates with other men. I went to gay bars in Memphis where I grew up, but I had a hard time going downtown. I lived in the suburbs, and the buses quit running too early. In those gay bars I was attracted to some men; I even went out to a few parks and a bathhouse in Memphis, but I didn't want to have sex with anyone there. I never had sex with anyone while I lived in Memphis.

Then I moved to Westminster, Maryland. I went down to Baltimore and had my first sexual experience in a bathhouse. That's when I opened up my gayness. But I still didn't express it elsewhere. I kept my gay profile low at all times. I wasn't even active sexually; I was passive sexually.

In fact, I used to identify myself as a preppy. A lot of guys were attracted to me when I was in my thirties at some of the "preppy" gay bars. I had a lot of sex with them. (This was long before the AIDS scare. Before AIDS hit, I usually had sex with one man each month; after AIDS, it went down to once or twice a year. I am in my forties now.)

Years ago, someone who was gay back in Memphis identified me as a gay man, but I refused to admit it. Then after I came out, I didn't know myself fully, but I thought I was preppy. Later on, here in Philadelphia, a man identified me as a leatherman [a person who is sexually into leather, but not necessarily involved with sadomasochism (S&M)], but I refused to admit that as well. In my life, I was always identified by other people as one thing or another, but I never admitted it *all* until later.

When I worked as a tutor at Gallaudet University in Washington, D.C., I went to the D.C. Eagle bar. I was curious, and I found that I liked it better than nonleather gay bars. I thought other gay bars were too flauntingly gay. But at the D.C. Eagle, the scene was low-profile — almost like those redneck bars back in Memphis.

Well, when I moved to Philadelphia, I went to the 247 bar and Post Bar (Bike Stop did not exist then), and I found that I liked the atmosphere there. A lot of deaf gays went to 247. I met a leatherman at Post and he asked me to go and have sex with him at his place.

That was my first sexual experience with a leatherman. We talked a lot about options, such as S&M, bondage, fistfucking, oral sex, and so on. We narrowed them down until we agreed on having anal sex and holding each other. That was the first time I learned about leather and S&M by talking about it. He was cautious, and he wanted to know about me, and we had to agree on what we wanted to do in sex.

Since then, I've gone to Equus. I had anal sex with the men there without discussing each other's sexual needs. We just did foreplay, and then fucked each other. Sometimes they wanted oral sex, but not me. They wanted me to fuck their asses. That's all I did.

When the punk style appeared, I started wearing a leather jacket with a black shirt and a pair of black jeans.

Sometimes I wore a white shirt with my black jeans. Someone came up to me one night and said, "It's about time you admit to yourself that you're a leatherman."

I insisted that I was only into classic punk.

But when I attended the National RAD (Rainbow Alliance of the Deaf, a social deaf gay organization) convention in Dallas last year, I took an S&M/leather workshop there and realized that I have been a leatherman all along. I also realized that if someone had fallen in love with me, we would have had a master-slave relationship. If we'd agreed on monogamy, I would have had to be in control of him. I know I can't control him at all times, but I can limit him when we're together. I am into light S&M. And I have a very strong fetish for rubbing very hairy legs.

Some hearing leathermen I've met in bars didn't mind exchanging notes with me, but most of the time they didn't approach me. I felt too much like a wallflower, so I joined the Philadelphians Men's Club.

At first they didn't know how to talk with me. But when I talked with them after a while, they understood my speech. I also taught them fingerspelling and signs, but it was hard for them to remember. There are a few leathermen there who can fingerspell and sign well. I also have a registered interpreter, and he teaches ASL to those interested in learning it.

In leather bars I've often talked with guys, but with the loud music and raised voices, they can't hear me well, so I have to write notes. I can't even read their lips in the dark, so they have to write notes.

Sometimes, when I found myself signing with some guys who could sign or with guys who wanted to know some signs, I wasn't aware that they wanted to learn sign language just to have sex with me and other deaf guys. After that, we'd never see them again, or if we saw them again, they'd say hi and then leave us alone. That's a real problem. In bars and elsewhere, we deaf gay people are invisible. They don't know about our deafness until they find out from us. Then sometimes they suddenly make excuses and take off.

Many deaf gay people are frustrated, almost desperate to find a lover. Very few deaf gay people are lucky finding lovers. Often, once they have sex with someone, they rush into becoming lovers even though they don't know each other that well.

All that's got to change.

FOUR

AMY BERNSTEIN

OF BREAD, LOVE

I GUESS I'M SO USED TO IT that when the man in the bakery asked me, I was caught off guard.

"Is that your friend or your roommate? The one who can't talk?"

I was so surprised that the only way I could respond was, "Uh, we, uh live together."

"She can't talk, right?" he asked in a thick accent with the unpretentious familiarity and concern that immigrants often display.

Having recovered somewhat, I managed to tell him, "No, she's deaf. She actually speaks quite well because she only recently lost her hearing."

"Only recently?" he asked from under his thick moustache. "What happened?"

This part was easy. I had done it so many times, the smooth speech about how Hannah had lost her hearing, and no, the doctors don't know why, and yes, she is awfully young to lose her hearing. This is usually followed by a short sentence or two about how she copes by using a combination of assistive listening devices, lipreading, and sign language.

The expected question came.

"What does she do for a living?"

"She's a graduate student."

This answer always elicits a wide-eyed "No kidding! What's she a graduate student in?" so I was prepared. After all, I have given this presentation a zillion times to store clerks, postal workers, co-workers, friends, new acquaintances, and strangers. So, through the speech I went, telling him how she's studying sociology and wants to study late-deafened adults because since she's lost her hearing she's become aware of how few services and how little understanding there is about this group of people.

The next question came on cue.

"But how does she hear in her classes?

I launched into a reiteration of the part about assistive listening devices, lipreading, and interpreters.

Now, the usual wrap-up.

"Well, anyway, if it had to happen to anyone," I said admiringly, "I suppose it was good that it happened to her, since she's very bright" — I always boast a little at this part — "and she has, thank God, learned to read lips and sign and use her deafness positively for academic study."

I paid for the bread and, saying good-bye, left the bakery.

It's been almost three years since Hannah began losing her hearing. Most of it's gone now, so the bumpy ride of continual adjustment to even more hearing loss is over. Still, situations come up constantly that require new adaptations and coping skills: a lecture we would both love to hear, but cannot; a noisy party with the possibility of meeting new and interesting people; a new movie that really should be seen on the large screen rather than waiting and hoping that the video version will be closed-captioned. We are constantly redefining our relationship, trying to preserve the balance as I change like a chameleon from partner, to interpreter, to enabler, to mother, and back to partner again. Wanting to be helpful, yet allowing her to learn to adjust to silence. And all at the same time trying to stay aware of my own feelings and needs.

There was the time we wanted to go hear Kate Clinton. Neither of us had heard her comedy before, and we happily anticipated the opportunity that accommodated both our schedules. A few phone calls revealed that the performance was not to be interpreted because there "had been no interest." Hoping to generate what the organizers would think was "interest," I asked all of our friends (whether or not they were going to the concert) to call and inquire if it would be interpreted.

On the day of the performance we drove two hours to Western Massachusetts for the afternoon show. When we got to the box office we were told that they had not found an interpreter and the show would not be accessible to the hearing-impaired! Hannah passed the afternoon in the library waiting for me. I spent the afternoon alone listening to Kate Clinton, trying to remember jokes so I could tell Hannah later, and feeling incredibly confused about whether to feel fortunate or guilty that I was a hearing person.

Hannah can't hear the radio. We awoke one morning to a snow-covered Boston. Listening to the radio while I dressed for work, I heard that there had been a subway accident and buses were being provided for commuters from Kenmore Station. Hannah was getting ready to take the subway to school. I told her about the accident, signing simultaneously and facing her so she could read my lips. We looked at each other for a moment.

Then she quietly said, "That affects me."

"Yes," I said. "It does."

Hannah can't use the voice telephone. We bought an answering machine to be sure that we didn't miss any calls. When I come home, I listen to the messages and tell her who called. One day, she said to me, "Who was the message from?"

"Just my mother," I replied.

"What did she say?"

"The usual," I said. "Wanted to know how we are. You know..."

"What else?" she asked again.

Irritated, I looked at her with confusion and said with a shrug, "The usual phone call. Nothing much."

"That can't be all," she insisted. "It was a long message."

I stared at her, refusing to believe that I had to spend energy giving her a blow-by-blow description of a simple message from my mother, who had called simply to chat, with nothing in particular to say.

"I want to know what she said. Don't just give me an overview," she said, her voice rising. "I want to know what she said!"

The urgency in her voice startled me. I suddenly realized that when you're deaf, being left out of even the most mundane experiences can make you feel cut off and out of touch. Apologizing, I recounted the story about how my mother said she and my father had planned to go to the mall that evening, but it was very cold, so they stayed home instead. But tomorrow they definitely have to go shopping to buy food for their cats, since it was almost gone. I felt both frustration and guilt. Of course I want her to know what's going on, but having to spend the extra energy to convey a simple "meaningless" conversation when I was tired seemed above and beyond the call of duty. What is my role as a hearing partner? At what point do *I* get to say, "I don't feel like it now"? What is the line between being supportive and being myself? Whose needs go first? What is the price of being a hearing partner?

As I rode the bus to work, I thought again about my conversation with the baker, surprised that he had even seen Hannah. She almost never goes into that bakery. I usually buy the baked goods myself. It was crowded and we stood in the corner signing to each other about what we wanted to buy. "How the baker even noticed us among all the other people I can't imagine," I thought and then caught myself sheepishly. I keep forgetting that people who sign stick out in any crowd. Hannah told me that deaf people are often embarrassed to sign in public. It was hard to believe — I had become so proud of the little bit of sign language I had learned.

Hannah says that the separation rate for relationships when one partner suffers hearing loss is very high. She looks at me cautiously when she says it, afraid of becoming another statistic. I think about that while I ride the bus to work, the fresh bread from the bakery on my lap. Flour, water, and yeast is all it takes to make bread. If you take away one of the ingredients, you don't have bread. A good relationship is not so simple. You can take away lots of the parts and still have a wonderful relationship. I think about the bread again. Just as the yeast turns the flour and water into something delicious, Hannah's hearing loss has ironically turned our relationship into something special. We have learned to communicate without speaking — in different, deeper ways — and have had to face the things in each other and ourselves for which many other people don't usually have the opportunity. As a result, we have gained a closeness that is ours alone. I can live with that.

HANNAH GERSHON

GOING THROUGH THE FOREST

Over the course of three hours I happened to look up and see Amy's mouth moving in speech for the fifth time. I gave up. You would think that after three years of living with a deaf lover she would remember to get my attention before attempting to say anything. There we were, just the two of us hiking through the middle of a forest. Who was she talking to, the chipmunks? I had to decide whether or not I should stop her yet again and make her start over from the beginning: "Sorry, I wasn't watching. What did you say?" But it was the fifth time this morning that this had happened, and I was already tired of struggling over communication.

I decided to ignore her.

And she continued to ignore me.

I watched her more closely now, waiting to see the look on her face when she realized she'd forgotten that I was deaf. Laughing to myself, I imagined how she would feel momentarily shocked that I had understood nothing of what she had said all morning. She would feel, as I felt, the loss of closeness between us when she finally realized that all those thoughts, feelings, and observations she was expressing were not being shared with me. Best of all, I imagined her apologizing when she realized that it was her fault for not communicating properly.

She continued to walk in front of me, gesturing as she spoke but never signing, talking to her heart's content but never making her thoughts accessible to me.

I felt hurt and angry. I interpreted Amy's talking without signing as a hidden message that she really didn't want to share her feelings with me. After all, if she wanted me to know what she was saying, she would communicate in a way that would enable me to understand. She knows how to speak so that I can read her lips. And she knows how to sign!

All she would have to do is stop and turn around, put down the binoculars she was carrying, wave to get my attention, wait for me to signal that I was ready to receive her communication: then she could speak slowly, sign, probably repeat what she was saying once or twice, and then she could do this every time she wanted to say anything so that our hike would take six hours instead of two and we wouldn't get back to our campsite before dark.

I felt guilty. I was asking for too much. When Amy and I began our relationship ten years ago, we were not then, and did not expect to become, a so-called "interauditory" couple. We were both hearing, and being hearing, of course, was the unnamed, asssumed perspective from which we viewed the world. The ability to communicate through sound was taken for granted. The idea of being deaf was some abstract, irrelevant concept at best, while representing some kind of vaguely threatening oddity and otherness at worst. The truth was that I had always had a mild hearing loss, but when I became deaf three years ago at the age of thirty-three, the unnamed assumption was forcibly articulated between us.

Just as I had to learn a new identity for myself as a deaf person, Amy had to learn that she was a hearing person. Living together as hearing people in a hearing world, we never had to stop and define the meaning of hearing. The ability to hear (at least sufficiently, if not well) simply existed without having to be analyzed. But when Amy began to interpret my phone calls, act as my ears during our socializing with friends, and intercede for me when ordering bagels at the local bakery, she did so as a hearing person. And why shouldn't she? She could still hear and I could not. Hadn't it become her responsibility as my hearing partner to do these things? And hadn't it become her responsibility to make her communication accessible to me?

As we hiked through the forest that morning, I vacillated between wondering why Amy wasn't doing her "job" to communicate effectively with me, and feeling like a criminal for making so many demands on her. She can no longer simply "talk." She now has to "work at communicating." I must work hard, too, of course. The deafness is within me, not her. She can walk away from it if she wants. Like other feminist couples both gay and straight, we had based our relationship on egalitarian principles. Neither one of us would ever have power over the other. Our design had been to combine our unique strengths to help each other reach our goals.

In truth, Amy has done much to help me. She has spent countless hours assisting me with speechreading, learning sign language, filling in as my interpreter, and generally doing all the things that she can as a hearing person to adapt to my deafness. She has agreed to changes in our lifestyle, such as substituting captioned videos for big-screen cinema movies, using a TDD, hiring interpreters, and even foregoing certain social events altogether because I would not be able to participate.

But what help have I been able to offer her? What happens to the egalitarian paradigm when one partner is deaf and the other is hearing?

I continued to wrestle with this dilemma all the way up and down the mountain we were hiking, past the waterfalls, back to the car, and all during the long drive back to our campsite. Amy continued to chatter away without signing or stopping to see if I was trying to read her lips. When we arrived at our campsite, she finally grabbed my shoulders and turned me around to face her. Signing and speaking slowly, she asked me why I had been so sullen and withdrawn all day.

I was surprised. How could she not know?!

I struggled to control my anger, and only when I was pretty sure I could speak calmly, I told her how much I was hurt by her failure to communicate with me. Didn't she *want* to talk to me? Didn't she think I was worth the effort it takes? What did she do, forget that I was deaf?

Yes. She forgot.

I was stunned. I never thought it could be forgotten.

All my interactions with the world are now based entirely and exclusively on visual communication. I never forget that other people cannot talk to me if their backs are turned, because no matter what I do I will never hear their voices. But hearing people can and do forget things like this. They interact with the world through sound that carries around corners, through walls, and behind people's backs.

Furthermore, they cannot turn off the sound. A deaf person can look away and choose not to see something, but a hearing person's ears are always "on." It's impossible for hearing people to understand how deafness affects one's experience of communication. They can be told about it, but they cannot directly experience it, any more than deaf people can have a genuine hearing experience.

I know this observation will seem silly and trival to most people who have grown up deaf. But I am only beginning to understand the meaning of the difference between being deaf and being hearing. For one thing, it means that hearing people, even those with considerable exposure to deaf people, will forget how to communicate occasionally. Specifically, I can restore the egalitarian balance to my relationship with Amy through my understanding of her as a hearing person.

In this society, hearing is assumed of everyone, and deafness constitutes a special case, an exception. Following that concept, I had thought that Amy had to do all the changing and accommodating for me and my "special" needs. I forgot that I would also need to see her needs in a new way because, from my perspective, hearing needs have become an exception to my norm.

Amy made this abundantly clear to me back at our campsite. I had been wondering all day why she didn't communicate with me. Well, she had been wondering exactly the same thing about me. Her question to me was, why hadn't I told her that I couldn't understand her? From her point of view, I was the one who had failed to communicate. And she was right. But I was also right that she didn't communicate with me.

We were both right, and we were both wrong. The good part is that each of us knows better now what the other needs for communication. We ended the day closer and more in synch with each other, but we wouldn't have achieved that without going through the forest first.

TALK OF THE TOWN: ON HEARING PARTNERS

NEW YORK CITY, *compiled by Phillip Green*

"BILL," age thirty-one

Before I met my lover "Tony," deaf people were mostly a mystery. I didn't know what they were all about. I was very curious about the language, though. I was interested in sign language and I had decided to take a class. I never really had an opinion about the deaf — I just thought they were mysterious.

My lover and I met through the Empire Rainbow Alliance of the Deaf (ERAD) [now defunct]. One of the members, who was in a sign language class, invited me to a meeting. It's funny — most people learn sign language because of their lovers. I met my lover *because* I learned sign language. Mine was backwards.

What helps me best in this relationship? Keeping the communication open. Never shutting down, and making sure that if he misses something, I repeat it. And I learned not to take his deafness for granted.

✦

"MARY," age thirty-three

I had worked with deaf people and knew them professionally and personally before my lover "Diane" and I ever met, so I didn't really have any new impression. I knew deaf people already.

I met Diane through a mutual friend. I was fluent in sign language when we met. I think for a lot of gay men, their hearing lovers didn't know sign language. But with women, it seems they already knew sign language when they met. And some of my hearing friends learned sign language so they could communicate on their own with Diane.

I think we dealt with the deaf/hearing issues right off the bat. So I don't feel that they're issues anymore. It's easy for deafness to become *the* issue in social or professional situations, or cultural events, or whatever. But it isn't so much anymore.

✦

"ERIC," age twenty-eight

Well, like other hearing people, I assumed that they're "deaf-mutes" who came over and handed you a card for a dollar. But more recently, even before I met "Frank" — well, my parents managed an apartment complex and had a deaf tenant. I had a conversation with him by pad and pencil. My parents couldn't handle *that,* so I had to do it for them. It was too much for them. That was the first time I ever "sat down" with a deaf person. I guess I had a stereotypical view of them.

Frank and I met at a local hot spot. He approached me first and asked if I would like to go to this club with him. He'd written this on a piece of paper. Then I realized he was deaf, but it didn't bother me or anything. I wrote back, "No thank you." After I thought about it, I ended up going back to that club and meeting him there. The rest is history.

Our first communication was the "universal communication." Well, I mean he's not a good lipreader, so it was the pad and pencil first. Then he taught me some signs little by little. The first signs I used were sexual. Then he bought me a book, and after a while he paid the tuition for me to go to a sign language class.

The only hearing friends who were aware of him were my roommates at the time. They thought it was really neat. First, they knew I was taking a sign language class — one of those adult continuing education things — and then later I got a TDD. They put two and two together, and then he was coming around a lot. I think they were intrigued. I didn't encounter any prejudice. Honesty is what helps our relationship best. Making sure we talk things out. Making sure I make my point, making sure we discuss things, because communication isn't always as convenient as it would be with a hearing lover. We can't just assume that someone will just *know* everything. You have to communicate. At first it was hard because it was pad and pencil, and that can only get you so far. You can only discuss superficial issues.

✦

RICHARD, age thirty-one

Before I met my lover "Greg," I had had little experience with deaf people. I was aware of the protest at Gallaudet in 1988, and I remember feeling supportive of the students' demand for a deaf president and disgusted by the insulting comments of the woman [Jane Spilman-Bassett] who was the chair of Gallaudet's board of directors. But I had never really given much thought to the deaf. I had little, if any, concept of deaf culture.

Once, on a trip, I met a guy in a gay bar, and he was deaf. I spent a couple of evenings with him, communicating by writing back and forth. He had a lot of family problems. He lived with his parents, who had never attempted to learn sign language. His alcoholic father was physically abusive and resented him because he'd never learned to speak. I felt sorry for him — not because he was deaf, but because of his family situation. It was awful. He made a very strong impression on me, and after meeting him I was interested in learning more about deaf people.

Greg and I met while we were both vacationing in Provincetown. He was standing on the deck of a bar with a group of friends, holding forth in sign language. I was very attracted to him the moment I saw him, both because he was cute and because he was signing with so much energy and vitality and enthusiasm. A friend of his, also deaf but with good speech, noticed me watching and came over and asked me if I wanted to meet him. Of course I said yes. It was awkward at first because I knew no sign language and he doesn't speak. But his friend interpreted for us at the beginning.

Greg and I spent the next four days together, and when we left Provincetown, we agreed to keep in touch when we got back to New York. At the time, I never expected that we'd develop into a couple.

Anyway, for the first day or two, we wrote back and forth. After the second day, though, we threw the paper away, and Greg started teaching me signs. He would sign a word or phrase, and then he would fingerspell the same word or phrase while speaking the letters. I would repeat the sign and the fingerspelling. I understood little of his speech, but I could clearly understand his pronunciation of letters and gradually learned the fingerspelling alphabet and ASL vocabulary. It took a lot of patience and good humor on our parts, but my lover has had experience in teaching ASL to hearing people and to foreign-born deaf adults. We found that, after a year, I am able to sign just about anything in a rudimentary way, though I am still learning ASL grammar and syntax.

Most of my friends have been supportive and even enthusiastic. Phrases like "That's so cool" have been typical responses. Greg is outgoing and unself-conscious around my friends, and most like him a lot and seem happy to communicate with him by using whatever works — writing, simple signs, fingerspelling, body language.

A few of my friends are perplexed and just can't understand why I'd want to deal with the "burden" of having a deaf lover. Sometimes they ask whether we can really communicate fully with each other, implying that our communication isn't somehow "complete." But they are a small minority. Some of my friends appear to feel uncomfortable trying to communicate with him, but we don't spend much time with them.

What's helped our relationship is my lover's good humor, positive attitude, understanding, flexibility, and honesty. He is simply one of the finest human beings I have ever met.

SAN DIEGO, *compiled by John Dibelka*

Lauri, age sixty-one

My lover "Evie" is thirty-seven years old. We don't live together, but we see each other one or two days a week, and we're in a committed relationship.

Before I met her, I didn't really have any impressions of deaf people. I had an aunt who was hard-of-hearing all her life, but that was just how she was.

Evie and I met about four years ago. She did a newsletter for a gay women's group where I gave a workshop, and my name was misspelled on the paperwork. One time, I figured, "These things happen." But when it happened again, though, and over and over, I called her to ask her to get the spelling right. I guess you could call it a "cute meet."

But it really took about two years for us to start seeing each other.

We met first over the phone, but I didn't know she was deaf. I could understand her, and she understood what I was saying.

Evie teaches ASL, so we practice together, but we don't use it much. Mostly in crowds, like at parties. We still communicate with speech most of the time. Evie has two hearing aids, although she was what she calls "stone deaf" from age nineteen until she was twenty-six. She doesn't know why she got partial hearing back. She identifies herself as deaf.

Being with Evie took some adjustments, but we're both willing to accommodate. The hardest thing for me was remembering not to talk with my back to her because then she can't lipread. I always look at her when I'm talking to her. Or if I don't, she reminds me. I try to maintain eye contact, and I don't talk too loud.

When we're sitting together, Evie is always on my right. It seems easier for her to read me from there.

I like to lie in bed in the dark and talk, but with Evie, when the lights are out, that means fall-asleep time or make-love time. She takes out her hearing aids when we make love, and then I talk close to her ear.

When I found out at first that Evie was deaf, I was curious. I felt sad: I thought it was such a pathetic thing for such a young girl. She was thirty-three at the time. Sometimes I can feel overprotective.

We had one bad incident when we were just starting to date and I gave a party. I saw Evie swivelling her head back and forth. She looked frantic, trying to keep up with conversations. She told me, "I want to be normal."

But when my best friend met her, the first thing she said about Evie was, "She can talk normal!"

SEATTLE, *compiled by Karen Bosley*

"SARAH," age thirty-six

Sarah became a sign language interpreter before she met her partner "Naomi," thirty-nine. She was comfortable in the deaf world and developed excellent communication skills, so communicating with Naomi wasn't a problem. I asked Sarah how becoming involved with a deaf woman affected her relationship with the hearing friends she had before she got involved with Naomi:

I found that my hearing friends were not very tolerant. They were not willing to make any sustained effort to get to know my partner. They did seem to enjoy Naomi, but communication was too difficult for them, so they didn't really try. No one tried to learn sign language and everyone talked a lot about me not having to interpret for them. But in reality I did become their interpreter.

Most of my hearing friends sign. I now have only a few hearing friends who do not sign, but even their attitude is more positive. I also limit my time with them. But when Naomi and I are both with them, they never offer to provide an interpreter. They also assume that because I am an interpreter, I chose a deaf partner.

Sure, we experience stresses. Some are connected to my role as the interpreter for Naomi in social situations. Often she will say that she doesn't want me to be responsible for interpreting. But when we are in hearing situations and there are no other interpreters, I feel that I should interpret for her.

The telephone is another stress point. We have only one line, so all calls — TDD and voice — come through that line. That means I have to be responsible for answering the phone all the time.

Sometimes I get resentful — not of Naomi when we can't do some of the same things together — but when the situation is not accessible to Naomi. For example, music concerts. They are not always interpreted, and that means I can't go with Naomi, though I would like to be there with her.

This relationship has given me a great opportunity to interact and be part of another culture. Also, Naomi understands me better in my professional role as an interpreter. Better than anyone else I know.

I think it's important that in a "mixed" relationship the hearing person should not expect the deaf partner to be the teacher.

✦

KAREN, age forty-three

Karen comments on her own relationship with Marilyn, forty-one:

In high school (1962–1966) we had a student teaching program and I was put in a class for deaf kids. They were four or five years old. When I look back on that experience now, I realize that it was an oral class. But that was my first real exposure to deaf people.

I had no other contact with deaf people until I moved to Seattle and met a prominent deaf leader at a conference. She had an interpreter, so I was able to communicate with her. I don't really remember how I felt about her being deaf, except that I realized I had met someone very different from me and I was excited.

I think I can say overall that I didn't really have any impressions of deaf people before I met them. I guess I had such limited contact that I didn't think about deafness or deaf people except the few times I ran into the woman in Seattle. And I knew absolutely nothing about deaf culture and deaf oppression. I didn't even know that a deaf culture existed.

How did I meet my lover? Well, I actually met her several times.

The first time she had called me on the phone at my workplace. I was the director of a local rape relief program, and we were not accessible to deaf women. Marilyn called me and was quite furious with our agency for not being accessible. I had only been with the agency for six months, and becoming accessible to deaf people was not something I had focused on. So her phone call was a "good kick in the butt" for me.

Then I saw her at a workshop, but we didn't really talk. Then I saw her again at plays, concerts, etc. I didn't really try to talk with her because I wasn't sure how to communicate with a deaf person, and I usually avoid people when I think they are mad at me (smile). So when I saw her I'd just smile and wave. When I think about it now, I think I must've looked rather ridiculous just standing there, smiling, waving, and never attempting to talk with her.

Finally, about six months after the "phone call," I was at a small party, and Marilyn was there and with an interpreter. I became very attracted to her, and when she took a smoke break outside I followed and began talking with her. We had a date several weeks later, but then we didn't see each other for three months. (I was out of town a lot and her father died, so getting together was hard.)

I didn't know sign language at first, so we had to rely on Marilyn's lipreading skills. She is quite good at lipreading, and now I can appreciate how much work it must have been for her to do this. Marilyn was born hearing and became deaf when she was six years old, so she is able to speak. When we started dating regularly, I began taking sign language classes. But it was several years before I felt that I could really communicate with her in sign, so I had to depend on her lipreading and speaking.

It has been very interesting for me to learn a new language and to have to express myself in it. I am a very verbal person. I like to talk and am more of a "thinker" type of person than a "feeling" type of person. So it was quite a challenge for me to learn to communicate in a second language. I find that I am quieter when I have to use sign language to express myself. But at the same time, I am excited to have learned a new language, both because I never thought I could and also because it has enriched my life.

We still have some miscommunications, because my signing skills need improvement. But basically our communication is fine. Over the years I have acquired many new and wonderful friends, both deaf and hearing people who sign. I have maintained only four strong friendships among those of my old hearing friends. None of them signs, but two of them make a big effort to make themselves understood and they also understand the energy that it takes for Marilyn to lipread them.

One friendship with a hearing couple that I developed during our relationship has floundered a lot. I think it's because neither of the women had bothered to learn sign language, and communicating for them is a struggle.

No one has ever said anything negative to me directly about having a deaf partner. I do discuss with all my hearing close friends the difficulties that Marilyn and I experience living in an inaccessible world.

And, actually, Marilyn and I rarely socialize as a couple with my hearing friends. It's too much work for me and Marilyn, and not much fun. Basically I've maintained some separate friendships, and the same is true of Marilyn. She also has several friends who are really her friends and not mine. But it is much easier for me to be included with her deaf or hearing signing friends than it is for me to include her with my hearing nonsigning friends. I think we have both come to accept this as the way it is, and it really is not an issue for us anymore.

I think that the hearing nonsigning friends I have will always remain my friends, but I doubt that I will develop any new hearing friends who don't sign or don't even try learning.

Our relationship is interesting for some other reasons. We have four cultures to deal with: I am Jewish and hearing, and Marilyn is gentile and deaf. We have both experienced a great deal of oppression in our lives as a Jew and as a deaf person. It helps as a couple having hearing friends who are part of the deaf community and who are also fluent in sign language, and having Jewish friends who can sign.

We have both taught each other about our cultures, and that feels great. I think we can each relate to the other's experiences with oppression, even though the ways we have been oppressed are different.

I also have to be clear about my limits and control my feelings about the world's unfairness to deaf people and to Marilyn in particular — feelings that can force me to do things I don't want to do. Then I start to resent her. For example, interpreting calls for Marilyn. I have to feel that it's okay for me to say no sometimes, and when I do say yes, really mean it. It has taken me time to work this out.

I love Marilyn very much. And part of what I love about her is her deafness and how it has made her into the person she is. I feel very honored to have been accepted by her deaf friends so easily, even though my signing was not always very good.

I have been blessed many times, and my life has been enriched by deaf culture and the deaf friends I have.

SAN FRANCISCO, *compiled by Frank V. Toti, Jr.*

"Stephen," age forty-five

Stephen met "Michael," then thirty-three, about ten years ago.

How did you meet?

On a Bay Transit Authority train.

Did you start a conversation?

There was no conversation. I was going away for the weekend and I had a suitcase. He walked up and got on the train. At the next stop, he saw me and nodded, kinda nodded again, and stood next to me. There was no need to stand, but he bumped my knee with his leg and kept pressing against it. He started talking, and that's how we met.

He chose me above all the other people on the train that day. I was the one.

Did he ride with you all the way to the airport?

He had to get off downtown because he was taking a bus back to where he lived.

Didn't you exchange phone numbers on the train?

Rather than give him my telephone number, I ... actually that's exactly what I did. He wanted my address, but I gave him my number. Since I was going away for the weekend, I thought, "Gee, I'm not going to give someone my address. There may not be anything there when I get back."

Did you know when you first met that he was deaf?

Well, I suspected it because he didn't speak clearly, and he also had a small hearing aid, so I figured this guy has trouble hearing.

Was he the first deaf person you ever met?

No. I had met several deaf people casually, but I never had them as friends. They were just speaking, lipreading, and hearing enough to communicate. It wasn't like I had fifteen deaf or nonhearing friends.

But for real purposes, meeting Michael was the first time you experienced an intimate relationship with a deaf person?

Yes, beyond "Hello, Oh hi, How are you, Do you work here?" So, yes, it was the first time.

Because he was able to speak, you were able to communiate freely right from the beginning and...?

It was an illusion that we could communicate freely by speaking.

Why was that?

I assumed that because he could hear a little bit, he could understand what I was saying, and what I meant by what I was saying. But that wasn't the case. We could communicate freely but we didn't know what the other was saying.

How did he feel about speaking to you as a form of communication between the two of you?

I don't know how he feels.

How do you feel about oral communication being the only way for a deaf person? Do you know any signs?

No, I didn't know signs, and I didn't learn signs. I'd say that the way we communicated was basically — just, how we maneuvered around each other. It was more physical. It was like animals who are used to being around each other.

So you operated on a nonverbal level. You just sort of knew intuitively how he felt, what he needed, how he responded to cues?

Yes, we mostly responded to cues. And simple verbal communication was okay. That worked.

"Get me the blue box," for example — that would work. But discussing something like, "I'm really troubled because work is bothering me," and "I can't work on this chapter tonight." Or, "I want to be alone tonight because I want to write." That kind of concept I couldn't relay in words.

Did you ever discuss the fact that you've never learned sign language? Has that ever come up in conversation?

He wanted me to learn sign and I didn't.

Why? Was that early on, or later on, in your relationship?

Oh, it was around midpoint.

And your relationship lasted?

We still talk to each other and see each other, but the intimate relationship lasted — oh, I have to think — about two and a half years.

So halfway through the relationship, he wanted you to learn sign language. It became an important point to him.

I didn't realize it at the time.

Was that because he didn't communicate to you that it was important to him that you learn sign language? Or was it something he never pushed you on, and you didn't realize how important it was to him?

It was the latter case. He didn't let me know how important it was, and so I didn't realize how important it was. I thought it was ... I was afraid it'd put me into a realm of people who couldn't speak, and that my circle of nonhearing friends would suddenly become bigger than it was. That was a fear of mine.

Was there ever an occasion when both sets of your friends met at your apartment? Or did you do things socially with one group and then with another? Was it "separate and apart, and never the twain shall meet"?

Oh Lordy. It's very complicated — this is really very complicated. Um, our mutual friends never met each other, *ever*. His friends never met my friends, and my friends never met his.

My friends all liked him, and the friends he introduced me to were all hearing. He never introduced me to signing deaf friends, or even just hearing-impaired like himself.

So it appeared to me that he knew nobody who was like him or deaf. That was the illusion he presented to me.

So the only people from his life you met were hearing like you?

Completely. It was almost as if he were the *only* deaf person he knew. I'm not going to start projecting what that could mean. The one big event he took me to was a major deaf convention in Boston — where there must have been thousands of people signing in a room — and he knew many, many, many people. It was almost like he had a secret life that I never knew about. And at that event I saw how many people he knew, how many people loved him, and how he related to them in a completely different way from how he related to me.

How did you feel that day?

I felt as though he had set me up as some kind of goal to attain, as if I was this hearing lover he'd won, like a prize. He got a hearing lover, and he was parading me around. It was an odd thing. But the convention itself was an interesting experience.

Was he feeling more secure at that point in your relationship? Was there a real sense of security between the two of you?

No, no. In fact, that part was getting even worse. I think his big fear was that I was going to leave him.

That's interesting. That at the point he thought he might lose you, he decided to show there were other sides to him.

Yeah. But it didn't deepen us. It didn't at all affect the other problems we were having. His wanting me to learn sign, or his taking me to this event and meeting these people — it didn't strengthen or weaken what was there.

When you were out in public together, did you notice that other people would look at you two?

No, I wasn't aware of anything like that.

So there wasn't any self-consciousness on your part?

My self-consciousness about him had nothing to do with his inability to hear as well as I could. It was founded on other things.

What was the best thing about your relationship with Michael?

There are so many things, but they all sound so trite.

Did you like his voice?

Yeah, that's a strange question. Actually, I liked everything about him physically — everything. I was completely enthralled with his body and everything about it. The sounds and the smells, the looks, the lines, and the textures — he was put together very well. For me, anyway. I suppose the physical side was the best part or the part that — yeah, I guess that's what it came down to.

Did Michael's being deaf make you look at things differently?

Oh yeah, of course. But I wasn't sure whether that was because he was deaf or because he was just the person he was.

For instance?

He picks fights very easily. I don't know if that has to do with his being deaf, or if he's just a tough little guy who picks fights. Plenty of people who are deaf pick fights, and plenty of people who are deaf don't pick fights.

Did he ever sign while he was talking to you?

He'd do it to make a point, but he wouldn't do it casually. But if he really wanted to confound me or to leave me defenseless, then he would sign without saying anything, like a secret language. Sort of what your parents would do, like "Let's say this, and they won't understand what we're saying." So it was like a little weapon.

So how did you feel when he did that?

I just figured, "He won that contest."

Did you ever ask him what he had done?

Yeah, and then he'd say, "Never mind," or lie.

How did you know that?

Because I know whatever he *said* it was, it didn't *look* like it was nice. Even if I didn't know, I'd get a sense of what was going on. There was never anything gentle or easy about our relationship. So there wasn't "I'd really like you to learn sign," during a chat over breakfast. It was mostly fighting and a lot of sex.

Did you ever live together?

No. That was one of the things that became a problem. He wanted to live together and I wouldn't agree to it. He was extremely possessive about my time. It was difficult for me to get time to do the stuff I was trying to do, so I couldn't even imagine together what it would be like.

Did you ever ask to meet some of his deaf friends, or wasn't it important to you?

No. I assumed that he was giving me the part of his life that he wanted to give me, and I wasn't hunting for more or less than that. That tends to be how I am with people. If he wanted to introduce me to deaf friends, that was fine; if he didn't want to introduce me, that was fine. I didn't try to interpret it. I never analyzed our relationship as being hearing versus deaf. Maybe that was a big blind spot.

I only saw him with his own set of neurotic behaviors, and I had my own set of neurotic behaviors. Sometimes they matched beautifully, and we got along perfectly. But other times we were the most opposite people in the world.

But I didn't attribute it to the fact that he didn't hear.

It didn't seem to be the problem. Maybe it was, but it didn't seem to be at the time.

✦

"Alan," age thirty-three

How old is your lover?

"Eric" is thirty-six.

How long ago did the two of you meet?

February 1989. Just a couple of days after Valentine's Day.

Did you know Eric before?

No, an interpreter friend of mine — I've interpreting since 1977 — invited me to a ski weekend at Tahoe with some of her friends. Her girlfriend at that time was deaf, and we went up for the weekned and that's where I met Eric.

Is your circle of deaf friends large?

It's varied, but I have few close deaf friends. Most of my close friends are hearing.

Why do you suppose that is?

Most of my close friends are ones I've had for years — a group of five friends. Of the people I've met along the way — who work with deaf people — I haven't met many who wanted to be friends. In my role as an interpreter, I try not to get too close to people. I try to maintain a professional distance. Also, I don't attend many purely deaf events.

Is Eric your first deaf lover?

Yes.

Given your professional distance, what was it about Eric that made you feel differently?

Well, it wasn't a professional setting; it was a group of friends. There was a storm on, so we couldn't ski. Eric and I got to know each other well. We clicked.

So deafness has not been a distinguishing characteristic in your relationship?

It is an issue in many relationships between a hearing person and a deaf person, but I had never thought I would have a deaf lover. I know several couples, both gay and straight, and I have seen some of their relationships fail. So I never had any intention of having a deaf lover, because I knew it could be difficult. By the same token, Eric wasn't looking for a hearing lover. Each of us just happened to be looking at the same time, mainly for companionship.

You say that deafness can be an issue? In what way?

Communication is at the heart of it. From what I have seen, hearing people who are pretty skilled with ASL are either interpreters, children of deaf parents, or both. Intermingling with a deaf spouse among hearing friends who don't sign can be difficult.

Such as?

Interpreting so that the the deaf person is never excluded from any situation. Interpreting a conversation that the hearing person initiates. It is also the difference between the two cultures. The hearing person grows up with television and radio, which are things deaf people don't have access to. It's also hard bringing a deaf person into a hearing person's family, especially if there is no deaf family member and no one signs.

Does Eric use his voice?

No. He was born deaf. Second-generation deaf — his parents, sister, uncles, and aunts — so he comes with a rich experience of deafness.

Have you met his family?

Eric is a first-generation American. His dad is from the Middle East, and he grew up during the First World War. He uses a unique form of ASL and is quite a storyteller. Eric's mom graduated from

Gallaudet in the 1940s, and she's passed on good English skills to Eric and his sister. That way I've been able to interact well with the family, particularly his mother and sister. But with his dad I mostly watch and listen.

Does that make you his favorite?

Anyone who sits still and listens at the time is his favorite.

Is Eric out to his family?

Eric is not out to his mom and dad. He is out to his sister.

When you mentioned English skills, what exactly did you mean?

His mother, on the TDD for instance, talks just like a hearing person. Eric has very good English skills as well. He was sent to oral school by his parents; then when he was ten, he went to the California School for the Deaf. In his junior year, he transferred to Gallaudet, went through the preparatory program there, and graduated with a B.A. He is a student, pursuing an M.A. in rehabilitation, here in the Bay Area.

What type of discrimination or ostracism have you experienced as a couple?

Here in San Francisco, it's common to see two men together. It is difficult, though, to have a private conversation like two hearing people. I can't just lower my voice so what I'm saying won't be heard. When people see us together, they will assume either I'm deaf or Eric's hearing. Sometimes I will play along with being deaf.

What is the biggest challenge in your relationship with Eric? Is it the same one as with your previous hearing lovers or unique to your situation with Eric?

I am a certified sign interpreter, and my previous lovers had nothing to do with deafness. It was hard to discuss with them the problems I confronted in my work, particularly when you have to explain all the things leading up to what it is you want to discuss and why you need their shoulder. That was one problem in the past.

With Eric, it's a different problem. Because the deaf commuity is so small, I can't come home and explain what happened in my day. He would know who I was talking about. So there is still that separation between home and work life. There is, however, more recognition of the difficulties I face, even if he doesn't know what the particulars are.

How does your family feel about Eric being your lover and his being deaf?

I am out to my brother and my sister. Because I have been involved in signing for so long, my sister took a sign language class a few years ago. In fact, she's very good with languages. My brother owned a restaurant in Riverside, and because of his interest in me, he hired deaf people from the deaf school nearby and picked up fingerspelling. So when they met Eric, they already had a communication springboard without having to have me there. Eric has only met my brother once, and my sister, whom I see periodically, communicates well.

Additionally, my previous lovers have also been from varied backgrounds. A lover of mine for six years was from Nicaragua. He spoke fluent English, but there still was a cultural division. Once again, my sister spoke Spanish, so she was familiar with the culture. There has not been a problem for my family in dealing with persons of different cultures.

A close friend of mine, from school, remembered quite a bit. Another friend, who no longer lives here, learned some signs from me and has a handle on it. Her hearing lover picked up some signs and we used to do things together.

Whose friends do you spend more time with?

Mine, usually.

Any reason for that?

Most of Eric's close friends live out East. We only visit there once a year. He doesn't have a close network of friends who live here in the city. When we go out to an event, it usually includes both deaf and hearing people, such as an interpreted play or a party.

Has it been your experience — and I recognize Eric is your first deaf lover — but does the degree of success depend upon what kind of common ground people find? Have some of the relationships lasted longer because the deaf person was able to voice, or the hearing partner made a strong effort to become fluent in sign?

I see two kinds of relationships. One is when the hearing person is already from a third culture — he is between the hearing and deaf worlds — so he is already on the periphery.

The other one is what I see with most gay couples. A hearing guy who knows nothing about sign language or deaf culture meets a deaf man in a bar, and they form a relationshop. I should say that I've seen one couple whose relationship lasted for years, even though the hearing partner never picked up any degree of sign. But for the most part, these relationships are failures.

Generally, I don't see that a deaf/hearing relationship should be any more or less successful than any other type of relationship. People break up all the time for all types of reasons. If people want to stay together, they will make the effort. At the same time, with all the straight couples I have seen, the hearing partner has always been fluent in sign language.

✦

"Lin," age thirty-seven

Lin was previously involved with a deaf lesbian woman for a year.

How did you first meet?

At a gay parade here in San Francisco. She was a friend of many people from the Rainbow Deaf Society. It was a place to socialize with other gay deaf people and also an important source of community spirit. I was an interpreter then, and I was not thoroughly integrated into the deaf community, but I was on the periphery and was certainly welcomed at many functions.

Are you still interpreting?

No. I had to quit because I had a repetitive motion illness, which still troubles me from time to time. I was doing some academic courses for English-based deaf students, and they wanted a lot of fingerspelling on subjects I knew nothing about. And so for two semesters my hands were more stressed than in the usual course of signing or interpreting.

Was "Jill" the only deaf woman you have been involved with?

Yes. There have been a couple of women, though, who were hard-of-hearing and were considering sign language as something they might rely on more.

Did Jill use her voice?

No, not at all.

Were your hearing friends comfortable with what you were doing? Did the idea of your having a lover and deaf friends seem strange to them?

It was unusual. Most of my hearing friends did not have deaf friends themselves, but they were very accepting. I was living with other people, and it was in that context of roommates that Jill and I had our relationship. My roommates were very accepting.

Did any of them learn to sign?

None of them tried to learn sign language, but they tried to picking up "home" signs from either one of us. At least they started picking up some signs or mime — something they could make up to express "Please stay for dinner," or "You're welcome," without using a formal language to do it. It was a series of polite but expressive gestures.

So you spent more time, then, with Jill's friends?

Yeah, I think we spent more time with her friends. Because everyone in the room could communicate. But sometimes I felt left out if the conversation went very fast. Though not as often as Jill was left out of conversations at my house. Either that or my roommate would feel she needed to leave so that I wouldn't have to keep interpreting what was said. It was easier to be with Jill's friends, but we often slept at my house. If we went out for the evening, we would do something in the deaf community; then we'd come back to my place.

So there was some interaction and Jill really liked my roommates a lot and enjoyed their company. And she tried to involve them in learning sign and teasing them. She had a lot of liveliness and humor and interest in getting hearing people to interact directly with deaf people in whatever way they could. She enjoyed pushing their buttons in a very friendly way.

Do you still communicate?

I haven't seen her for probably three years.

What did you like best about your relationship with Jill?

There were two things: the fun we had in being playful and teasing, and the sex ... What unnerved me during lovemaking was having to be creative to communicate. Or sometimes we'd need to stop and turn on the light and talk a little bit. After some experience we got better at that, but it still unnerved me not to be able to say things. We started to sign into each other's hands. That was quite romantic. I also did some fingerspelling against her throat. We liked to play a lot.

Does that mean you now feel completely comfortable with deaf culture? I mean, is it fully a part of your life?

I've never felt completely integrated into the deaf community, because I can hear. However, I think a number of people would consider me a friend of the deaf community, and while I had a deaf lover there was more acceptance of me in deaf home situations than has been the case lately.

Do you have any words of advice for someone who didn't know sign but was attracted to someone who is deaf? What would you say to a hearing person who wanted to become involved with someone who is deaf?

Oh, I don't know. I'd say something different, depending on what appears to be their motivation.

When you say motivation, you mean...?

Well, I think there's a range of things. There are some people who meet a person, they really like this person, and it turns out that person is deaf. There are other people who feel as though they like — or are drawn to — that inability to communicate. They don't know how to sign and don't have to deal with a lot of arguments because they don't have a common language. I think some people are drawn to that but I'm not sure that's a good motivation.

There are some people who think it is an extension of their helping profession. I'm not too crazy about that myself, but I know some deaf people who like having a hearing person because it is more convenient in some ways. Other deaf people don't feel that way, but some do. I have no objection to a couple composed of a deaf person who finds it convenient to have a hearing lover and a hearing lover who likes having a deaf lover.

I think it all depends on the individual. Some very complicated relationships are really wonderful; sometimes they are more complicated than most people know how to deal with, and they don't deal with it very well. I don't have anything universal to say on this subject other than that it is often complicated, and that can be truly wonderful.

FIVE

W. JAMEY WINKLER

ONE NIGHT STAND I

waking up at dawn,
groggy and nauseous,
slowly becoming aware
of those cold cheeks
against your own.

being afraid to move.

wondering where you are.

straining to see
the dim lights
of an unfamiliar clock
through the early morning
light.

creeping out of bed,
grabbing your socks,
wondering how far
is your car.

tiptoeing across the room,
trying to find
the door.

wanting so badly
to be alone,
unfazed,
in your own place...

as far away as you can
go from this stranger's home.

W. JAMEY WINKLER

THE HARVEST

THE WRINKLED OLD WOMAN stood at the door,
absorbing the sights of the harvest.
All nine of her children gathered
around her, playing on the floor.
She stood there in languid silence,
mesmerized by the young migrants
plucking apples from the trees.

The wrinkled old woman stood at the door,
admiring the sweaty pickers.
All nine of her children gathered
around her, singing songs of the poor.
She stood there, enchanted
by the bare-chested herculean virileans
picking apples and swatting at the bees
dancing through the leaves.

The wrinkled old woman stood at the door,
entranced by her lascivious view.
All nine of her children gathered
around her, telling gory stories.
She stood there—
compelled by the vision of brawny workers
drenched in their rain of sweat
as they withdrew sharpened hatchets
and held them high in their quivering hands.

The wrinkled old woman stood at the door,
her attention commanded by this sensous display.

All nine of her children gathered
around her, playing a game of War.
Oh, what a sight to see—
the glistening hatchets flying
through the cool autumn air.
And the trees fell,
one by one,
until no more stood for miles.

The wrinkled old woman stood at the door,
open-eyed and gaping
at the rape of her land.
Nothing was left, not even a trace of life.
Every square of her nature
stood defaced,
stacked into lonely piles
and set aflame.

The wrinkled old woman stood at the door,
staring at the remains of her vestal orchard.
All nine of her children had disappeared—
running to the fires, gathering
around the flames with open palms,
feeling the crispy heat of the cold air.
The men had taken the harvest with them.

W. JAMEY WINKLER

YOUR HIDING PLACE

August 1981

ACROSS THE DOCKS and the Hudson River, over in New Jersey, the neon Maxwell House Coffee sign flickers. In the river itself, a nearby boat falters while three men struggle with an unusually large box. They manage to push it overboard and it floats for a bit before it sinks into the murkiness below.

You began coming to the piers back in June when you found a hiding place of your own, concealed between two railroad beams where you could keep out of sight for hours. It is only in this place, the only place in New York City, that you feel protected and secure.

You first met Brad here in your hiding place and you can remember his wide grin as he gazed about the dank piers. Etched in your brain is the moment he turned to you and you leaned forward, consumed with curiosity, wanting to know every single thought this man had. And his gentle lips soon met yours.

Later he held you and murmured how beautiful you were. He ran his fingers through your sandy blond hair and kissed your ruddy cheeks. He peered at your dark eyebrows and asked if your hair had been dyed. You shook your head no. His hand then moved down to your waist while he commented on your boyish build. When you told him you were twenty years old, he gave you a devilish grin and remarked he liked his men young.

Brad was slender but muscular. His chiseled features were accentuated by a pair of coal black eyes and dark wavy hair. His thin nose was set precisely in between two prominent cheekbones. His wide grin exposed a set of flawlessly white teeth.

The men wandering about do not see you crouched in the shadows as they navigate through a large pile of scrap metal. The moonlight catches their faces, illuminating their peculiar features.

Your back begins to ache so you change positions. You lean against an old sofa cushion tucked between the beams, a cushion that was molded by the former owner's ass. Sometimes if you hugged the cushion hard enough and inhaled its air, you could catch a whiff of Brad's Grey Flannel cologne, but tonight there is only the smell of dried urine and stale whiskey.

Brad was extremely hairy, which was the only thing you could've done without. Hair covered his entire body from his back to his balls. You were constantly pulling those elusive strands out of your mouth.

But you and Brad met in your hiding place every Friday night for several weeks. Then he stopped showing up.

You haven't given up hope, though. You keep returning.

As the rotting boards creak loudly beneath you, you wonder whether the pier is actually able to hold your 140-pound frame. And you watch through the cracks the river surging below.

When you last saw Brad, you said your parents would be off in Europe for a few weeks, and you'd have the house all to yourself. He shook his head and said he'd be very busy over the next couple weeks. You asked for his phone number, and he laughed, saying he didn't even have one.

That night he seemed distant. You wondered if he was somebody truly important ... someone who wanted to hide his own identity. Perhaps he was a millionaire; or even a millionaire's son. Or even better yet, an elderly millionaire's only son.

You sigh, and return to watching the men walk about slowly. They all hold deathlike masks as they file by, one by one, in their somberness. Everyone looks so sad, you think, as you light up your joint and inhale deeply.

In your haze, you begin to wonder about them: Were these simply ordinary men with perfect wives and children? Would any of their wives wonder where their husbands were at this very moment? Or...

A spasm quickly shoots up your thigh. As you massage your leg gently, you accidentally kick over an old can of beer. One of the men nearby looks up, sees you, and gives you a toothless grin under a bulbous nose, leering eyes, and thin grayish hair in disarray.

The Ugly Man slowly makes his way toward your hiding place. You do not move. He stops right in front of you and strokes the bulge inside his pants. You do not hide your expressions of repulsion. You look away, wishing he would just disappear.

Scanning the piers, you see someone who looks very much like Brad. The Ugly Man sees him too, and you both watch him in the distance as he crosses the West Side Highway toward you, slipping between cars.

As he comes closer, you see The Man is much taller and walks with a slight limp. But he does have Brad's build, and his grin seems familiar. You stand up so he'll remember your hiding place.

The Ugly Man steps closer to you, but you give him a glare that sends him off into the dark shadows.

You return your gaze to The Man, who still hasn't seen you. As you stretch your arms in the moonlight, a movement beside you catches your eye.

A fat man stands nearby in a pair of sweatpants and a white t-shirt with the words "Fuck Me" in big black letters. You cringe at the idea of him bent over, legs open, moaning loudly for you to move in faster. He waves to you eagerly. You stare at him for a long moment before you give him the finger. He looks at you, surprised, and then swings his own arm up with his middle finger. He turns and waddles over to the other side of the piers.

After scanning the area for a few minutes, you spot The Man talking to an older man in leather. You raise your arms again, pretending to stretch. He looks up, but you can't tell whether he is looking your way. You smile, and for a second he seems to smile, but you are not sure.

Two other men walk by and dissolve into a shadowy spot nearby. You ignore them, and you watch The Man shake the leatherman's hand.

The Man lights a cigarette, and as he slowly walks over to you, a rush of anticipation rises in your body. He is the one, you tell yourself.

When he stops in front of you, you struggle for words but he motions you to keep quiet.

He pulls you to him. And you feel Brad's lips touch yours.

You feel your pants dropping and his hot breath panting on your neck.

You look over his shoulder and all you can see are a few pairs of blinking eyes in the shadows.

January 1982

Even though it's very late and cold now, you climb the steps out of the Christopher Street subway stop onto Seventh Avenue South. The intersection bustles with cars honking and people scurrying between them. You glance at the familiar sights: Village Cigars, the Lion's Head Restaurant, and the blinking World Trade Center.

You moved into the city three months ago after finding a job in a deli and a rare cheap deal of a studio apartment on West Seventeenth Street. But the thrill of living in the city has already worn off. You have become tired of your phone not ringing, your TV set not working, and your cat not purring. In fact, your cat doesn't want your attention and has been hiding behind the stove for a few days now. The world seems to have forgotten about you — everybody has something else to do, and their lives are moving forward. So you've set out once again for the piers.

A young man approaches you, asking if you wanna buy dope, but you rush by him, crossing Seventh over to Christopher. The sidewalks are coated with a thin layer of melting snow. The air is brisk with an odd touch of warmth in it. The cold dampness seeps into your torn sneakers and you curse yourself for wearing the wrong shoes on such a cold, wet night.

You walk all the way west on Christopher to the familiar highway. When a gap finally appears in the traffic, you skitter through. You make your way over to your hiding place. It is empty. You scan the men: it's only a crowd of Ugly Men, Fat Men, Bald Men, Short Men ... On a night like this you may have to settle for whoever's available: a mediocre-looking man could come across as very striking as long as he looks better than the others. But whenever a better-looking man comes by, all eyes go to him. Competition is very fierce when every man wants someone better-looking.

Suddenly you see someone jump out of his truck parked in the parking lot across the highway from you. He is tall and muscular, with a thick shock of hair and a stride that reminds you of Brad.

You step out of your hiding place, watching him as he walks toward you. Up close, he is actually heavyset with a pockmarked face and a desperate smile. His thick shock of hair turns out to be a flat hat. He exemplifies the reason no one should size up anyone from afar. He motions you to follow him to his truck.

You step backward away from him and turn around. You stand there for a long time without feeling. Facing the fading lights of New Jersey, you have become a river with a lost sense of time. Finally you notice the men everywhere are trying to escape the morning light.

When you turn around at last, the man is waving at you from inside his truck. He flashes his headlights three times.

Your throat turns tense. You struggle to breathe as your legs carry you over to the truck. You disappear inside and when the door clunks shut, his strong hands roam over your body in the comforting warmth and darkness. You try to think about Brad and you realize you can no longer envision what he looked like.

March 1982

The icy sheath of winter is finally eroding. On the way over to the piers, you stop at the Christopher Street Bookshop for poppers. You haven't used them in quite a while because they burn the insides of your nose and make the skin under your nostrils peel. But a whiff now and then wouldn't hurt, you figure; in fact, it seemed a great way to welcome spring.

Outside of the All-American Boy Store, you notice a man stepping out with a few packages under his arms. He is so remarkably pure-looking, with stylish blond hair, deep-sea blue eyes, and a clear complexion. He glances at you briefly, and you smile. His eyes dart away as he passes right by you. You stop and turn around, waiting for him to do the same. He doesn't, and you watch him as he pauses to talk to another beautiful man leaning against a stop sign. They put their arms around each other and stroll away together.

You arrive at the piers and scan the small crowd. The men aren't very attractive. You decide to wait, so you head over to your hiding place. On the way there, you pass several men. You check out each one and notice that not one of them has looked your way. You wonder if it's the way you look or what you're wearing. Blue jeans and a varsity jacket can't be *that* much of a turn-off.

At least nothing seems to have changed in your hiding place.

You step down between the two railroad ties when a pair of eyes squint back at you.

He stands up. He is muscular and lean, with a dark beard. You smile at him, knowing he has to be yours because of the slim pickings out there.

You sit down next to him while he looks away, bored, at the downtown skyline.

Suddenly he looks at you.

You are startled, and then you smile again.

Displeasure crosses his face as he looks away.

A cold moisture collects into tiny droplets on your forehead, and a dribble of sweat rolls down your side from your armpit to your waist. "Umm, are you from around here?"

He shakes his head.

"Where are you from?"

"Why d'you wanna know?" he asks.

You shrug. He looks at you blankly as you offer him a vial of poppers. He looks at the brown vial curiously. "What is it?"

You try to tease him. "Room odorizer."

He gives you a ha-ha frown and looks away.

You look at him for a while. "I think you're very good-looking," you say at last.

He looks at you as if he's been insulted. "What did you say?"

"I like you."

A short laugh escapes from his throat.

"Well, I'm a lot better than the others out there."

He observes you for a long moment. "Not really," he says thoughtfully.

You cringe, barely holding yourself up as a strong wind rushes in. You feel a little queasy. You wonder if he is also seeing Ugly Men, Fat Men, Bald Men, Short Men ... and which one he's labeled you as.

He smiles at someone walking nearby, and his smile catches your eye. You lean forward and realize quickly he is Brad — he is Brad! You grin and whisper into his ear.

He looks up, surprised. "How'd you know my name?"

"It's me." You smile. "Remember?"

Brad shakes his head. You notice some gray in his hair and creases under his eyes.

He sighs as you glance at your watch. It is close to dawn. Even though the piers are still black with shadows from high fences and buildings across the highway, the first slice of the rising sun cuts through the darkness of your hiding place.

"We met here last June."

Brad nods. "Is that so?" He checks out a man walking by.

You put your hand on his thigh, and he looks up at you angrily. "Look, why don't you leave me alone? I was here first. You're not my type, okay?"

Your muscles tighten and ache as you begin to feel very stupid. You just leap up and run in no particular direction.

You find yourself right on the pier's end as tears slide slowly down your cheeks. You smell the putrid morning dampness below along with the urine and broken cheap cologne bottles near your feet.

The sound of waves sloshing below is very soothing.

You give in to that sound, wanting to be free of your own pain, and somehow you feel the shiveringly cold river rushing all around and inside you ... You are so tired, so tired of struggling. The mucky water fills your mouth, but as you are being carried away, you know this is a compromise you can live with.

After all, no one wanted to share your hiding place.

"GEORGE"*

SMOOTH SKIN, SMOOTH TALK

EVEN THOUGH I WAS BORN DEAF, I find myself very frustrated with ASL. I had good experiences with speech therapy through my parents and the John Tracy Clinic materials sent from Los Angeles, so I didn't learn sign language until I was ten or eleven.

So many deaf people — when they use ASL — often don't slow down for me, or even repeat for me. Also, the syntax of ASL can be a little confusing. But I do love sign language.

I envy straight couples who can have children of their own. I guess it comes from having been straight until I was thirteen or fourteen, when a hearing friend made me realize that I was gay after all. Even though I prefer men, I find I still want a child of my own.

I've always had mixed feelings about gay bars.

They're always filled with sluts, but then again, if you want to pick up a man, they're the best place to go. I always feel edgy when I bring my lover to a bar for drinks with friends, because I'm afraid that someone else will steal him away from me.

Sometimes when there's a fight between deaf people in the bar, I'm usually asked to calm them down.

The first time I drank beer, something really funny (and very embarrassing) happened.

---

*This interview was conducted by the editor on July 11, 1992.

I was wearing a pair of white shorts, and I had just drunk some beer. It was all right, and I got used to the taste. I put my beer on this stand in the bar where a deaf friend of mine and I were talking and signing away. My lover was nearby; I was having a great time. Somehow or other, my hands in the middle of their signing knocked my mug of beer all over my shorts.

Imagine this — my shorts were very white, and there was this brownish-yellowish stain all over. Worse yet, it was all over my crotch, and I had to rub it all off. Everyone watched me trying to rub it off, and I was too embarrassed to continue.

So I ran out, disappeared, and never went back that night.

The seventeenth person that I had sex with was my first love. I was then twenty-five years old and in my second year of college. It was also my first gay bar, and there he was. Looking back, I know that falling for the first person you saw in a gay bar was a big mistake, but what do you know when you've never been in a gay bar before?

My first love was hearing and Hispanic. (I've always liked men with smooth skin.) And then right after him was this gorgeous Italian man who turned out to be married. His lies hurt me, and when he finally admitted that, yes, the rumors about him were indeed true, I walked away from him.

But I could tell he really liked me because I was deaf and different. Very easygoing and relaxed — that's me. I've learned that my ideal lover has to have a sense of humor, respect, and self-confidence. (Of course, he has to have smooth skin too!)

I wish the entire hearing gay community could learn sign language so I wouldn't have to deal with the same old thing — we meet, and I have to teach him signs, only to find him forgetting everything all the time. It's tiring. And I find it just as frustrating that other deaf gay people in the Boston area — and outside of Boston — are so hard to find. Perhaps living in the wrong neighborhood has something to do with it.

"RICKY"*

GOING THE OTHER WAY: INTERVIEW WITH A DEAF GAY BUSINESSMAN

HOW DO YOU SEE YOURSELF FIRST: as a deaf person or a gay person, or are those labels equal in your view?

I view myself more as a deaf person than a gay person. Gay is such a small part of me these days — I'm open to everyone and don't live in the closet. Since I'm an owner of a manufacturing company [in St. Paul, MN], I don't have to worry about being gay or hiding in the closet. So I look at myself more as a deaf person because it's a frustrating world out there for me. Being deaf is very difficult on a day-to-day basis.

From your own experiences, how do you think the straight deaf community feels about gay people now? Are they still homophobic?

Where are they? I don't socialize with any of the straight deaf people. I haven't seen any of them for years. Are there still straight deaf people around? I have no idea. Honest, I don't hang around them at all. I don't bump into them, or maybe I just didn't know many to begin with. I only have a few deaf gay buddies — that's it — but I have a lot of hearing gay friends.

What was your work life like before you started your company? Were you happy working for other people?

Nawwww. I was such a great worker, and they knew it. They did appreciate me, but I was underpaid. Imagine doing a job worth ten dollars an hour for three-fifty an hour for a year. Anyway, I realized

*This interview was conducted by the editor via TDD.

that I was good, and that I could really do anything, so I quit.

I searched for an answer: what kind of a business could I start? I went to New York City and lived there for two months. I found my answer there — it was written on the wall: a greeting card company.

Just like that?

Yes!

But weren't you scared when you started your company? Weren't you afraid of losing all that money, time, and energy you'd put into it? How long ago did you start your company?

It's been over twelve years now. In the beginning I did not understand many things, but I grew and learned the hard way. I did not understand the term "fear" in the business sense, because all I knew was that when you borrow money from the bank, you are playing with the bank's money, not your own, and if I lost, it'd be the bank's loss, not mine. So I knew that from the beginning. I was lucky, very lucky, to be right every time. I made new products, and customers love them. If your product can speak for itself, it will sell by itself. And I grew up with this philosophy: "Where people go, I go the other way."

Hasn't the deaf gay community helped you in this enterprise?

Nope. There's no cooperation. Deafs are very easily jealous of each other, and they won't let you win. I'm not that way. I've helped out a lot of deafs. The problem is that some have a tendency to back-stab others. It's a very old and famous story in the deaf community — for any deaf person who is successful. So I was very careful in the beginning, and I've looked out for the last twelve years. My only true friends for a long, long time were hearing. But in the past year, I've begun to socialize with some deaf gay people, and I find they are good friends.

Our mutual friend told me, when I first proposed to him the idea of interviewing you, that you'd be reluctant because you had been written up in the gay press, and you found that it didn't help your company. Do you find that still to be true today?

Sometimes. It depends. If the story is about the greeting cards themselves, then it does help sell the cards. But if the story is about me owning a gay greeting card company, nope. It doesn't help my business. That's why I don't bother with it anymore. It just doesn't help.

You've told me before that you have hearing people working for you, and they are mostly straight; you don't tend to hire gay people. Wouldn't that be construed as homophobic?

Ha. The truth is, I have two straight people and two gay people working for me, adding up to a staff of four. I've always had both straight and gay people working for me. I hire whoever comes out best in the interview, not based on whether they are gay or straight. I'm much more interested in their skills. If they can handle the job, that's most important. Their backgrounds are not as important to my company.

Do your hearing workers know signing — a little or a lot?

My manager is very good with signs. He's been going to sign language classes. He wanted to go, so I offered to pay for him. He was so thrilled.

Starting up your own company — let alone keeping it going — must require quite a few particular qualities to succeed. What qualities do you find have helped you the most?

Humor. People need humor. Humor is the best medicine in this cruel, ever-changing world, and my cards contain mostly humor.

Humor is the only quality required for a successful business? What about good financial sense?

Oh, yes. The product must have a great sense of humor, and must be innovative in some way — for example, the scratch-and-peek cards, which I invented, and other ideas which were very original. But for business sense ... Hmmm. I guess I've been lucky enough not to have to worry. I usually just dove in. Whenever I wanted something to which my accountant would say, "No, no, no. You can't afford it" — I just dove in and did it. I believed that my reward would come later. And usually, it did.

Have you had other deaf people — gay or straight — come up to you and say, "I'd like to start a new business of my own"? What would be your advice to them?

Hmmmm. Actually, I'm still waiting for someone to come and ask me that question. So far, no one's asked me. Shucks!!! Hmmm. My advice? I'd ask them, "Do you understand the product you want to create or sell?" Or, "Are you willing to work so hard for nothing for three to five years, and then be happy with the reward after the fifth year?" If the answer is yes, then they should give it a big try.

ROBERT I. ROTH

BOY SCOUT OF AMERICA

AS THE PINK OLDSMOBILE HEADED NORTH on the Sunshine State Turnpike, its chrome gleamed in the Florida sun. In the passenger seat, I looked at the map, giving my dad directions in a loud voice on how to get to Sebring. At ten years old, I was excited to be off on my first experience away from home to spend a week with other Boy Scouts from all over the state.

In the backseat were two boys, Denny and Charlie. Denny was from the North Miami troop that I belonged to; Charlie was a friend of Denny's from another troop. I knew in some indistinct way that I was different from Denny and Charlie: I wanted to be their friend, to be liked. I knew they were hearing and I wasn't.

I was taught, however, at school and at home, that being deaf didn't make a difference. Though I had hearing friends in my neighborhood, I never thought of them that way. They were just kids on my block. I went to school on a small bus with other kids who were deaf, blind, or disabled. The yellowness of the bus screamed out, "There's something wrong with the kids in this bus! Come and look!" I was ashamed that I didn't go to my neighborhood school, only two blocks away. At my school, among the kids who moved their hands in a combination of sign and voice, I had many friends. Confronted with the occupants in the backseat, I hadn't the slightest idea of how to befriend boys who could hear.

In between looking at the map and watching for the road signs to make sure we were going in the right direction, I would study the boys in the backseat. They were visibly talking: their jaws were moving up and down, punctuated by what looked like giggling or laughing. I marveled at their familiarity with each other: hands lightly poking Denny's thighs to point out some happening in a passing car, or elbows nudging Charlie's chest provoking laughter at an unheard joke. Their loud laughing my hearing aid could pick up; it was their conversation I couldn't understand. My dad was too busy driving to repeat what was being said. (My mother always repeated everyone's conversations to me at family gatherings; she became rather famous for her loud voice.)

I desperately wanted to know what the two boys were talking about. I had long ago mastered the art (or had I?) of pretending to understand what was going on, by laughing at the right moments. I always made sure that I looked like I was listening, and I laughed when others laughed. The secret was to have the beginnings of a laugh on your face. It may appear like a perpetual grin, but at the right time, it could be interpreted by others as a laugh. This took care of that split-second between the time that others laughed and the moment when you realized that yes, true to business, they were laughing. So, pretending to understand Denny and Charlie, I was laughing away without the slightest clue as to what I was laughing about. It often seemed, from their curious glances at me and each other, that they didn't have a clue as to what I was laughing about, either.

In between figuring out what the boys were saying and looking at the map, I focused on the rocket ship perched on the car's broad hood. Or I counted off the white stripes on the road that the rocket seemed to be whooshing over. After several hours of counting white stripes, we finally arrived at Sebring.

Dad dropped us and our backpacks off at the main building. My sense of adventure overcame the momentary terror of seeing the Eighty-Eight drive off, its tires spewing a trail of dust. I didn't know anyone except Charlie and Denny, and they didn't really count.

A man seeming years older than Dad walked up to the three of us; he had the look of authority about him. He talked with the two boys; they started following him, so I did too.

After several attempts at conversing with me, the man pointed to some tents grouped around a clearing and tried to tell me that I should go there, as if I should pick a tent and get settled in.

I chose a tent in one corner because it seemed empty. Inside were two canvas cots. I laid out my sleeping bag and got out the *Mad* magazine I'd bought the previous day. I still remember the cover clearly; it had the numbers "1961" printed boldly across the cover along with the words, "The most upside-down year since 1881!" Turning the magazine upside down confirmed that the numbers still read "1961." I felt upside down, too. What was I doing at Sebring? Who was going to talk to me here? No one waved their hands to talk. Those who did try to talk with me curtly waved me away whenever I responded with a "What?"

I remember little of that week. Nothing made sense to me; nothing was explained to me. I figured out the activities by following along with whatever anyone else was doing. The first night, I followed the others to an odd building with no roof; upon entering I discovered it was a communal shower.

I was horrified at the thought of taking my clothes off in front of other people; no one had prepared me for something so unthinkable. I walked out and went a week without taking a shower, preferring instead to sponge myself at the washbasins near the latrines. Otherwise, the week was a blur of obtaining badges for cooking, canoeing, whittling, and so forth. These badges were for a pea green sash that was part of the Scout uniform.

I don't remember how Robert and Brad, the two Eagle Scouts, knew that I was lonely. I had seen them before during the week; they always seemed to be together. I had wanted to befriend Robert, but with Brad always around, there never was an opportunity. Robert was the taller of the two, with broader shoulders. His hair was black, cut longer than the crew cut that Brad and other boys had. The fact that Robert and I shared the same name appealed to me — we had something in common. Surely, I thought, he would like me and be a friend if I could somehow meet him.

I remember walking back to my tent alone when Robert and Brad caught up with me. Robert asked how I was getting along.

Surprised at their sudden interest in me, I said, "Fine" — my usual denial when there was a problem related to my not being able to hear.

Then they suggested a prescription for making friends; it was used by world leaders and immediately bonded people together. Did I want to know that secret to making friends? I was so lonely and desperate to have friends in this place miles away from home that I was game for anything.

Robert described to me the secret, while Brad nodded in assent. The secret was to get on your knees and take the other person's penis into your mouth and blow it. I was surprised; like the communal shower, no one had ever told me about "blowing." Brad, seeing the look of incredulity on my face, followed Robert's lead and picked up on the world leader story: "That's how President Kennedy and Premier Khrushchev get along. It's done all over the world." Well, that seemed like irrefutable evidence to a ten-year-old mind. It took a few more minutes for them to overcome whatever doubts I had left.

They led me to their tent, which of course looked just like mine, but without my things in it, their tent lacked the security mine had.

Robert told Brad to go first while he stood lookout in front of the tent.

I continued standing, at a loss what to do. It was Robert I wanted to be friends with. I looked up at Brad's face. He seemed to stand at least two feet taller than me. He motioned for me to kneel.

I hesitated, not sure of what he had said.

His hand moved to my shoulder and insistently pushed me down.

I bent down on the dirt floor. I felt a burning in my cheeks. I faced his belt buckle emblazoned with the words "Boy Scouts of America." His hands blocked my vision as they fumbled with the buckle. Then the zipper glided down, revealing his white underpants, their brightness in contrast to his dark green pants.

As his hands pushed down both underwear and pants to his knees, I was intrigued by the downy hair just below his navel.

Then I saw his penis. It was odd, different, and larger than mine, surrounded by smallish hairs. I'd never seen another penis before, aside from my brother's when we took baths together.

Brad pushed his penis against my lips. I was surprised by its soft, silky texture. I didn't know what to do, but I felt a growing sense of confusion. I realized that I shouldn't be here, yet my body remained fixed, unable to move. I felt, again, harder, his hand on my shoulder. Looking up at his face, he broke his leer to tell me to just blow on it.

Fingers from his other hand seemed to pry my mouth open. His penis went into my mouth. Oddly, it grew firmer and hotter inside. The heat of its skin felt strange and, for some nameless reason, comforting. I blew on it, as instructed, inhaling and exhaling through my nose. I willed myself not to touch the penis with my tongue.

After a few minutes of steady blowing, Robert came inside the tent. Brad released me while Robert took his place. Robert's pants were already down around his knees; his penis was already hard.

I felt defeated. I finally understood that Robert's intentions were not friendly.

My mouth accepted Robert, as it had Brad. I felt Robert's hands at the back of my head. They were insistent, pushing my head forward. My tongue inadvertently touched his penis, reveling at its smooth texture. My saliva wet the bottom of his penis. A sudden release of pressure, coupled with the natural tendency to pull back, slid my mouth backwards over his penis.

This was followed once again by pressure moving my head toward his body. As my nose nestled momentarily in his sparse hair, the light aroma of sweat made me dizzy. As Robert held my head firmly, I continued this motion for what seemed an eternity.

Then Robert stopped, pulling out of my mouth.

I looked up.

Robert told me to go, waving me out. I got up and pulled aside the tent's flap, surprised at the sudden sunlight. No one was out there.

I walked toward my tent. Inside, I tried to figure out what had happened. This hadn't made any friends for me — what had I done? In a panic of regret, I grabbed my drinking glass and ran out of the tent toward the washbasins.

At one of the sinks I filled up my glass and rinsed my mouth. Did I do that? I rinsed again. Why don't they like me? I rinsed again and again.

The day came to leave camp. I was glad to see Charlie's dad. He said, "Hello," the first nice word anyone had said to me in the last few days. When Denny and Charlie backed away from me and were only too happy to let me sit in the front seat of the red Chevrolet, I realized that the whole camp knew what had happened.

I felt my face burn.

But I consoled myself with the thought that my dad's car was a year newer and an Oldsmobile...

A few months later, I came home from school and picked up the mail on the way into the house. My heart raced as I noticed the "Boy Scouts of America" logo on the envelope, and it was addressed to my dad.

I had not gone to a troop meeting since camp ended, refusing to go whenever my mother suggested it. I was sure that Denny had told the whole troop what happened. Fear ran through my body: My secret was known to all the Scoutmasters and now my father would be informed of the sordid truth! He would be totally disgusted with me and never look at me again.

I went into my bedroom, locked the door, and stared at the envelope. With trepidation, I opened it and read the letter. The top of the paper announced in small letters, "Founded 1908 by Sir Robert Baden-Powell."

Fear, relief, and revulsion went through my body as I read these words: "Your son recently had the time of his life Scouting at Boy Scout Camp in Sebring, Florida. A contribution to continue the work of the Boy Scouts of America would be appreciated so that other boys may also enjoy scouting."

I tore up the letter into small pieces and threw it away.

ROBERT I. ROTH

SAY THE WORD

IT WAS DIFFICULT TO SEE the audiologist. The window was a series of glass panes with about an inch of air between each pane. Although the window was designed to reduce noise coming into my space from her room, the effect was that of multiple shadows and diffused light. Unless the desk lamp shone directly on the audiologist, it looked like three audiologists were testing my hearing. She was busy looking at some books and adjusting dials. I was born with a "profound sensori-neural hearing loss, with damage to the cochlea, etiology undetermined." I had enough residual hearing, it was agreed, for speech lessons to be beneficial.

This was my twelfth annual hearing test.

While waiting for her to begin, I looked around my room. It was an airless room about five by seven feet. Tiny holes no bigger than a pencil point punctured the walls and the ceiling in a diagonal pattern, as if the room was wallpapered in perforated metal. In one corner of the room was a small child's chair. In the other corner was a box of various toys, some *Cat in the Hat* books, and old issues of *Look* magazine. Above the box was a satin banner with the word "RADIOEAR," and underneath it, the phrase, "World's Finest Hearing Aid."

My first hearing aid was a box as big as a car battery, connected to headphones that I wore on my head at home and at school. My parents' friends said I looked like Arthur Godfrey.

Then I had a hearing aid, a Sonotone, that was the size of a transistor radio, strapped to the middle of my chest with white straps. Neighborhood kids called me a girl because it looked like I was wearing a bra. Following that, for a short time, I had a Zenith. My mother tells me I flushed it down the toilet.

I sat facing the window on an armchair made of metal, but upholstered generously in a dark green vinyl. In an effort to make the hour go faster, I helped myself to one of the headphones and, after adjusting it on my head, I was ready for the testing to start. Finally, my left ear could discern a deep humming. The testing was about to begin.

The tests always started with a series of tones for the left ear, then the right ear. Then a series of words followed, again starting with the left ear. I believed that if I heard all the words and gave the correct responses, my hearing would miraculously improve to the point where I'd no longer need a hearing aid.

The audiologist explained, as she had the year before and the year before that, that I should raise my left hand if I heard something in my left ear, and my right hand if I heard something in my right ear. Each year, I was always eager to show that my hearing had improved. I really tried my best to be cooperative. Often, I heard the same tone, two or three times: Was the audiologist deliberately repeating the tone or were my ears ringing?

Then it was time for the words. This was a test designed to determine the amount of residual hearing I had for speech comprehension. The more residual hearing I had, the more I could comprehend the speech of other people, and therefore the better I could replicate that speech. The audiologist read the words from the list, and the list never changed from year to year.

"Say the word 'airplane.'"

I visualized one of those new DC-8 jetliners. "Airplane," I said in my high, nasal voice.

"Say the word 'baseball.'"

"Baseball." In my mind's eye I saw my brother swinging the bat in a game with the kids on my street.

"Say the word 'cowboy.'"

I thought of Will Hutchins, the hero of "Sugarfoot," my favorite Western on television. I never understood the stories on the show, but I liked his easygoing manner and his lopsided grin. "Cowboy."

"Say the word 'hot dog.'"

"Hot dog."

"Say the word 'sidewalk.'"

This one always confused me: Was it "sidewalk" or "sideway"? Or was it "sideboard"?

"Sideboard." Better to play it safe.

I watched her as she wrote in her notebook.

"Say the word 'railroad.'"

"Railroad." It came out sounding like "wailwoad."

The words were then repeated in my left ear, with which I couldn't hear as well as with my right ear. I had to do a lot of guessing.

Finally the words were over, and she left her room. I took off my headphones and clipped my hearing aid, a Radioear, to my belt as the audiologist pulled open the door to my room. The door, which was at least a foot thick, let in a flood of fluorescent light as it opened. After she made adjustments on some switches on the wall, I followed her outside.

We walked to her office, where we joined my mother. The audiologist explained the results, which were of course the same as last year's. And the year before. My hearing didn't get better, it wasn't going to get better. As I listened to the audiologist, I willed myself not to cry as the truth hit me: I would always be deaf.

✦

Martin Morrisey was my speech teacher. Not too long after my deafness was diagnosed, my parents hired him to teach me how to speak. Mr. Morrisey taught me how to blow out a match with my nose as a prelude to learning how to blow my nose. And he taught me how to play Chinese checkers. As we played, I had to clearly say what my next move was going to be.

We lived in Chicago at that time: I loved my Saturday trips to the Loop. After an hour with Mr. Morrisey, my mother treated me to English muffins at Marshall Field's. Afterwards, we'd shop or visit the Art Institute. When I was eight, my family moved to Miami and we left Mr. Morrisey behind.

As my bar mitzvah approached, my mother asked me if I thought Mr. Morrisey might enjoy coming. Because bar mitzvahs, for a Jew, are a rite of passage into manhood, the year leading up to my thirteenth birthday was spent studying Hebrew, discussing ethics in Sunday school with the rabbi, and practicing reading excerpts from the Torah and Haftorah.

I was excited by the prospect of Mr. Morrisey's coming; he'd see how well I had progressed in my speaking abilities. He had moved to California a few years before, but my mother kept him informed of my progress. I had liked him, and agreed that he should be the guest of honor.

He arrived several days before the bar mitzvah on a train from Los Angeles. My mother took me to the Trade Winds Motel, where he was staying. The three of us visited for a while, and then she left to do some errands.

The television was on, and "Sugarfoot" was playing. I watched Will Hutchins mount his horse and turn toward the camera, flashing that lopsided grin.

I sat on a chair facing Mr. Morrisey, who was sitting on the bed. I was aware the dynamics were different now: he was my speech teacher, yet not my speech teacher — this visit was not going to be a speech lesson. He didn't look much different from the way he had looked five years before; however, for the first time I noticed his features. He was slightly overweight, but not unusually so; the word used at the time was "portly." His face, framed by jet black hair, was clean-shaven, except for a pencil-thin moustache. He was easy to lipread, for his teeth were white and straight.

Although he corrected me a few times on my pronunciation, I relaxed and began to relate to him as a person, as someone who had come all the way from California just to see me. By this time, he was relaxed as well, lying on the bed on his side, with his arm bent at the elbow and his hand propping up his head. We caught up with where he lived, who my friends were, and how the bar mitzvah preparations were going. He was different from other men my parents' age: he seemed interested in what I had to say, and he conversed with me as an equal.

In between watching Will Hutchins on TV and talking with Mr. Morrisey, *something* was happening to me. The room's temperature was getting warmer, even though I could see that the air conditioner under the window was on, its breeze gently billowing the drapes away from the wall. I wanted *something* to happen: My penis was getting hard. I was aware of my giddiness, the warm yellow light from the lamp, the flickering black-and-white glow from the TV — and yet I had no idea what this *something* was.

I got up from my chair, took a few steps, and got on the bed. While lying there, my hand held up my head, as if I was mirroring Mr. Morrisey.

I looked into his blue-gray eyes. I wanted to describe my feelings, but I had no words for them. I waited for something to happen.

Nothing happened.

Mr. Morrisey got up and changed the channel.

✦

The Eternal Light shone as I walked beneath it and turned to face the Ark. Beside me, Rabbi Jaffe reached to the left of the Ark and pushed a small button. Slowly, the gilded doors of the Ark open to reveal the Torah, sheathed in deep blue velvet. With a slight nod of his head as my cue, the rabbi gave me permission to take the Torah out of the Ark. I gingerly placed one hand on one of its wooden handles, and with my arm I cradled the Torah as I gently lifted it out of the Ark. Triumphantly, I turned to the congregation and lifted the Torah for all to see.

It was my moment.

I walked the few steps toward the pulpit. Rabbi Jaffe steadied me by cupping my elbow with his hand. I turned slightly to look toward the left of the Ark, where Mr. Morrisey was seated. He got up from his chair and walked toward me. As the guest of honor, it was his privilege to remove the sterling silver breastplate from the Torah. He removed the pointer and held onto it as I rested the Torah gently on the pulpit and unrolled it to the appropriate passage.

As Mr. Morrisey handed me the pointer, he placed his arm around my shoulder and gave me a reassuring squeeze, wishing me luck.

After the bar mitzvah, I never saw or heard from him again.

✦

"Sh'ma yisroel adonoi elohenu adonoi echod. Hear O Israel, the Lord is God, the Lord is One."

The rabbi was concluding the service. I glanced at the front row, where my family was. Mom wore a pink dress and a pillbox hat with a veil. To her left were Ricky and Eileen, my older brother and sister, Nanny and Papa Geiser, Nanny Greenwald and her husband, Uncle Harry, and then, my father, in his dark blue suit. Behind my family, relatives, friends, and members of the temple filled the sanctuary.

But what I noticed most was the obvious distance between Mom and Dad.

✦

Two weeks after I turned twelve, Ricky and I were watching TV in the Florida room when Dad came in to announce that we were going for a ride. Mom joined us as we got into the Chevy station wagon. It was their wedding anniversary, and we were going to do something together as a family, except for Eileen, who was working that day.

It was an overcast day. We went east on the causeway, toward the beach. At Ocean Drive, we turned left and kept going. In the backseat, Ricky and I played Flinch, a hand game of feint and surprise: you had to trick your opponent into removing his hands from your palms to avoid being slapped, and the penalty was a free slap, usually delivered as hard as possible.

Somewhere north of Hollywood, after riding for half an hour, we turned into a parking lot overlooking a deserted beach. It was quiet.

Mom and Dad talked a little bit.

"Just say it," I saw my mother saying.

Dad looked at my brother and me, and then they continued talking in low voices.

I got bored. I looked out the back window and watched as two men walked down the street. A car coming in the opposite direction caught my attention, and I followed it with my eyes until it disappeared from sight. I heard Dad's voice, but I wasn't paying attention to him.

Suddenly I heard Ricky crying. But he wasn't just crying, he was weeping and struggling to breathe.

I turned to my parents. "What's wrong? What happened?" Suddenly I noticed that Mom was crying, too, and Dad looked unbearably sad.

If there was anything I could've done differently that day, I would've spared Dad the pain of repeating himself.

"What's going on? Why is he crying?"

Dad looked at me. The back of his hand wiped away a tear at the corner of his eye. He looked helplessly at Mom.

"Don't look at me, Phil," she said. "This is what you want. *You* say it."

Dad faced me again. He spoke clearly so I could understand him. "Your mother and I have decided to separate. I'll be moving into my own apartment tonight."

I looked blankly at him until the enormity of what he said hit me. I opened the door and bolted from the car.

Mom called out after me. I pretended not to hear. I didn't want to hear anything. I didn't want to hear the world. I reached down to my belt where my hearing aid was attached, turned it off, and kept on running. Halfway down the street, I looked back at the car. No one was coming after me.

I slowed down to a walk. They had been arguing for the last several weeks, but I couldn't understand what they were arguing about.

Once, in the bedroom we shared, Ricky shushed me, trying to listen through the wall to their bedroom. When I asked what was happening, he said, "Never mind," probably to protect me. I finally realized why Dad didn't buy the traditional roses for Mother's Day a few weeks before, even after I reminded him. This was why Mom was crying at the Publix Market a few days ago, when she turned to me and asked, "Robert, am I a good mother?" I was unnerved, but I assured her that she was.

Even then I didn't have a clue to what was going on. I never dreamed that their marriage was anything but perfect.

After a few minutes of walking, Dad caught up with me and put his hand on my shoulder. I turned my hearing aid back on.

We turned back to the car.

"Why are you doing this? Don't you love us?"

He insisted that he loved Ricky, Eileen, and me as we walked back to the car. His eyes pleaded with me not to ask about Mom.

As I got back into the car, Mom looked at me and squeezed my hand. Ricky's eyes were red as he turned to me and made an effort to smile. I told him that everything would be all right. He responded with a few nods, but then he began to cry all over again.

Except for Ricky's crying, we rode home in silence. All I could do was to hold my brother's hand and look out the window.

RAYMOND LUCZAK

HOW TO FALL FOR A DEAF MAN

DO NOT BE AFRAID of your face.
Move into a beam of light
in the bar. Smile openly.
Watch his hands move
quicker than strobe lights
as he surveys the crowd with his friends.
Try not to think of how hard
it might be to have a casual
conversation.

When he comes across the floor,
do not ask his name with
exaggerated lip movements.
A simple How-are-you will do.
Try not to feel lost
in his eyes, worn thin by years
of guessing lip movements of strangers
and wondering for weeks afterward
exactly what they had said.

Try not to look insulted
if he takes out a pad and pen.
Write your name clearly.
Point to him and ask with your eyebrows
his name. Watch him write it
and take his hand up in the air.
Point to his name on the pad
and feel his fingers pull yours
this way and that until he nods.

Point to him in the chest and
tell him with your face, You are cute.
Ignore how much you are sweating
from this effort of introduction.

Watch the tips of his fingers slip
off his chin and his lips mouth the word CUTE.
Feel an erection coming on when he points
to you and signs, CUTE.
Watch him write on the pad YOU ARE
VERY NICE TO ASK. Nod again
not because you don't know what to say
but because you don't know the signs.

Try not to feel embarrassed when
you ask, How do you say, Thank you?
Repeat the question. Try
not to feel frustrated when he shakes
his head no. Try not to scribble furiously
on the pad HOW DO YOU SAY THANK YOU?
Watch him sign, THANK YOU. Follow his hand
and again until he signs, YOU'RE WELCOME.
Realize how much elegance hands can possess.

Try not to ask him the sign for FUCK.
He is tired of showing how. He wants
some sincere attempts to talk.
Try not to ask him to tutor you for free
in American Sign Language. He is not
a teacher. He is tired of teaching.

Ask him where you can take classes in ASL.
Write it down on his pad
and tear off the page for your pocket.
Try not to be bothered by his wary eyes.
You are just another one who says
he wants to learn but never gets around to it.

Try not to look away from how
much eye contact he requires.
Do not be afraid of his face.

Try not to feel surprised
when you call him later on the TDD relay service
and find how clearly you understand him.
Try to feel comfortable with telling a stranger
how much you miss him while listening
to the sound of her typing on the TDD to him.
Wait an eternity before she returns with,
I'M SO HAPPY YOU CALLED...

Ask him later how much TDDs cost and
invest in one of your own.
Learn to picture on the phone his face
when he types KISSES ON UR NOSE.

Practice fingerspelling license plates,
store names and TV program titles.
Remember to keep your palm out.
Do not think like T-H-I-S
but as one word, THIS.

As you drive home alone, notice how rhythmic
telephone poles and corner signs are.
Wonder why no one ever thinks of making music
for eyes alone.

Try not to feel left out at parties
when his friends sign quickly to each other.
When he introduces you to them, say
NICE TO MEET YOU. Try not to feel
overwhelmed if you cannot read their names.
Ask again until you get their names right.
Try not to resent it when he says you are
HEARING.

Keep an indifferent mask on when your friends say,
Oh he's so cute, I mean, really,
you two are getting along?, and then never talk
to his face. Count how many of them
return your calls. Your real friends
won't need a sign language manual.
They will care enough to find ways to communicate.

Attend foreign movies and hold his hand secretly.
Learn not to whisper or demand his eyes.
Learn instead to enjoy the clarity of subtitles.
Realize that was how he had always watched TV
and movies: foreign movies without captions.

Read a few books on deafness. If he doesn't know
which ones are good, ask
his friends. Try to ignore the longing in their eyes
when they see how serious you are.
Realize how few hearing men have deaf lovers.
He is a very lucky man to have you.

But try not to protect him all the time.
Allow him to fumble with his speech
when he points out his choices on the menu.

Never holler his name. Do
not lash out when he doesn't turn
around as you repeat, Can you get over here?
Instead, touch him gently on the shoulder.
Sign, YELL-YELL NOT MEAN. ME-SORRY.
Watch him kiss your hands for forgiveness.

Do not worry whether you should
continue buying audio cassettes
or listen to the radio in the morning.
Your ears and voice are a gift
as much as his eyes and hands are.

Discover how much water and sun it takes
to sow, and how much can sprout in your hands.
Do not be afraid of its face.
It is no longer a plant. It is a tree
now taking root in each other's eyes.

RAYMOND LUCZAK

ELEGY FOR BUZZY CONTRERIO

HOW CAN I EXPLAIN the seeming insignificance of you
in light of all that had gone before? You stared once, twice
when I was eighteen. I was so afraid,
so stilled I never let on. But if you knew, well...
Why didn't you? I would've liked your salt-and-pepper stubble
a coarseness against my red beard, an entwining of sweaty fingers.
We would've wrestled madly the scent of desire out of each other
with your two spotted dogs roving outside your bedroom door.
Instead we continued talking and ... Oh, nothing.
I wish more than anything to see you wink just one more time.

RAYMOND LUCZAK

THE CRUCIFIXION

I WAS ONLY AN INNOCENT boy at the time.
My parents tried to explain to me
what the word "crucifixion" meant,
but I could not lipread them.
As I trailed after them for Jerusalem,
they chatted amiably with each other,
and met a caravan of speech
therapists who chatted amiably too.
They frowned on every gesture I made
when I tried to speak more clearly.
My voice was not good enough. I turned
my hearing aids, but all I heard was
their seamless chatter.

Ravens leaped from their olive trees,
wings spreading wide for the winds.
They were also coming to Jerusalem.
My parents always covered their ears
when they let out a series of caw-caws.
I loved them because they were so *loud*.
And their wings! They were a joy to watch,
their chest-beating show of power.
Some distance behind us there were people
laughing and pointing at the ravens.
They did not talk, but their bodies sang
with their hands: the most beautiful caw-caw.

My parents saw them too, and promptly turned me
around to the front. I imagined

speech therapists whispering to them:
He must learn to speak right. I practiced
my *st*'s, *r*'s, and *w*'s with fervor.
They clapped hands whenever I got them right.
You're saved from those barbarian hands.
My parents' eyes had never been so full of relief
they almost cried. Over the last hill before
Jerusalem, I saw the smooth mound of Calvary Hill
rise high. While my parents pointed at it,
I stole a glance back at those weird people.
They must be gypsies, I thought. There,
an older man winked at me, his gnarly hands
gesturing I should throw away my hearing aids.
I riveted my eyes back to the road.
My father tousled my hair,
for I now knew better than to stare;
he'd said gypsies always kidnapped children
like me, and they never saw their parents again.

As I scampered down the dusty road, I tripped
and knocked a boy down. Our hearing aids clashed
like jolts of volts: We got up and looked
at each other. I pointed to his hearing aid,
wondering why he had one when I had two.
He pointed to his empty ear and shook his head.
He turned abruptly still when our parents stood
behind us. I looked up at the angry faces
of our speech therapists. My mother compared notes
with my friend's mother while we hungered
after each other's hands. Finally — and
suddenly — my father said, "We mustn't be late."
We hurried on, before the gypsies could come
close. They became quiet when they recognized
our speech therapists surrounding
the two of us. I gave them a smile:
Their hands flurried suddenly into wings.
We doubled our pace, and so gained quick
admission into the city. I looked behind
and saw the gates closing on them.
My friend and I looked at each other, suddenly lost.

Huge ravens alighted on the eaves of roofs
and clotheslines bouying on the wind. My caravan
melted into the crowd's clamor for the death
of Laurent Clerc, the gypsy who'd claimed to be
the king of us all. As we pushed our way closer,
the road became covered with broken shrapnel pieces
of hearing aids. They smoked like burnt cinders.
My parents didn't even notice, they were too busy
chanting. I looked around and caught a woman
whose mouthing didn't fit in with the crowd's chants.
Then I saw there were many of *them,* mouthing
without a sound. My friend's eyes also blinked:
There were gypsies right in our midst!

The crowd's electricity changed when the Roman
soldiers shoved to clear the way for Clerc.
I bent low and followed my friend to the forefront
where we could see him better. There he was:
dragging along a cross made of piano boards.
Sweat dripped from his chubby body,
soaking his loincloth of a hearing aid harness.
His double chin sagged from awkward speech,
his throat swelled from a thousand therapists' hands,
his naked feet bled from the sharp metallic cinders.
Right behind his heels was King Alexander Graham Bell.
I quaked in his stern presence, his long gray beard
flapping in the wind. Ravens stretched their claws
back and forth while they circled above him.

I watched King Bell flay Clerc's crisscrossed back
with a whip of piano strings, and saw his eyes glow
when he saw how Clerc couldn't speak. His hands
were wild with rage, trying to let go his cross.
I saw a thousand tears in the eyes of disguised gypsies.
King Bell whipped him again, and again,
proclaiming, "You must speak! You must speak!"
The crowds picked up on this, chanting along.
Clerc fell at last, his face now ruptured by the sharp
edges of broken hearing aids. I broke out of
the crowd and pulled the cross off his back.

Clerc's eyes spoke with tender thanks
as King Bell stared at my hearing aid harness.

"How dare you do this to him? He doesn't deserve
your pity." I tried to answer,
but the words came out all wrong. He drummed
his fingers on his elbow as I tried again,
and again. He smiled whenever I got a word
right, and said, "Good. Say it again, but remember
to make your *t*'s clearer." The crowd turned
enormously silent as I spoke slowly:
"You ... don't ... have ... to ... hurt ... people."
They clapped furiously while King Bell hugged me
and shouted, "See? He speaks so well!
This boy will be my heir." He tousled my hair
as he beckoned me to step aside. I watched him
brandish his whip before Clerc twitched again.
Bits of hearing aids dug into his flesh.
King Bell kicked his sides until Clerc turned over.
He bent down and said slowly into his face,
"Do you understand what this boy said? He said,
'You don't have to hurt people.' That's a lot
more intelligent than you could say with hands!"

Clerc took a deep sigh and heaved himself up.
His eyes locked on mine as he mouthed slowly
so I could lipread. His gestures said:
You like talk? Your-hands easy—
King Bell whupped his hands short.
"I understood every sign you made!"
The crowd turned to watch his queen Mabel's hands fly:
It's true, he's right— *"No."* He looked
around, and signed very bluntly *something.*
It looked like a whip. Her face dropped, grim.
King Bell ordered his soldiers to lift the cross
back on Clerc's shoulders. As I watched the two
dissolve into the following crowds on Calvary Hill,
I felt a man's hand stroke my shoulders softly.
He had to be one of *them.* I followed him
through a maze of alleys to a tiny room upstairs.
The windows were covered with burlap curtains

as he lit a candle. The room burst into gypsies
surrounding my friend, who had no harness on.
He was the happiest boy I had ever seen.
They imitated animals and all sorts of people,
and he laughed. I couldn't help it either,
and found our fingers groping for their signs.

Later that day we stole our way toward Calvary Hill.
Alice Cogswell's face looked sad as she prayed
nearby until she recognized one of us. Her face
lit up with unspeakable joy as she looked around
to make sure no one was watching our hands
flickering near our waists, away from our faces.
Babies future same again never. Proud my s-o-n.
We nodded, not looking directly into Clerc's face
while his flabby arms sagged on the cross. We tried
not to feel the rusty nails staked in the heart
of his hands. *Say last words couldn't.* I looked
into her eyes, hardly silenced with rage.
I watched the bored gazes of King Bell's guards
before I said, *I-f he-can't, many-many future-will say
last words his.* The gypsies tried not to appear
too excited as they led me out of the city. Ravens
swooped playfully all over us, caw-cawing noisily.
As I walked past the front steps of the king's temple,
I noticed the frantic footsteps of speech therapists
paid to convince parents teaching Speech was the Way,
the Only Way into the larger world. After I'd left
Jerusalem, I looked back on Calvary Hill.
Clerc's cross was no longer a shadow looming starkly
in the evening sun. Instead outstretched hands reached
higher into the sky, and they were all our own.

RAYMOND LUCZAK

YOU FEEL BEAUTIFUL

IN THE TIME THAT IT TAKES Tom to return from the bathroom, Michael looks around Tom's tiny apartment near Dupont Circle. The walls are almost bare, the furniture's arrangement is almost geometric, the pile of unopened bills and junk mail sits in the center of the kitchen table. He looks at the red-and-white cane with its folded silver joints near the foyer; he still feels warm from Tom placing his fingers lightly over his hands. As they continued to speak in the bar, a sweaty intimacy arose from feeling each other's hands as they talked. Michael had been wondering all evening about the color of Tom's eyes behind his orange glasses when Tom asked, "Me-feel your face?"

He looked about himself. "O-k."

Michael stood still as Tom's fingers felt the contours of his face. "Not-know you n-i-c-e b-e-a-r-d."

"Thank-you."

"You-must v-e-r-y handsome. How old you?"

"Twenty."

"W-o-w-w-o-w. You lonesome tonight?"

Michael was not sure how to answer, but he knew he wanted to feel more of those fingers touching his face; it was amazingly comforting not to worry about being poked in the eyes. "No. Not really..."

✦

In the time that it took Tom to unleash his cane into a long stick and to swing lightly from side to side in front of his feet, Michael felt Tom's intermittent squeezing of his elbow as Michael led him along. It was a strange but wonderful sensation to feel so needed, and to feel so trusted to keep him away from the cars whizzing by in the hot August night. "Turn left 16 S-t four doors more big pink house."

"We-arrive."

"You w-o-n-d-e-r-f-u-l guide. Can't believe you never guided deaf-blind man before." His hand reaches out in the air until it finds Michael's face. "B-e-a-u-t-i-f-u-l you."

Michael is still not sure what to do, lying naked on Tom's bed and watching him walk from the bathroom to the bed. How does one let a deaf-blind man know what he wants to do in bed? Michael's bedroom eyes had always made it easy for him.

Tom feels for the edge of his bed and sits down in his underwear. "Where you?" Michael reaches over and guides Tom's hand to his cock, and is surprised when he smiles. "Not-yet. S-a-v-e best for end."

"Not understand."

"Me show-you." Tom's fingers are feeling their way down to Michael's toes. "Tell me color h-a-i-r here."

Michael sits up and looks at his own toes with a Martian's eyes as he signs into Tom's left hand. "Not-yet b-l-a-c-k, will change soon." He watches Tom change expressions from happy to concern to chuckle. "What you do-do?"

"Know your body must. Color your skin?"

"White."

"No. People say they're white, not-true, they really p-e-a-c-h. You p-e-a-c-h? Look. Have f-r-e-c-k-l-e-s. L-o-o-k." Tom points to his shoulders. "Not white."

"Same. Have. F-r-e-c-k-l-e-s." He takes Tom's hands to his face, to his shoulders, and to certain parts of his arms and legs. "M-o-l-e on b-a-c-k have also."

"Where?"

"You-search." Michael feels the light strokes all over his back until Tom finds the mole.

"T-i-t, color what?"

He looks down at his chest. "A-little pink, t-a-n most."

"Exact where is p-i-n-k?"

He guides Tom's tongue with his index finger and finds it licking both his finger and nipple.

"Feel-like orange s-h-e-r-b-e-t."

He tries not to laugh. "Like ice-cream?"

"Of-course!"

"But orange s-h-e-r-b-e-r-t?"

"Favorite ice-cream me." Tom smiles.

"O-h. Thank-you."

"Color what?" Tom rubs Michael's chest hair.

"Black."

Tom feels Michael's wavy hair. "Color what?"

"B-l-o-n-d. No, s-t-r-a-w-b-e-r-r-y strawberry b-l-o-n-d. Dark red with little yellow."

Tom smiles and kisses him on the forehead. "You-smell n-i-c-e. You-use S-e-l-s-u-n B-l-u-e?"

"How you know?"

"Experience." Tom grins."Color what?" He nudges his nose into Michael's beard.

"Red. Both orange-red same-as old fire."

"Same-as hot-dogs cooked too-long?"

Michael laughs.

"You-tremble n-i-c-e laugh. You-t-i-c-k-l-i-s-h?"

"Yes. But—"

"I-know. Won't." He smiles. "Me-same t-i-c-k-l-i-s-h. Color what?" He strokes Michael's pubic hair. "H-a-i-r you-have lot. Me-like."

"Why question-question? Let's j-u-s-t do it."

"Do what?"

"You-know. T-h-i-s." Michael guides Tom back onto the bed. His mouth zeroes into the space between Tom's thighs.

✦

After his economics class the next day, Michael takes a pair of jeans off the rack at Hecht's and steps into the dressing room. He has never looked closely at his naked body in a full-length mirror, never looked really at how skinny he is, and he'd rather not look. Besides, why should he when he had to look at it every day? Yet he can't stop thinking of Tom's comment, "You-feel beautiful."

Leaving his jeans on the hook, Michael stares at his body in the full-length mirror. He stares at himself so hard it does not register in him that his standing naked behind two shutter doors is quite ludicrous.

"Feel-feel beautiful?" He closes his eyes and lets his fingers wander as lightly as Tom would all over his chest and feels those ridges and indentations of his body. He wishes to describe to Tom just how b-e-a-u-t-i-f-u-l he feels right now.

JAYE AUSTIN-WILLIAMS

NGENE'S VOICES

A novel excerpt*

1971

ON THE DAY NGENE WAS BORN, there was a large celebration, for Nkulela Dlemanzima's had been a difficult pregnancy. Her husband Mbotane had paced the floor for hours, listening to Nkulela's screams, not knowing what to do. The village doctor, Damani Isizwe, had become concerned when Nkulela took ill. He told Nkulela and Mbotane that their baby might be born early, and that Nkulela should stop working, and certainly stop taking the long walks required to get her there.

Sure enough, Ngene came to them three months early. She was terribly small, but seemed well otherwise. The only unusual thing was that Ngene did not cry when she greeted the world; only squinted. Though Mbotane thought this odd, it was a passing thought.

He rushed outside to the front of their house and yelled, "A daughter! We have a baby daughter!" And there was a party like none they'd seen in a long time on Fergaasten Street in Soweto.

* *Ngene's Voices* is a novel in progress about a young deaf girl growing into womanhood in South Africa, and spanning thirty years — from her birth in 1971 to her thirtieth birthday in the year 2001, some ten years after apartheid is declared officially dismantled. Ngene is plagued with the ability to hear only the voices of the white men who oppress her people, which this excerpt illustrates. The remainder of the novel treats how she deals with this particular ability in order to bring about an understanding of the internal workings of the system of racism in South Africa.

✦

Inside the house, Nkulela rested comfortably, but her mind was heavy with suspicions about this child.

At first they marveled at how quiet an infant Ngene was. Nobody they knew had been able to sleep peacefully, night after night, during the first three months of their children's infancies. But when she hadn't uttered a sound by the time she was three months old, they summoned Dr. Isizwe to examine her. He looked in her eyes and ears, and said he could see nothing wrong. But when he clapped his hands, snapped his fingers, and made sounds from the opposite side of the room, the child just stared up at the ceiling or glanced randomly around the room, oblivious to everyone except her mother.

Mbotane burst into tears. He and Nkulela looked at each other, remembering the night, about halfway through Nkulela's pregnancy, when Mbotane had awakened from a sound sleep and sat bolt upright in bed, drenched in sweat.

"Mbo!" she said. "What is it? What has frightened you so?"

He buried his head in her breast and rocked like a baby until he calmed down enough to talk. He told her he'd dreamt they had two children. In the dream, the police broke into their home and bludgeoned the son to death as the rest of them looked on.

As they beat him, one of the white policemen kept yelling, "Stinking, bloody keffirs!"

The boy continued screaming for his life.

"Listen to him," the officer said. "They make sounds like sows!" The other officers laughed, and then he glared at Nkulela. "And they breed like rabbits! Why, hmm? Why do you keep making babies?"

The boy's screams grew louder and louder, until the girl covered her ears and began to scream, too. "Daddy, make it stop! Please, make it stop!"

The officer looked at the girl. "We'll make it stop, little keffir-bitch. Don't you worry!"

Mbotane wept as he recounted the dream. But he hadn't told Nkulela everything.

"What else, Mbo?" Nkulela asked gently.

Mbotane shuddered. "When the boy was dead, they asked you to put on a big pot of water. You did so. They asked me ... to dismember the boy's body. I refused, and they beat me. So—" He wept uncontrollably. "—so, I did so. They each grabbed pieces of his body, dripping with blood, and put them into the pot of boiling water. They laughed and joked about which parts of a 'keffir' were more tender to eat than others, and whether they'd die if they ate keffir meat. I remember then turning to the girl — our daughter — and..."

"Come, Mbo. Tell me," Nkulela said, softly.

"She was ... a portrait capturing a horrible moment. She stood with her hands over her ears, her mouth wide open, as if she was screaming, but with no sound. That's when I awoke."

They both cried as Dr. Isizwe looked on with empathy, when they remembered what Mbotane had said that night: "Oh, my God! Oh, 'Lela. If we ever do have a child, I pray from the deepest part of my soul that baby will never hear the ugly sounds of hatred the white men utter!"

1983

Nkulela was curious at Ngene's behavior lately. It was as if the child couldn't get close enough to her. A fleeting thought she'd had one day now plagued her. If I didn't know better, Nkulela mused, I'd swear the child was trying to crawl back up inside of me.

Every little thing seemed to give the child a start these days. It wasn't as if there was no reason at all to be afraid. They had stopped counting the number of neighbors who had been gassed, dog-mauled, or shot to death over the last twelve years. But time's passing did not soften the edges of the pictures scalded into her brain: Her brother Mantulo's four children had all been murdered by the police in Sharpeville. And then, of course, there was Mbotane's left hand, from which the thumb and three fingers had been severed when a colored police officer had raided their home one morning, and beaten Mbotane bloody, and nearly to death.

When Ngene was not yet seven, a young colored boy wandered onto the Dlemanzimas' street one day, and spotted Ngene and other children playing a game called Chase. The children used hand and body gestures which they'd made up so Ngene could be included. They were intrigued by the boy's name, very different-sounding from theirs, which were Zulu.

"My name is Thomas Banziwe." He told them he had been named after Thomas Jefferson from America. It was because "Mr. Jefferson was a very intelligent and wonderful man." His parents had taken one look at him when he was born and decided he would grow up to be a great politician, and so named him after the great Thomas Jefferson.

One of the children, Kuleni Seseseko, said, "Oh yes. I've heard of Mr. Jefferson from America! My mother's great-great-great-grandmother rode a ship to America and worked for him! My mother says Mr. Jefferson had a very big mansion in the southern part of America, and that African people there lived very much like we live here in South Africa today!"

"Wow!" the children all exclaimed.

Ngene then taught Thomas the gesture for "chase," and the game was on. Some children played the police, and others were villagers. One of the police counted to ten. If you were caught by the police, you were hit over the head and rounded up in an area where you were "shot" and played dead. Later that evening, Thomas told his father, police officer Mbeli Banziwe, about the new game he'd learned and about the girl Ngene who spoke with her hands.

Early the following morning Officer Banziwe, along with three white superior officers, Lofgen Platternik, Hanz Pedersen, and Chief Leftenant Luther Janssen, arrived at the Dlemanzima home. They pounded on the door.

Mbotane opened the door, and the officers barged past him, demanding to see "the mute," as they'd called her in their language.

"What is the problem, Officers?" Nkulela asked in her decidedly poor Afrikaans, which Native Africans were required to speak in the presence of their superiors.

"*We* are asking the questions here," Janssen snapped. "Don't flap your black-bitch tongue at me."

"Our daughter is still asleep," said Mbotane calmly, and in a slightly smoother dialect of Afrikaans.

Janssen glared acidly at him. "Well, wake her up, keffir-ass! Go on! We don't have all day to chat with you!"

Mbotane started toward Ngene's room.

The officers whispered among themselves in Afrikaans. Then, in a mocking Zulu, Janssen yelled, "Wait! Call to her from here."

Mbotane and Nkulela looked at each other.

"DO IT!!!" Pedersen hollered, startling Mbotane and Nkulela.

Nkulela looked down. Mbotane paused, and then called — not very loudly at all — "Ngene!"

"What the bloody hell was that? Call to her like she's bloody deef and dumb, man," hollered Janssen.

Fire raged in Mbotane's eyes as he looked up at Janssen, who stopped laughing abruptly, and looked coldly back at him, the hungry question in his eyes: You challenging me, keffir-boy?

Janssen looked at his fellow officers, and then slowly turned to Mbotane. "That's what she is, isn't she, black-sow-bastard! She's deef as the wall she's lying behind, isn't she?"

No response.

"ISN'T SHE!!!"

Nkulela jumped, then spoke quietly. "She was born early, you see."

"Don't give me any sad story, sow-bitch. And when you speak to me, you speak civilized people's language. I don't care how hard it is for you, jungle whore."

The officers snickered.

In a broken Afrikaans, Nkulela spoke barely above a whisper. "I'm sorry, Officer. My Dutch is not very good." Seeing the officers' heads hanging from trees in her mind, she looked away for fear her eyes would betray their grotesque reflections and invite further wrath.

"Go and get her out of that room," Janssen growled to Officer Banziwe.

Officer Banziwe left eagerly.

Nkulela spoke louder, and with desperation. "Please, Officers, she's really very normal. There's nothing wrong with her."

Crescendoing over her pleading, Janssen's voice gradually drowned hers out: "Shut your bloody keffir-SOW-BITCH MOUTH!!!" The scream stopped Officer Banziwe in his tracks. Janssen looked at him.

"GET HER OUT OF THAT ROOM!"

"Yes, Leftenant, sir!"

Then, in a mockingly courteous change of tone, Janssen addressed Nkulela. "You see, my colored friend there works very hard to counteract the pollution in his blood lines. He tells me his son had occasion to visit with the little deef devil in there. Seems she showed the boy some monkey gestures, and with great pride, the little ignorant thing came home and boasted the primitive hand drivel to his father." Then, with a nod to Officers Pedersen and Platternik, he continued, "Is not the colored blood torment enough? Now the man must endure a gesture-monger polluting what there is of his boy-child's mind as well?"

They all laughed.

Officer Banziwe brought a sleepy, yet frightened, Ngene into view.

There was silence as the men looked at her, and she looked at them with a familiarity that made them shudder.

Janssen moved and gestured in an apelike manner, overenunciating his words. "Officer Banziwe" — pointing to the colored officer in a large, cartoonish fashion — "says you were showing his boy how to talk your language." There were no words for the horror and confusion crossing Ngene's face. Mbotane and Nkelela looked at each other, also confused.

Janssen stopped and looked curiously at Ngene. "Do you understand me? Can you ... hear what I'm saying?"

Ngene looked to her parents for guidance, for some explanation of what was happening to her, but there was none.

Nkulela spoke haltingly to Ngene and without sign, just to see if what they'd all suspected was coming to pass. But once again came the familiar look of patient confusion that wrinkled Ngene's button nose ever so slightly whenever anyone forgot to sign or gesture when they spoke with her. She obviously still could not hear. What was it, then, about Janssen that distorted her face with this new, horrified confusion?

Janssen now slaughtered this moment in which everyone was compelled by the same mystery — what had just happened on Ngene's face? — with a dismissal. "Let's get on with this so I can get back home and poke the missus before the day gets away from me."

The officers laughed jocularly, and laughed even harder when they saw the unintended irony of Nkulela instinctively putting her hands over Ngene's ears to protect her from such foul language.

"Hey, papa," Janssen growled to Mbotane, who was trying to hide his desire to kill him. "Come on over here."

Mbotane obeyed.

Janssen gestured mockingly to Ngene, saying as he performed a bizarre dance, "You gonna teach your papa to talk with his hands like you?"

Ngene, horrified, began to cry.

"Come on, looky here, deef little keffir-girl," Janssen continued as his fellow officers egged him on with jeers and laughs. "Come on. Talk to your dadda."

Ngene obeyed and signed, "Daddy, I don't understand. Please make them go away."

"I would if I could, precious little one." Mbotane's hands spoke gently, trying to comfort her.

"Hey! Hey, hey, hey! Don't get carried away with that jungle crap," Janssen barked. "Dadda. Come here."

Mbotane hesitated, sensing something horrible was about to happen.

"Hold out your hands."

Mbotane did not move.

"I said hold out your bloody hands, nigger-dog-man."

Mbotane did so.

Pointing to his left hand, Janssen asked, "You use this one a lot?"

"I am right-handed."

"Oh, so you're going to be cheeky and answer me roundabout, are you? I'll ask you again. Do you use this hand a lot?"

"Yes."

"How much?"

"I am a laborer ... sir. I use my hands."

Again, in his now-familiar, mockingly cordial tone, he continued, "Mmm-hmm. Would you say that you use it more or less than your right hand?"

Mbotane suddenly felt his bladder give way, and the urine ran down his legs, inviting an onslaught of laughter.

Janssen jested to his fellow officers, "Ah! See here, the bloody keffir's pissed himself!" He turned to Mbotane. "But that's not going to get you out of answering the question of the day: Do you use it more or less than your other hand?"

Mbotane stammered, "Less."

"Good. Then you won't be needing it."

With that, Janssen grabbed Mbotane's left hand, and motioned to Officer Platternik, who then pulled an eight-inch gutting knife from a small scabbard concealed under his uniform jacket.

Mbotane struggled and pulled his hand free.

Janssen flashed a look to the others, and they converged on Mbotane, bringing him to the floor.

Officer Banziwe's eyes pleaded with Janssen to let him give the beating.

A smirk stretched across Janssen's acid face.

Officer Banziwe glanced toward the kitchen table and chairs, and picked up one of the chairs. He then slammed it into Mbotane's head, and when Mbotane fell, pounded him across the back. Blood squirted everywhere, splattering everyone present.

A surreal pause overtook the room when Officer Banziwe put the chair down at last, placed one of his hands to his face, and with two fingers, wiped away some of Mbotane's blood. He looked at his fingers, repulsed — it was not so much the idea of the blood but the reminder of the color of his own skin. He looked down at Mbotane, now unconscious, and let out a scream so anguished, it paralyzed everyone for a moment.

Janssen then laughed uproariously at the picture of Officer Banziwe trying to beat the color out of himself by pummeling this pathetic black man. He motioned to Officer Platternik, already kneeling eagerly next to Mbotane's limp body, who in one swift motion, sliced into Mbotane's hand. With the hungry anticipation of one cutting up bite-sized portions of steak, Platternik systematically severed Mbotane's thumb and three of his fingers. The redness of her father's blood and the pain and horror on her mother's face screamed so loudly into Ngene's eyes, she wanted — needed — to shut them, but could not. Her mouth agape, she stood, mimicking her mother's gesture — hands over her little deaf ears, a vaguely familiar vibration caught in her throat, unable to escape through her mouth.

Ngene bolted out of the house and ran away. No one could find her until morning.

1986

Ngene stood looking out over the river and watched the fish scatter and converge just beneath the surface. The pleasure she found in her visits to the river was turning to compulsion now that these sensations, which ripped from one side of her skull to the other, had begun to increase. She took off her dress and laid it down next to her, and walked closer to the edge of the river. She smiled sadly and curiously at her reflection undulating, beckoning her. What was it about the water that drew her as never before?

Ngene walked into the water, letting it gradually embrace her body. When she was totally submerged, she opened her eyes and watched, through the gray-brown haze, the fish and water life swim and dart, oblivious to her. She stood virtually still, moving ever so slightly with the current, and held her breath. Waiting. But the sensations did not come when she was underwater. Things seemed more normal here.

Before her head had begun to go crazy, Ngene had never known what comfort could be found in not being able to breathe. She was bitterly afraid to come up for air; afraid the combination of sunlight and soft wind would jar loose whatever was causing the terrifying clatter.

She did not know "words" — only the symbols dancing back and forth between the eyes and hands of her and her family — so she didn't know there was a word for the intermittent tumult inside her head. She knew two things: it had been her unwelcome companion since she was about seven years old, and it terrified her.

The word was "sound."

"BRIAN SEAMAN"*

A WORLD-CLASS TRAVELER

I WAS A COLLEGE STUDENT when I went with five other deaf friends on my first trip to Europe many years ago. It was a disaster — rivalries soon developed among us, and I got really sick from food poisoning in Italy. What's more, my friends saw all of Florence and I saw nothing.

But even though I was sick and bedridden, I really wanted to see Michelangelo's *David* more than anything else. If I couldn't see *David,* I couldn't feel I had seen Europe. My friends agreed to bring me to the museum where *David* was, and guess what? It was closed. The museum was closed on Mondays, but my friends brought me up close to this big old keyhole so I could peer through to look at *David.*

The irony is that at the time, I thought I was the only one who was gay in the group. I've learned since that *four* of us were gay.

I didn't go to Europe again until fourteen years later, and I've been going there every six months ever since.

✦

I remember this one time in Switzerland — in Bern, I think — where the center of the town had a huge square. Underneath this square was a very nice shopping mall, and because the traffic above was so congested that I couldn't walk through, I went underground instead. Besides, a woman friend of mine was going to arrive there. Another friend who'd been to Bern had recommended a nice restaurant located right underneath this square for our other friend's surprise birthday dinner.

---

*This interview was conducted by the editor on October 6, 1992.

After we made a reservation at the restaurant, I had to go to the bathroom. In there I saw this man looking at me, and well, we had quick sex — a "quickie." I went out, and met up with my friend; while we were walking to the place where our friend was supposed to meet us, I saw the man I'd just had sex with walking toward us.

I walked as if I didn't know him, and he came up to us and just put his hand over my crotch. I thought, "No."

My friend banged and banged her purse against this man. He stumbled off and left. It's one of those things you have to laugh about when you look back, but at the time it wasn't funny.

I refused to tell her about us until a few years ago.

She said, "Yeah, that was so awful."

I told her with a straight face, "I want to tell you something. We had done it fifteen minutes before."

She didn't know what to believe. "You did!?! Why did he grab your crotch?"

I don't know why he did that in front of us, but I suspect that either he wanted to inform my "wife" that I was a screaming queen, or that he wanted to say, "Thank y-o-u."

✦

This also happened in Switzerland. In a very small town near the border of Italy, there was a train station way up in the mountains. I tried to find two cabs to take five of my friends and me and our suitcases up to the mountains. But all the suitcases filled up one cab, and the other cab was full with my friends. I was the sixth person.

So I told my friends to go on ahead with my suitcase, and since the train wouldn't be arriving for about three hours, I decided to walk up by myself the thousands and thousands of stairs that went straight up to the train station itself.

About halfway there I saw this building that looked like a toolhouse, and the door was ajar. I went in there, and I couldn't believe my eyes. There was a real orgy — I mean, a *real* orgy — going on. They stopped for a second, unsure of what to make of me. But when they saw the bulge in my pants, they let me join them.

As it turned out, I stayed there for too long. When I finally arrived at the train station, my friend asked me, "What took you so long?"

My excuse was, "You think it's easy to climb up those stairs?"

✦

In Germany, I stayed with a deaf gay German friend in a small town near Koln. I found it very hard to learn German Sign Language because it was so much like Cued Speech [a system of pointing to various places on the face for certain sounds to help lipreaders make the distinction between sounds like *p* and *b, f* and *v,* etc.]. They'd sign, and for names and places, they'd point to their lips and mouth the name.

I found many deaf Germans to be very intelligent, but it was so strange to see so much mouthing along with their signs. They found the idea of my fingerspelling the alphabet on one hand rather strange.

I said, "That's how we Americans do it."

They said, "We never fingerspell in German Sign Language."

I asked, "Then how do you know which city or name the other person is saying?"

They said, "We point to our lips. That's never a problem."

I wanted to insult them a little, so I asked, "What about those long, long last names?"

They said, "We don't have problems with that either. We just point to our lips and mouth the last name."

Anyway, that's part of deaf German culture.

✦

I should add that many European men have uncut cocks. I don't mind uncut cocks *if* they are clean. If I could smell them before they open their pants, I'd just take off. I can't stand "head cheese" [smegma].

Even though Europeans have uncut cocks and tend to keep themselves clean, I don't understand why Americans can't keep their own uncircumcised cocks clean. Perhaps American doctors were right to start circumcising most male babies in the forties and fifties. There have been people who want to stop the practice of circumcising male babies. That is a nice idea, but it's not realistic in America.

First of all, in this country there is not much communication between parent and child on how to keep clean. In Europe, people are more open and honest about sexuality, and they do tell their children that sexuality is not a filthy thing. I blame the religious people in America for making sexuality into such a horrible thing when it's not.

✦

In spite of their small physical stature, Frenchmen do have big cocks and they know how to have sex. They're much more casual about these things — "Wanna have sex? Let's go ahead." I think it's because in the French culture, there is no such concept as "gay," "straight," or "bisexual." What's more, it's legal for boys from the age of fifteen to have sex with adults. While of course there are some anti-gay groups in France, the French government won't allow them to speak out against homosexuality.

What's more, you can't really tell the difference between straight and gay men in France. The only way you can find out if they're gay is through eye contact.

✦

In Paris there are two types of trains. The Metro is the local in the heart of Paris, and the RER is an express train that goes outside the center of Paris but still within the city boundaries. I found this amazing toilet on the RER line. I should say that many toilets have been closed since then.

Anyway, when I went in, there were two corridors — on my right was the men's restroom, and on my left was the women's restroom. On both sides was a long wall, and on the other side of this wall were three toilets. There were always six men standing there, and there was this long, long line waiting to use the toilets. Of course, some of them would just have quickies and leave.

The female custodian at the entrance to both bathrooms knew exactly what was going on in the men's restroom, but she couldn't put a stop to it. If a little boy came to use the bathroom, she'd come in and close her eyes and wave her hands around with a broomstick to stop the sex. The little boy would then go to the bathroom, and once he left, the sex would resume.

That place — the walls and the urinals — have since been removed. (Sigh.)

✦

Before I went to Egypt, I read in a book that Arab men there were very open about sex even though the Islamic religion is vehemently against it. They were reportedly crazy over blond hair, which I don't have. But they were also crazy about blue eyes, which I have.

I thought, "Okay."

My Yugoslavian friend went with me. We are not lovers, but we are more than friends. We do not sleep together, but we are very, very close, because we are *so* alike in our interests. Even though he is a deaf Yugoslavian (and comes from a deaf family), he has one-fourth Turkish blood in him, and he looks very Turkish. And because he is very good-looking, he never has any problems picking up men.

When we arrived in Egypt, I discovered that "blond hair" in their book also included a light complexion. I was mobbed, and many men actually lifted their robes at me. It was nice in a way, because I could pick the handsomest ones or the biggest cocks.

But that was a very sticky situation. For one thing, the men who chased me were very yucky. I mean, blak! They were ugly, with brown teeth, and totally uneducated. Even though I felt very uncomfortable with them, I was surprised at how they kept themselves very clean. Their bodies didn't have any smell. But they were really too much for me. I mean, some of them stroked their crotches with big smiles on their faces right in front of people there on the street. That really turned me off.

I guess the minute they saw me, they just forgot their own culture and upbringing and went after me. (Smile.) My friend was hardly mobbed due to his Arab looks — he seemed to be of no challenge to them.

✦

In Egypt, I rode the first-class train from Alexandria to Cairo. The two-hour ride was beautiful, and air-conditioned, which was perfect for me. The second-class train? Don't ask. It was more like tenth-class: It looked like it hadn't been cleaned since the day it was built. The seats had leather — or maybe plastic — covering that was so thick with dust that if you slapped it, a cloud arose. I know that in Egypt the air is dry and dusty, but still it was pretty ridiculous. The windows were even more shocking — each window had two panes about two inches apart. I don't know how they got in, but you could see *millions* of dead bugs in the bottom of each window. The third-class train was nothing but wood; its seats were like benches, and the whole thing looked very rickety.

Anyway, on the train, a very good-looking Egyptian man sitting opposite me waved his hand down to get my attention. I looked around myself, and I was the only one there. (My Yugoslavian friend had gone off for a quickie nearby.) I pointed to myself, "Me?"

He flicked his tongue out a little, as if he wanted to lick something, offering sex. I felt embarrassed, partly because I just didn't feel it was the right time and place. He went all the way around to me and pulled out a small card. I read it and did a double-take. On it was the word "deaf" in both English and Arabic.

In my own mind I did a double-take. "You're deaf?" I asked.

"Yes, I'm deaf." Right there he faltered and forgot the fact he'd been trying to pick me up. I still *really* wanted him because he was so good-looking and because he was deaf. He learned that I was an American, and he got *so* excited over that.

My Yugoslavian friend returned from his quickie and he wouldn't believe me when I told him that the Egyptian was deaf. I showed him the card and found that it was printed by the British Association of the Deaf or something like that.

Anyway, we all talked, and the deaf Egyptian was quite intelligent. He worked as a baker's assistant for three dollars or so a day. He said that most deaf people work at different kinds of jobs for the same kind of money. (I learned later why so many deaf people do not succeed as well as they do here in America: the Arabic language is based on sound and does not have an alphabet at all, so how can they learn to communicate? Turkey used to have the same problem, but when they changed over to an alphabetic system for Arabic, the literacy rate for that country went right up. But then again, I noticed on Egyptian TV that people were reading the newspapers out loud. Apparently hearing people there have a very hard time with Arabic so it's not just a deaf problem.)

And yes, I did sleep with him. He was — wow — wonderful. His penis was eight inches long — which was very unusual in Egypt; most penises I saw were rather small, about four inches.

I also learned from him that in general, Eypgtian wives do not open their legs for sexual pleasure but only for conception of children. When women in Egypt begin to menstruate, their clitorises are removed surgically. You know when the male foreskin is circumcised, the penis becomes less sensitive, yet the lust for sex remains. But for the Egyptian woman who undergoes a clitorectomy, her lust dies down. She feels much less desire for sex, so she is content to stay home and raise the children. What's the rationale for clitorectomy? It appears that men there want to keep women under control by making sure that their wives don't want to have sex. And these women never think that their husbands are capable of being fucked by other men, but it happens all the time. They'd never admit it, but men turn to each other for sex. They may call gay sex disgusting in public, but they don't go around back-stabbing each other the way some hypocrites do here in America.

Another thing about gay sex in Egyptian culture is that if you want to fuck a man in the ass, you must pay. And if he wants to fuck you in the ass, he has to pay you. I think it is because they are so poor they just need the money. Or they might feel that to be fucked is a bit too much, so money should be involved. This is not like hustling at all; it's just a part of their culture.

When you have sex with an Egyptian man, you cannot ejaculate in the air. You must come inside his ass, or in his mouth. Why? Because they believe Allah has said so. Semen is used to create life, and to waste it is a sin. I couldn't accept that, because it was so unsafe. But the deaf Egyptian I had sex with happened to be flexible enough. But all the *hearing* Egyptian men I had sex with were pissed off whenever I pulled off when I knew they were going to come. They prayed to Allah and apologized to Him profusely in Arabic.

✦

I had two of the most embarrassing experiences of my entire life in Aswan, Egypt — and they both happened the same night. It was a beautiful and hot night in October, and it was starting to feel cool. Even then my AC wasn't very good. It just wheezed some, so I told my Yugoslavian friend that I was going to go outside and cool off.

I sat down right by the Nile River with the hotel right behind me. I watched the passersby and then I sensed a cab coming to a loud stop near me. I thought I heard a loud honk, but I didn't turn my head around right away. When I finally did, I saw that a cabdriver had gotten out of his car and he was standing right in front of me with a growing erection poking through his long flowing robes. He just stood there, staring at me, and I could see the shape of his erection through the cloth. I felt terribly embarrassed by the whole thing because other people had noticed him.

I just sort of sat there, feeling very uncomfortable but not showing any expression, because he was also really fat. His body was like water balloons underneath. If he'd been skinnier, I might've gone off with him. But what made it worse was that he tried to "help" me, offering me a cigarette. I refused, since I don't smoke. He was somehow really smitten with me, so I gestured that I was married and indicated that my wife was in the hotel behind me. He even gestured back that we should join him in his cab and have a three-way.

Finally, I gave up and went back to my hotel. The guy even followed me right into the lobby, and I indicated to the manager there that I didn't want him to follow me. He finally went off, and I went upstairs. I found my Yugoslavian friend crying from having laughed so hard. He'd actually *watched* the whole thing. He thought it was the funniest thing in the world.

Later that night, when it was much darker out, I decided to go for a walk with my friend. Of course, I made sure that cabdriver was not around. There were many cab cars and horse buggies that night, and one cab stopped for me. The driver said, "Come on, come on, get in."

I was not impressed with him. I'm the type of person who wouldn't sleep with anyone for the sake of — sure, sex is sex — but I have to feel comfortable with the person first. So I told that driver, "No."

But the driver and my friend had this little conversation. My friend told me that the driver wanted me to come into his cab for a free ride. His cab kept following alongside me, and when I changed my direction, he went off and came around the block. That bothered me, and people were looking at us. I thought then, "Well, he's not too bad-looking."

I got in, and he didn't want me to sit in the back, so I sat out in front with him. He took me straight out of Aswan, which was not a very large city. It was not long before we were outside Aswan in the dark at some hiding place.

We blew each other, and then that's when I noticed a line of Egyptian men outside the buggy waiting for me to blow them too. They were also horse cabdrivers. I felt so embarrassed, but I have to admit that a few were good-looking, and so I did have sex with them too. Finally I gestured, "No more. It's really late. My cock can't take any more."

They didn't care. They only wanted my mouth.

I gestured that my jaws were exhausted.

Then they started arguing among themselves.

I got fed up with them, so I got out and started walking back to Aswan. When I looked back at them, they were already having sex with each other. But the same driver caught up and took me back to my hotel.

I thought the whole experience was so bizarre.

✦

Greece was a very different experience for me. A book about gay people in Europe had said that there are many gay men in Greece, but they never ever show it with their eyes or show any emotion to you, so you're always doubting whether they are attracted to you. So it was very hard to pick up men there. I was often riddled with doubt as to whether a man had noticed me, so I had to pursue him for blocks and blocks and blocks until I gave up when I realized the whole situation was ridiculous. I thought, "Why should I follow him like a stupid dog who doesn't know any better?"

Greek gay men are so closeted; they don't want *anyone* to know they sleep with men. They are also very vain. Even my Yugoslavian friend, who is very good-looking, had the same problems I had.

I've gone four times to the island of Mykonos, where there are allegedly a lot of gay people. But there are so many foreigners, mostly Germans. That's fine with me — I happen to like German men myself. But when I'm in Greece, I want Greek men, you know? That was so frustrating for me ... I've always been so attracted to Greek men. I even went to a few gay bars on Mykonos, but even then, the bars didn't seem gay at all.

I'd like to go back to Greece again, but I hope to find next time a deaf Greek person who'd show me where all the gay places are.

✦

In Italy it was easy for me to pick up men. You know the cliche that Italian men are supposed to be crazy over fat women? That seems to me especially true, and many men there are upset that Italian women rebel against them by staying thin. So whenever I went into a porn movie theater or a gay place, I was always mobbed. I am not exactly thin, you know, so they kept feeling my body and gesturing, "You have *something.*" They want to feel *something* — some meat on the bones. That turned me off, because I want them to want me for what I am, not for what I have.

✦

One time in Italy I went into a train station to go to the bathroom — it wasn't for sex — I really *had* to go to the bathroom. Guess what I saw there? I saw a priest — or something above the title of priest, I think. He might've been a bishop, but I'm not familiar with the clerical hierarchy of the Catholic Church. Anyway, he stood there with a smile on his face and lifted his robes to expose his cock bobbing in the air.

I was surprised, because I'd thought they preached against gay people. Yet he had this big nice smile on his face. I gave him a blow job, and he gave me a blow job too. I guess I could say I was blown by a bishop.

Oh, that reminds me of this one time when I was in Athens, Greece. I was walking with my Yugoslavian friend through this beautiful park near some ruins, where there were many homeless cats. I had to go to the bathroom, and I noticed a Greek Orthodox bishop running up and past me into the bathroom. I thought nothing of it until I went inside.

There he was, with his robes lifted up and his cock exposed. I was turned off because — I don't know — there was something funny about the whole thing. He was so desperate, and he had these robes on.

When I got out of the bathroom, I told my Yugoslavian friend that the man behind me was gay. He didn't believe me, so he went in to find the bishop jerking off like a pig.

✦

One night, a deaf Italian friend drove me around in his car, showing me all sorts of places, among them a street full of prostitutes with these huge breasts. They wore mini-*mini*-skirts and ten-inch-high heels, so they really strutted. He said, "You know they're all men?"

I shook my head no.

He nodded yes.

I shook my head no.

He said, "Watch their breasts."

I did. They were false breasts — they were so perfect and did not jiggle at all.

My friend explained that most of them came from Brazil. Because the economy there is so awful, they come to Italy to work as prostitutes for a few months so they can earn enough money to buy a home of their own in Brazil. Unfortunately, many of them eventually got AIDS.

✦

I went to Norway because it was an emergency. That's a long story, but the point is, I was there. I met a few deaf people there, both straight and gay, and they were all very nice. A deaf gay friend showed me the special places for sex, which I found to be truly wonderful.

Picking up men was pretty easy. But my deaf gay friend warned me about this ultrareligious woman who worked near this particular tram stop bathroom. It was located on an odd incline, next to a florist's shop and other little shops. She'd go right into the men's bathroom near her office with her eyes closed, waving around a crucifix, and rant about how sinful homosexuality was. A few gay groups there protested her actions, but neither they nor the government had been able to do anything because she had been working there for many years. She'd keep an eye on whether one or two men went into the booth, and if two went into the booths, she'd physically prevent one of them from going in until the other one came out.

Well, that was where I saw the biggest cock of my life. I just opened a stall door and there he was. The man was in his late twenties, but his cock was cut — which was surprising — and twelve inches *soft* with huge balls, and very thick. He happened to work in the florist's shop next door to the bathroom. He explained that after five o'clock, the shop was closed, so we could go there in its back room and have sex. It was a *magical* quickie, and even more so when his friend came in. He lifted his legs, and the man entered him without *any* difficulty. I couldn't get over that. Anyway, our three-way was wonderful.

A few days later I saw him on the street. He refused to recognize me. Apparently he didn't like to sleep with the same person twice.

✦

Turkey was similar to, but also different from, Egypt. One could get away with touching asses and crotches right there in the streets in Egypt, but in Turkey, one *just can't.* It's really that much stricter.

One night, in Istanbul, my Yugoslavian friend and I were walking in a park near our hotel. It was dark, but I could see a man with a beautiful beard. I could tell he was hot, even from a distance. I started to tell my Yugoslavian friend that I was going off with him, but then I couldn't wait — I just went off. And the second my friend turned around to say something, he found I'd disappeared. Of course, he knew I'd gone off for a quickie nearby, so it didn't bother him. We don't have to talk about these things — we're so close that we understand without having to talk about it.

The park was on a steep incline, so when he saw the bearded man and this other person taking off together in a cab, he didn't know it was me. I tried to wave to him, trying to tell him that I was leaving with the driver. He thought it was odd, because most Turks are dark-skinned and the waving arm wasn't, but he didn't think much about it. (Later, when I returned to the hotel, he told me about this strange incident where he'd seen this white-skinned man waving his arm. Then he realized it had been me!)

Well, anyway, our cab went up this steep winding road, which bothered me a little. Remember, I had little money on me, and I knew I wouldn't know how to get back to the hotel. Sure, the name of my hotel was in my pocket, but I knew I wouldn't know how to get back there from a strange place. Naturally, I was a little afraid. The bearded man patted my thigh, gesturing that everything was all right.

We arrived at a quiet place. I think it was a lover's lane. Below us was a huge parking lot filled with taxis, and there was no one else around. We got out of the cab, made out, and then opened our pants. He had a beautiful cock, and we began having marvelous sex.

Suddenly I saw two men below, and they walked up toward us.

The cabdriver gestured, and we got in the cab. I didn't pull my pants all the way up, but I didn't tuck in my shirttails either. (My shirttails covered my cock.) He drove the cab down to them, and when they came over to us, we saw that they were cops.

I thought immediately of the movie *Midnight Express,* and I thought that was how I would end up: in prison, in all that filth. My life was finished, over and out. I kept thinking, "What do I do now?"

The cabdriver and the cops spoke rapidly and furiously in Arabic, and eventually they realized that I was deaf. The cops tried every which way to make sure that I was indeed deaf. One of them gestured that I should give them my passport, but although I knew exactly what they wanted, I played dumb. I pulled out my novel, which was in English, and that made them even madder.

Finally I "understood" that they wanted my passport. The cop looked at each line, and at each country stamped in my passport, to find anything related to being thrown out of any country. In other words, they wanted to ban me from their country, but they had to have some kind of evidence to do that. He saw only that my passport was almost full, and that I'd traveled a lot.

Finally, the cop gestured to me, asking why I was with this cabdriver.

I gestured that I had come up here to look at the scenery, and that I had wanted to cool off in all this heat.

The cop then gestured fucking by putting his index finger into his fist.

I repeated his gesture with a dumb look on my face. I knew what he was asking about, but I just *had* to play dumb. I had to make it clear that the concept wasn't in my vocabulary. But I should say that if the cop had thought of lifting the front of my shirt, I would've been finished. (You see, the cabdriver hadn't blown me yet.)

The cabdriver got the drift of what I'd said before, so he explained that he'd done this many times for other tourists who wanted to see a mountainside view of Istanbul. Somehow he was able to give the cops some money — something like ten dollars — and they gave him back some other amount. I'm not sure how that system worked, but in any case, the cops eventually left us.

After they'd left, the cabdriver indicated that this kind of thing happened all the time. He still wanted to have sex with me, but I had just sort of lost my desire. He wouldn't listen to me — he just continued to drive us further up into the mountains outside Istanbul. Eventually, we parked on the shoulder of a two-lane highway and he led me up this steep hill into the woods. We went ahead and had wonderful sex.

After that, I paid him about twenty dollars to take me back to the hotel. By the time we got back there, it had been about three hours since I'd seen my Yugoslavian friend.

He asked me, "Where have you been?"

I explained everything that had happened. You know what? He refused to believe me. He thought I was lying.

I tried to warn him about the cops, but he shrugged it off.

The next night I was so tired from sightseeing and wandering all over the city that I wanted to go to bed early, but my friend didn't. He was in the mood for some sex. I tried to warn him again about the cops.

That night I read Margaret Mitchell's *Gone with the Wind.* (Whenever I travel, I like to bring thick books, because the train rides all over Europe tend to take forever, and because it's the only way I can catch up on books I've been meaning to read. Also, when I'm finished with them, I can throw them out to make room for the other things I've bought along the way.)

Anyway, eighty pages later, my Yugoslavian friend showed up. His face was very white, even though he was dark-skinned.

"Cops caught you, right?" I smiled.

He nodded slowly. And it turned out that his experience was much worse than mine had been the night before. To make a long story short, he was picked up by a man in the park, and the two of them didn't realize it, but cops followed them. And the second my friend touched the other man — even without opening his pants — they were arrested right there on the spot. The other man was clearly used to this kind of situation, because he slipped away so fast that my friend was left there alone. After a long argument between the cops (one of whom seemed to be understanding and would've had sex with my friend), he was at last let go.

So I sat there and smiled at him coyly. You see, he hadn't believed me.

✦

Hungary is world-famous for its steam baths. Both men and women go to them, but the bathhouses are always sex-segregated. For example, a certain steam bathhouse was open to men only on Mondays; the same place would be open to women only on Tuesdays, and so on; all bathhouses are closed on Sunday. That way each bathhouse has three days for each gender.

So when I arrived in Hungary, I checked my guide for gay bathhouses. I thought, "Fine," and then I asked Tourist Information for their listings of the particular schedules for bathhouses. I compared the two lists and saw that they were the same. In Hungary there is no such thing as a gay bathhouse, but I can assure you that there is *plenty* of action. But you have to be careful.

At one bathhouse, I went into a room to take off my clothes and I was given this incredibly flimsy apron. It was about one square foot that I could tie around my waist with very skinny strings. The material was cotton, but it reminded me of Kleenex.

I didn't know what to do with it. They could tell immediately that I was a tourist. So they showed me how to wear it, which was to put it on in front and tie it in back. If I wanted to take a shower, I could take it off, but I was to wear it elsewhere in the bathhouse.

I felt so odd wearing it, but I saw other men wearing it too.

Pretty soon, I noticed that men standing with the water up to their shoulders were jerking each other off, though without showing any emotion toward each other. A few were even resting their elbows on the pool's edge and leaning back so they could be jerked off in the water.

Later, a deaf Hungarian friend told me which bathhouses on the list were good, and at which times and which days the action would really heat up. Sure enough, he was right.

It struck me that it was very difficult to make eye contact with other gay men anywhere outside these places. A lot of these men don't consider themselves gay at all. Many of them are married and have families of their own, but if they have sex with other men in these places, it's not because they consider themselves to be gay at all. They just enjoy it.

✦

Among Yugoslavian deaf people, there are two kinds of their attitudes toward gay people: the older deaf people really look down with disgust on gay people, while the younger ones are very open-minded. Some of the younger deaf people are even curious to try gay sex once or twice, but it's not a big deal to them. I never talked about my being gay at all with them, because we were too busy talking about other things.

On the other hand, the older deaf people kept asking me why I am not married. They brought it up throughout our conversation, even when we were talking about something else completely different.

Why do they do that? It's just none of their business.

Their second question after they learn where you're from is always, "Are you married?" They don't even ask which school I'm from, as many deaf people do in America.

I've found this to be true when I've come across deaf Yugoslavians visiting America.

You might think I travel all over the world for sex, but that's not true. It's just that if the opportunity is there and if I'm attracted, I take the opportunity. If the sex doesn't happen, that's fine with me.

I'm really much more interested in learning about other cultures. Sex just enhances everything I learn on my travels, and these stories I've just told are only a tiny drop in the pail.

GIGI DORAN*

CONSTANT MOTION

I HAD MY FIRST LESBIAN EXPERIENCE when I was twenty-one. I took acid, which blew my mind. This was in the seventies, when taking drugs was the thing to do at college. One woman convinced me to follow her to her room, and somehow we began making out. She was a deaf student from Gallaudet; she's now married and straight.

So we slept together.

The next morning I woke up, and I was so confused. I was in a different bed in a different bedroom. When I woke up, she told me, "We made out last night."

"We *did?"* I couldn't believe it.

"Let's do it again."

So we made out.

I thought, *Wow,* and I enjoyed it very much. It was better than making out with men, where I had to worry constantly about getting pregnant. Sex with her was both sexual and sensual — a comforting feeling all over my body. It was thrilling.

And I should add that was my first real orgasm. (Smile.)

✦

Even though I learned ASL at age nine when I went to Fanwood, a deaf residential school in White Plains, New York, I call ASL my native language. I love ASL!

✦

When I was living in California, my mother reached under the car seat and found a letter a girl had written to me. (I'd forgotten about it.) She got very upset and hurt.

* This interview was conducted by the editor on July 11, 1992.

So my parents flew out to California and confronted me. "I can't understand that you could be gay," my mother said. Then she went into a long list of questions like, "Where did I fail you?"

My father was very cool the whole time. "She's just a college girl. She's just curious. She'll get over it."

I told her that my two sisters may be curious, but they'll be straight.

She was still upset and emotional.

But you know what's happened now? My father still has a hard time accepting me as gay.

The women in my family — my mother and sisters — ask me questions about AIDS and my relationships. They even get excited when they learn that I have a new girlfriend, and they've sometimes sent gifts to me in both our names, which was very nice.

But my brother, like my father, won't even talk about it.

It's just odd how things have turned out, that the women in my family are much more open-minded. They ask me all kinds of questions, and I explain everything in detail. It's wonderful.

✦

In Boston the deaf lesbian community isn't really unified. It's made up of tiny little groups and individuals, whereas in L.A., deaf lesbians make a point of getting together regularly. That's why I miss California so much — there are so many deaf lesbians my age there.

I should add that some lesbians here in Boston are really neat.

✦

My first lesbian bar was called Phase I in Washington, D.C. Whether it's still there, I don't know. It was in the southeast part of the city, straight down on Eighth Street from Gallaudet. A friend had invited me along, and I was curious.

Phase I was a small bar with really butch and large women. I looked around and found it interesting. I found that those real big dykes — wearing caps and looking really tough — were really sweet. It's just a front for them.

Soon a new big lesbian bar opened some distance away, and I went there instead.

Then other bars cropped up all over the city. In them I found lesbians, bisexual women, and a few straight women who were curious.

Intermingling among them was always nice.

And going to bars has helped me define my own self-identity. I can see how other women behave, dress, and interact. From them I piece together the little things they have taught me in different ways, and I become what I am.

✦

Hearing people need to recognize that changing expressions on deaf people's faces don't always mean that they're mad. It's just part of them, a part of ASL and deaf culture.

Also many deaf people like to be in constant motion. Why sit still? They have things to do.

Hearing people often think deaf people are rude. They are offended when a deaf person pounds or slaps the table just to get the attention of another deaf person at the other end of the table. And when they stamp on the floor or pound on the table, it's all for the same reason — attention.

I had two different first loves — with two different women. The first one was when I was eight or nine, and I followed her everywhere she went. We're still good friends today, and I find that when I see her I feel love, still. We've talked about it, and nothing will happen because I respect her so much. She's straight and I'm gay. But we still give each other silly laughs and heartfelt hugs.

The other first love — which involved sex — was Barbara. (She was also the first woman I ever slept with.) That first morning when we woke up and made love, I felt, Wow! What a different experience. It was radical. It didn't fit in with society's expectations.

And with her my heart just fluttered. We shared each other's secrets, we found out what the other liked, and we stayed together. It was just like two becoming entwined as one.

That lasted two years.

But do I regret that? No, not at all.

When I was younger, my ideal woman would've been blond with blue eyes. She'd be about my height, and her body would have a nice shape. She'd be smart, strong-willed, and nice.

Nowadays, I don't have an ideal woman. All I care about is her personality, her character, and her independence. I don't want her to bow down to anyone — that I will always respect. She should be well-read, intelligent, and employed.

The important thing is harmony: we must love each other. Looks aren't that important. What's important is personality, character, and intelligence.

Whether she is deaf or hearing doesn't matter.

Looking back on my relationships, I wonder if I'd want a hearing lover. Well, the older I get, the more I prefer having a deaf lover. I wouldn't have to teach her signs, or explain deaf culture. We'd just get on with the relationship.

Of course, many hearing lesbians were fascinated with sign language. I had sex with many of them during the 1970s, and — this is really interesting — they asked, "How do deaf people make love in the dark?"

I said, "We leave the lights on."

They were shocked.

And so they learned that *that* was how we deaf people need to see more.

In a way, I was educating my hearing lovers that having the lights on was an enjoyable twist in lovemaking. And it helped us to communicate more with our hearing partners.

Looking back on the 1970s, I find it really funny that many hearing lesbians thought that deaf women were really hot in bed. I say, "Not always — it all depends on the individual."

If deaf people could join the military — the Navy, the Army, the Air Force, and the Marines — it would be nice. The benefits are truly great. I wish the officials would stop thinking "ears." They should substitute that with "eyes." Deaf eyes catch even the slightest movement.

For example, what if a hearing soldier had to maintain a vigil and started to fall asleep? A deaf soldier could catch a slight movement on the enemy side and signal an alert.

Once, when I was younger, I went into a bar and noticed a woman whose hair from the back made me think she was a good friend of mine.

I went up to her, turned her around, and kissed her on the lips.

It was the wrong woman.

I was deeply embarrassed. "I'm so sorry."

Her lover, furious, came up to me.

"Wait a minute — let me explain." I told her about my mistaking the back of her for someone else. "I'm so sorry — I'll buy you a drink."

That I did, and then I took off.

Her lover had gotten the wrong idea, and I know I could've gotten beaten up. But lucky me — nothing happened.

I'll never forget that.

People need to stop making assumptions and to accept cultural differences. That's why unity is so important to the deaf gay community. And hearing people need to know that deaf gay people are okay. I hope someday we will be one big happy family.

KEITH R. MITCHELL

LOVE ENCOUNTERS OF THE CLOSE KIND

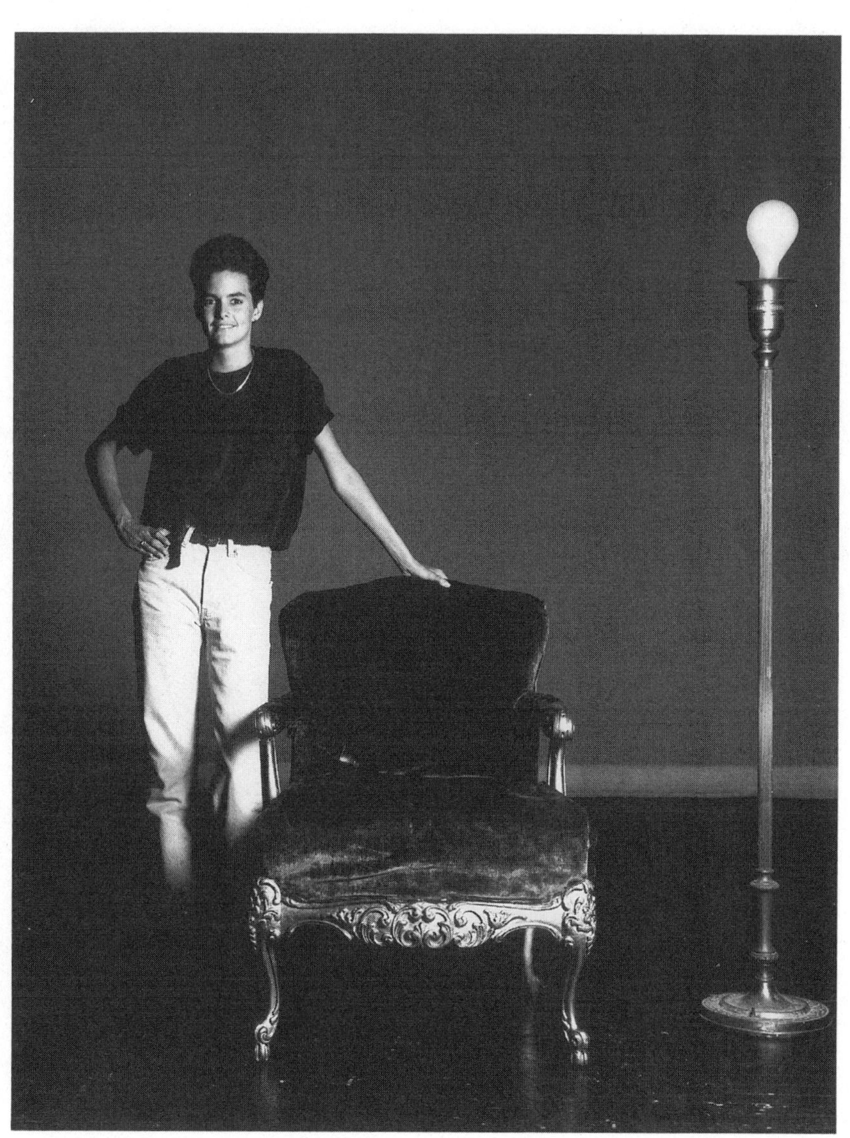

EDWARD M. SCHWARTZ

BLACK HOPE/WHITE HOPE TOGETHER

BLACK HOPE
White hope
Together here we are
We can sign a song
One song to sing for everybody

No more struggle
No more trouble
No more hate feeling

Black hope
White hope
Again we are together
We all can sign a song
One song to sing for everybody
One color
One world of ours

We are able to leave the hate feeling
We are able to feel free at last
Free at last for one world
Black hope and white hope are binding
Together one color
One world of ours to sign and sing a song

EDWARD M. SCHWARTZ

STORM

THERE IS A BIG STORM out there:
clouds intense with the power of lightning all over.
They might assault me badly when I walk through
the deep woods. I encounter the thundering sounds
but I do not have any fear. I will walk
through the storm. My battle is not, not yet over.
Storm will make me strong enough to walk through.

EDWARD M. SCHWARTZ

SAVED

I'M SAD, SICK, AND SCARED
with no hope, no faith, and no confidence.

But I can't let myself do this.
I know someone who could save me.

He is a man of mystery.
He would come to save me if I ask him:

Save me, please. My chance,
my desire, my density to live.

Life is so precious.
There is so much work I have to do.

I'll live to the day I can live.
Thank you. I am saved.

EDWARD M. SCHWARTZ

FAITH

I HAVE FAITH in everything you say.
Anything you say, I believe you.

You've shown your faith in me.
In return I trust you in my heart.

But I must warn you: If you ever try
to destroy your faith, then

distrust and disbelief will destroy you.
Keeping the faith is important.

ABOUT THE CONTRIBUTORS

"MARY ABERNATHY" has a B.S. in psychology from Gallaudet University. She is currently an in-residence counselor for a group home in Washington, D.C. Even though she hates to write, she is a voracious reader. Mary enjoys people watching, sign chatting, and the outdoors, especially the marine environment. She resides in Washington, D.C.

"ALEX" lives in Park Slope, New York.

JAYE AUSTIN-WILLIAMS is a director, actress, playwright, screenwriter, essayist, and short story writer. She has served in the past as an ASL consultant to the Theater Development Fund, working with various interpreted Broadway productions and with Hands On, an organization that provides interpreted performances for Off-Broadway shows. Her work is committed to celebrating the lives and works of both African and African-American women, and lesbian and gay people. She has appeared in the anthology *Women Writing,* and in the magazines *Knitting Factory Knotes* and *Spectrum.*

AMY BERNSTEIN has been a native of Massachusetts all her life except for her six years living in Israel. Today Ms. Bernstein is an administrator at Harvard University. She spends her free time trying to learn sign language.

KAREN BOSLEY has been a community activist for the past twenty years. Professionally she is a fundraiser for a local community clinic organization in Seattle. Now president of the Deaf-Blind Service Center there, she has been involved in the deaf community for nine years, and in a loving and caring relationship with Marilyn.

GREGG BROOKS, a longtime resident of Los Angeles, California, has been actively involved in the TV broadcasting and movie industry for many years. Winner of the 1974 Los Angeles Emmy Award for Most Outstanding Individual Achievement for a Weekly Television Series, he has written a book called *The Cracked Tune,* two screenplays, and several stage plays. He was also the editor of *The Visual Media Resource Book* (1984–85).

"DEAN" lives on the West Coast.

JOHN DIBELKA is a contributing editor at *Bear* magazine, in which his social analysis column "Bare Pause" appears. He is currently working toward certification as an ASL interpreter at Mesa College, San Diego, California.

GIGI DORAN is currently working on completing her graduate studies in counseling and psychology in Cambridge, Massachusetts.

"DWAYNE" lives in Canada.

JACK FENNELL died from AIDS on December 18, 1992.

"FINNEGAN" still lives in a prison in California.

"GEORGE" lives in Boston, Massachusetts.

HANNAH GERSHON moved to Massachusetts with her partner Amy Bernstein after living in Israel for several years. Deafened four years ago due to unknown causes, she is currently working on her Ph.D. in sociology at Brandeis University, where she is examining the relationship between disability and cultural identity.

PHILIP J. GORTON will graduate from the Model Secondary School of the Deaf (MSSD) this June; he plans to attend college this fall and study both psychology and theater arts.

PHILLIP GREEN lives in New York City.

ERNEST HOFFMANN lives in Washington, D.C.

"IVY" lives in New York City.

"JADE" has written poetry all her life and lives in New York City.

TOM KANE has given lectures and talks on being deaf and gay at the Deaf Way Conference at Gallaudet, and he's traveled all over to explain deaf gay culture (but not deaf lesbian culture, since it's quite different). He has also set up the Deaf Names Project in order to collect names of deaf people who have died from AIDS and include them in the Names Project. He recently received an award of recognition for his fifteen years of outstanding service by the Capital Metro Alliance of the Deaf (CMRA), and he chaired a national retreat for deaf people with AIDS last October.

RAYMOND LUCZAK became deaf at the age of seven months as the result of double pneumonia and grew up in Michigan's Upper Peninsula. After graduating from Gallaudet University, he moved to New York City, where his play *Snooty* won the 1990 New York Deaf Theater's Sam Edwards Deaf Playwrights Competition. Since then his essay "Notes of a Deaf Gay Writer" has appeared in *Christopher Street,* later reprinted in *Deaf Life* magazine. Along with his story "You Feel Beautiful" here, other stories from his forthcoming novel *A Collage Of Hands* have appeared in George Stambolian's *Men on Men 4* (NAL/Dutton) and Jill Jepson's *No Walls of Stone* (Gallaudet University Press). His play *The Rake* was produced; he is now writing a new play.

"JAMES MACKINTOSH" is a New York–based writer and administrator.

DOROTHY MARDER, a late-deafened lesbian, is a free-lance press and portrait photographer. She has been actively engaged in the movements for social change. Her photos of civil rights, peace, anti-nuclear, feminist, and gay and lesbian events have been widely published in the alternative press. She is now attending graduate school, working toward a degree in social work. In 1989 she suffered a sudden hearing loss resulting from the use of a powerful antibiotic administered at the end of a life-threatening illness. Since then she has continued to cope with not being able to decode spoken language, even with the inadequate help of hearing aids and other assistive listening devices. She has read much about the deaf community and studied ASL; like many other late-deafened lesbians and gay men, she'd like very much to be a part of the deaf gay community.

"MICHAEL" is a social worker and works specifically with clients who are deaf or have other communication disorders. When not working, he loves to ski and swim.

KEITH R. MITCHELL was born in Cincinnati, Ohio; he began shooting photographs at the age of ten. When he was thirteen, he moved to North Carolina. After graduating from high school, he attended Gallaudet University, where he received a B.A. in psychology in 1986. Ever since becoming serious about photography at Gallaudet, he's worked with Annie Leibowitz. He lives in Washington, D.C.

"NANCY" lives in New York City.

"NICKOLAS" is actively involved in establishing the Big Apple RAD, a new club for deaf gay people in New York City.

"PABLO" lives in the Washington, D.C., metropolitan area.

"PATRICK" exists somewhere in Philadelphia.

DRAGONSANI RENTERIA is a multilingual Mexican/Italian-American Deaf dyke who grew up in El Paso, Texas. For many years actively involved in the Deaf gay and lesbian community, she is an activist, filmmaker, and journalist. She is the director of the Deaf Gay and Lesbian Community Center in San Francisco, where she currently resides. She is also the publisher and editor of *Coming Together News.* Involved in a number of organizations including the Northern California Leather Association of the Deaf, she holds a B.A. from the University of California at Berkeley, and will soon be working toward her degree (J.D.) in juvenile law.

"RICKY" resides with his partner of four years in St. Paul, Minnesota.

ROBERT I. ROTH grew up in Chicago, where he was born, and in Miami. He attended special education programs until sixth grade, when he began attending regular school. After learning ASL in his late twenties, he became involved in producing plays in sign language and curating exhibits about deaf art. He currently lives with his life partner in Seattle, Washington, where he works as an arts administrator, and paints and writes in his spare time.

EDWARD M. SCHWARTZ was the first deaf cabdriver in New York City, where Joe DiMaggio, Jack Cassidy, Dustin Hoffman, and Karl Malden were among his many customers over his 60,000-plus miles on the job. In 1973 he began working for Avon Products, where he stayed for seventeen years. He was promoted from offset operator to accountant, thanks to hard work and his degrees from both Rochester Institute of Technology (RIT) and Long Island University (LIU). Also a founding member of the New York Deaf Theater, he died from AIDS on May 9, 1991.

DAVE SCOTTON says, "I chose to be me." He is now back in L.A. and is continuing his education there. He lives in Boys' Town, a.k.a. West Hollywood.

ANN SILVER has continuously battled deafism, sexism, anti-Semitism, and homophobia from the day she was born. She is a Deaf Art-ist, writer, and Deaf rights advocate. During the 1970s, she was one of the original members of the Deaf Art Movement and also the only Deaf member of the Furies, a lesbian-feminist think tank of legendary standing within the national women's movement. Her drawings and paintings have been exhibited in the U.S. and abroad, and many of her logos can be found in graphic design textbooks. Author of over one hundred published essays and articles on the arts and culture of Deaf people, she is currently working on Deaf Art/De'VIA (Deaf View/Image Art), both as a genre and as an academic-scholarly subject. Having lived in D.C., Tokyo, and New York City for many years, she is back home in Seattle. "School Essay" is an homage to her Deaf friends and interpreters whose lives have been existinguished by AIDS.

TANIS lives in Vancouver, British Columbia.

EDWARD THERIAULT (a.k.a. "E.T.") lives in Massachusetts.

FRANK TOTI, JR., was born and raised in Rhode Island and currently lives in San Francisco. An avid conversationalist and a good listener, Frank leapt at this chance to put his "ears and mouth" to work. This is his first published effort.

"VICTOR" lives in Boston, Massachusetts.

W. JAMEY WINKLER, a 1991 graduate of Trenton State College, has backpacked through Europe for a few months. Currently sharing a house with his lover of four years in Lawrenceville, New Jersey, he is working on his third screenplay and has begun his first novel.

"YVETTE," a graphic designer, lives in Brooklyn, New York.

A LISTING OF ORGANIZATIONS FOR DEAF LESBIANS AND GAY MEN

Because this listing comprises only what I was able to find, it is by no means complete, but I do hope that it provides a link to others in the deaf lesbian and gay community itself. I have not had the opportunity to check whether each organization still exists, so find out for yourself (smile). Because many of these organizations are often short of funds, show your support by enclosing a SASE (self-addressed stamped envelope) with your inquiries.

UNITED STATES

✦ *COMING TOGETHER NEWS*
P.O. Box 5669
Berkeley, CA 94705-0669

A bimonthly that aims to bring together the deaf, hard-of-hearing, and hearing-signing lesbian, gay, and bisexual communities everywhere. Write for suscription information. Also, CTN is publishing the first edition of *International Deaf Lesbian and Gay Resource Directory* later this year, and in it various organizations helping deaf people with AIDS will be listed. You can also write to the same address above if you wish to learn more about the National Deaf Lesbian & Gay Awareness Week Project/Committee.

✦ *DEAF LIFE* MAGAZINE
Box 63083, Marketplace Mall
Rochester, NY 14623-6383

While this monthly does not focus on deaf gay issues, it is certainly gay-affirmative and very informative on what's happening out there in the larger deaf community in America.

CALIFORNIA

Los Angeles/West Hollywood

✦ SOUTHERN CALIFORNIA RAINBOW SOCIETY OF THE DEAF (SCRSD)
P.O. Box 2686
Van Nuys, CA 91404

✦ LOS ANGELES LEATHER ASSOCIATION OF THE DEAF (LALAD)
c/o Kevin DeWindt
10701 Moorpark Street, #4
Toluca Lake, CA 91602

San Diego

✦ SOUTHERN CALIFORNIA LAMBDA ALLIANCE OF THE DEAF (SCLAD)
P.O. Box 3840
San Diego, CA 92163

San Francisco

✦ RAINBOW DEAF SOCIETY (RDS)
P.O. Box 421606
San Francisco, CA 94142-1606

✦ THE DEAF GAY & LESBIAN CENTER
25 Taylor Street, Suite 701
San Francisco, CA 94102
(415) 885-2341 (TDD)
(800) 735-2922 (Voice, California Relay Service)

Established in January 1992 with the help of DCARA (Deaf Counseling, Advocacy, and Referral Agency) and the United Way of San Francisco, the Deaf Gay and Lesbian Center provides "proactive" support through advocacy, community education, counseling, and referrals. The Deaf Gay and Lesbian Center works with the Rainbow Deaf Society (RDS), the Deaf Community AIDS Project (Deaf CAP), the Deaf AIDS Center (DAC), and DCARA. This is the first deaf gay and lesbian community center in the United States, and as far as I know, probably the first in the world. They also sponsor an outreach number for deaf lesbians and gay men in the Bay Area; that number is (510) 465-0927.

San Jose

✦ SAN JOSE LAMBDA SOCIETY OF THE DEAF (SJLSD)
P.O. Box 90035
San Jose, CA, 95109-3035
(619) 392-1139 (TDD)

COLORADO

✦ MILE HIGH RAINBOW SOCIETY OF THE DEAF (MHRSD)
P.O. Box 86
Denver, CO 80201

DISTRICT OF COLUMBIA

✦ CAPITAL METROPOLITAN RAINBOW ALLIANCE (CMRA)
P.O. Box 33275
Washington, DC 20033-0257
(202) 649-4332 (TDD)

✦ LAMBDA SOCIETY OF GALLAUDET UNIVERSITY (LSGU)
Gallaudet University
800 Florida Avenue, NE
Washington, DC 20002

LSGU is a deaf gay and lesbian club for its students.

FLORIDA

Miami/Fort Lauderdale

✦ COCONUT CITY SOCIETY OF THE DEAF (CCSD)
P.O. Box 100545
Ft. Lauderdale, FL 33310-0545

Tampa

✦ GASPARILLA ALLIANCE OF THE DEAF
2310 Southview Avenue, #57
Tampa, FL 33629

GEORGIA

✦ PEACHTREE RAINBOW DEAF SOCIETY (PRDS)
P.O. Box 872, 977 Montreal Road
Atlanta, GA 30021-0872

ILLINOIS

As of this writing, Windy City Rainbow Society of the Deaf (WCRSD) is no longer in existence; however, Thomas at (312) 738-9755 (TDD) is trying to set one up. Chicagoans, please show your support!

✦ RAINBOW BRIDGE
P.O. Box 42
Itasca, IL 61043-0042

A social-support group for people with disabilities who are gay, lesbian, or bisexual.

LOUISIANA

✦ ACADEMIA RAINBOW SOCIETY (ARS)
P.O. Box 57166
New Orleans, LA 70157
(504) 889-0138 (TDD)

MARYLAND

✦ BALTIMORE LAMBDA ALLIANCE OF THE DEAF (BLAD)
241 West Chase Street
Baltimore, MD 21201

MASSACHUSETTS

While there is no established deaf gay or lesbian club, it has been reported that deaf gay people get together on the first Thursday night every month at Club Cafe on Columbus Avenue in Boston.

MICHIGAN

✦ RAINBOW GREAT LAKES ALLIANCE OF THE DEAF (RGLAD)
c/o Affirmations
195 West 9 Mile Road, Suite 110
Ferndale, MI 48220

MISSOURI

✦ KANSAS CITY RAINBOW ALLIANCE OF THE DEAF (KCRAD)
P.O. Box 10252
Kansas City, MO 64111
(816) 531-6706 (TDD)

NEW JERSEY

✦ NEW JERSEY RAINBOW ALLIANCE OF THE DEAF (NJRAD)
P.O. Box 596
Rockaway, NJ 07866

NEW YORK

✦ BIG APPLE RAINBOW OF THE DEAF (BARD)
39 St. John's Place
Brooklyn, NY 11217
(718) 399-2664 (TDD)

By this time BARD should be fully established. Call for more information.

✦ EDUCATION IN A DISABLED GAY ENVIRONMENT (EDGE)
P.O. Box 305, Village Station
New York, NY 10014
(212) 749-9438 (TDD)
(718) 723-6620 (Voice)

While this is not a deaf gay group, they do provide an interpreter at their monthly meetings at the Gay and Lesbian Community Center on West 13th Street.

OHIO

Cleveland

✦ BUCKEYE RAINBOW SOCIETY OF THE DEAF (BRSD)
P.O. Box 6253
Cleveland, OH 44101-1253

Gahanna

Deaf gay men into leather can become part of the Deaf International Chapter of the National Leather Association. NLA: Deaf also sponsors Deaf International Leather Festival Weekends.

✦ NLA: Deaf
P.O. Box 30286
Gahanna, OH 43230

OREGON

See Washington State for the Northwest Rainbow Alliance of the Deaf (NRAD).

PENNSYLVANIA

✦ PHILAMDEAF (Philadelphia Lambda Society of the Deaf)
c/o John Flynn
3518 Ainslie Street
Philadelphia, PA 19129-1630

TEXAS

Dallas

✦ DALLAS RAINBOW ALLIANCE OF THE DEAF, INC. (DRAD)
P.O. Box 225661
Dallas, TX 75222

Houston

✦ ASTRO RAINBOW SOCIETY OF THE DEAF (ARSD)
P.O. Box 66136
Houston, TX 77266-6136

WASHINGTON STATE

✦ NORTHWEST RAINBOW ALLIANCE OF THE DEAF (NRAD)
250 N.E. Northgate Way
Seattle, WA 98125

Its members also come from Oregon and Vancouver, B.C. (Canada).

✦ SEATTLE LAMBDA SOCIETY OF THE DEAF (SLSD)
c/o Brian L. McDanel
2442 N.W. Market Street, Suite 252
Seattle, WA 98107

WISCONSIN

I have tried to get ahold of the address for the Southeastern Wisconsin Rainbow Alliance for the Deaf (SWRAD) in Milwaukee, so I am not sure if it still exists.

AUSTRALIA

✦ KOALA DEAF FEDERATION
P.O. Box 1014
Carlton, Victoria 3013
Australia

Sydney/NSW

To my understanding, Waratah Deaf Association exists for deaf gay men and lesbians, but I have been unable to track down its address.

Melbourne/Victoria

✦ MOOMBA DEAF ASSOCIATION
P.O. Box 1014
Carlton, Victoria 3013
Australia

Perth/West Australia

✦ KANGPAW DEAF ASSOCIATION
P.O. Box 55
North Perth, WA 6006

CANADA

Montreal, Quebec

✦ ASSOCIATION DES BONNES GENS SOURDS, INC.
C.P. 875
succursale <C>
Montreal, Quebec H2L 4L9

Toronto, Ontario

✦ TORONTO RAINBOW ALLIANCE OF THE DEAF
P.O. Box 671 Post. Stat. F
Toronto, ON M4Y 2L4

Vancouver, British Columbia

See WASHINGTON STATE, U.S.A.

EUROPE

DLAGGS is responsible for keeping this list of European deaf gay clubs up-to-date (see United Kingdom for the Coordinator's address). Addresses marked with an asterisk (*) are not group addresses; they are personal addresses of contact people. The Coordinator has helped pull together a very successful first European Deaf Lesbian and Gay Conference in Paris in December 1992.

BELGIUM

✦ "Manneken-Pis et Jeannke-Pis" Tels Quels
rue Marche-au-Charbon, 81
1000 Bruxelles, Belgium

DENMARK

✦ Regnbuen
Knabrostraede 3,3. Sal
1007 Copenhagen K., Denmark

FRANCE

✦ ACGLSF (Association Culturelle des Gays et Lesbiennes Sourdes de France)
c/o Maison des Homosexualities
25 rue Michel-le-Comte
75003 Paris, France
42-72-91-13 (Fax)

GERMANY

There are reputedly two groups in Dusseldorf and Dortmund, but no addresses were given for them.

Berlin

✦ "Gemeinschaft der 'verkehrten' Gehorlosen Berlin 1985 e.V." bei Mann o Meter
Motzstrasse 5
1000 Berlin 30, Germany

Frankfurt

✦ "Charlie's friends" Gehorlosen Gruppe Frankfurt am Main
Ralf Barthel*
August Schneidel Str. 9
W-6000 Frankfurt A.M. 50, Germany

Koln

✦ "Gehorlsengruppe Koln e.V. 1989" SCH.U.L.Z.
c/o SCHULZ
Bismarckstr. 17
5000 Koln 1, Germany

ITALY

✦ Mauro Prattella Monastra*
Viale Brenta, 16
20139 Milano, Italy
(039) 20.22.963 (Fax)

NETHERLANDS

✦ "Roze Gebaar" — landelijke werkgroep van dove homofielen en lesbiennes
Postbus 9204
3506GE Utrecht, The Netherlands

NORWAY

✦ Geir Brodal*
Feltspatveien 43
1155 Oslo 11, Norway

PORTUGAL

✦ Carlos Martins
Praceta joao Faria Borda
Ne 4-1o DTO
2700 Amadora, Portugal

SWEDEN

✦ "REGNBAGEN"
c/o RFSL, P.O. Box 350
10124 Stockholm, Sweden

SWITZERLAND

French-speaking Region

✦ Janine Reymond*
Ave de Valmont 15
1010 Lausanne, Switzerland

German-speaking Region

✦ Tomaso Jannotti*
Langmoostr 10
8135 Langnau AIA, Switzerland
01-713-05-80 (Fax)

UNITED KINGDOM (U.K.)

In the U.K., deaf lesbian and gay groups are known as DLAGGS. Address all correspondence regarding DLAGGS (especially for updates on the DLAGGS that follow) to:

✦ The Coordinator, DLAGGS
c/o 7 Victoria Avenue
South Croydon
Surrey CR2 0QP
081-660-2208 (Minicom, eves. only)

Birmingham/West Midlands

✦ CENTRAL RAINBOW
Hon. Secretary
P.O. Box 2221
Birmingham B4 7AS
021-429-3986 (Minicom)

Brighton/South Coast

✦ PUNCH AND JUDY CLUB
Secretary
P.O. Box 394
East Bourne, East Sussex
BN20 9RF
0323-416197 (Minicom)

Cardiff/South Wales

✦ DRAGONS CLUB
Secretary, "Way Past Heaven"
147 Coed-y-Gores
Llanedryn, Cardiff
South Wales CF3 7NH
0222-733379 (Minicom)

Greater Manchester/Northwest

✦ TRIANGLE CLUB
Hon. Secretary
c/o Gay Centre
P.O. Box 153
Manchester M60 1LP

London/Southeast

✦ BROTHERS AND SISTERS CLUB
Hon. Secretary
4 Abersham Road, Flat A
Hackney
London E8 2LN

✦ DAHLING (Deaf and Hearing Lesbian Group)
Hon. Secretary
54-56 Phoenix Road
London NW1

Nottingham/East Midlands

✦ EASTERN RAINBOW
Pat* 0623-662585 (Minicom)
Kev* 0602-279704 (Minicom)

ADDITIONAL INFORMATION ON DEAFNESS

If you wish to learn more about deafness, you should write the following publishers for their catalogs as they all advocate a strong deaf cultural perspective.

✦ DEAF LIFE PRESS
c/o MSM Productions, Ltd.
85 Farragut Street
Rochester, NY 14611-2845
(716) 328-6720 (Fax)

✦ DEAF MEDIA, INC.
2600 Tenth Street, #101
Berkeley, CA 94710
(510) 841-0165 (TDD)

✦ GALLAUDET UNIVERSITY BOOKSTORE
800 Florida Avenue, NE
Washington, DC 20002-3695
(202) 651-5271 (TDD/V)

✦ NAD BOOKSTORE
814 Thayer Avenue
Silver Spring, MD 20910
(301) 587-6282 (TDD)
(301) 587-6283 (V/TDD)

✦ T.J. PUBLISHERS, INC.
814 Thayer Avenue, #206
Silver Spring, MD 20910
(301) 585-4440 (TDD/V)

BI ANY OTHER NAME, edited by Loraine Hutchins and Lani Kaahumanu, $12.00. Hear the voices of over seventy women and men from all walks of life describe their lives as bisexuals. They tell their stories — personal, political, spiritual, historical — in prose, poetry, art, and essays. These are individuals who have fought prejudice from both the gay and straight communities and who have begun only recently to share their experiences. This groundbreaking anthology is an important step in the process of forming a new bisexual community.

BROTHER TO BROTHER, edited by Essex Hemphill, $9.00. Black activist and poet Essex Hemphill has carried on in the footsteps of the late Joseph Beam (editor of *In the Life*) with this new anthology of fiction, essays, and poetry by black gay men. Contributors include Assoto Saint, Craig G. Harris, Melvin Dixon, Marlon Riggs, and many newer writers.

THE PERSISTENT DESIRE, edited by Joan Nestle, $15.00. A generation ago, butch-femme identities were taken for granted in the lesbian community. Today women who think of themselves as butch or femme often face prejudice from both the lesbian community and the straight world. Here, for the first time, dozens of femme and butch lesbians tell their stories of love, survival, and triumph.

BUSHFIRE, edited by Karen Barber, $9.00. Amidst many differences, all lesbians share one thing: a desire for women. Sometimes intensely sexual, other times subtly romantic, this emotion is always powerful. These short stories celebrate lesbian desire in all its forms. The authors portray a lazy affair set against the backdrop of Venice; a small-town stone butch being "flipped" by a stranger with painted fingernails; an intense but destructive relationship between a reporter and a mysterious dancer; and a holy encounter between a birthday girl, a call girl, and her rosary beads.

A LOTUS OF ANOTHER COLOR, edited by Rakesh Ratti, $10.00. For the first time, gay men and lesbians from India, Pakistan, and other South Asian countries recount their stories of coming out. In essays and poetry, they tell of challenging prejudice from both the South Asian and gay cultures, and they express the exhilaration of finally finding a sense of community.

LEATHERFOLK, edited by Mark Thompson, $13.00. There's a new leather community in America today. It's politically aware and socially active. This ground-breaking anthology is the first nonfiction, co-gender work to focus on this large and often controversial subculture. The diverse contributors look at the history of the leather and S/M movement, how radical sex practice relates to their spirituality, and what S/M means to them personally.

LEAVE A LIGHT ON FOR ME, by Jean Swallow, $10.00. Morgan is a computer instructor who doesn't understand what exactly has happened to her long-term relationship with Georgia, nor what exactly is happening to the rest of her when she stands near Elizabeth. Georgia, forced into exile from the South she loves and from the alcoholic family she both loves and hates, doesn't understand why, after six years of recovery, she still hasn't found her way home. And Elizabeth, the rich and beautiful doctor, doesn't understand why she can't keep a girlfriend. But Bernice, who watches and waits, understands a lot by just being herself. Together, they move from a difficult past into a passionate and hopeful future.

CHOICES, by Nancy Toder, $9.00. Lesbian love can bring joy and passion; it can also bring conflicts. In this straightforward, sensitive novel, Nancy Toder conveys the fear and confusion of a woman coming to terms with her sexual and emotional attraction to other women.

ONE TEENAGER IN TEN, edited by Ann Heron, $5.00. One teenager in ten is gay. Here, 26 young people from around the country discuss their experiences: coming out to themselves, to parents, and friends; trying to pass as straight; running away; incest; trouble with the law; making initial contacts with the gay community; religious concerns; and more. Their words will provide encouragement for other teenagers facing similar experiences.

YOUNG, GAY AND PROUD!, edited by Sasha Alyson, $4.00. One high school student in ten is gay. Here is the first book to ever address the needs of that often-invisible minority. It helps young people deal with questions like: Am I really gay? What would my friends think if I told them? Should I tell my parents? Does anybody else feel the way I do? Other sections discuss health concerns; sexuality; and suggestions for further reading.

REFLECTIONS OF A ROCK LOBSTER, by Aaron Fricke, $7.00. Guess who's coming to the prom! Aaron Fricke made national news by taking a male date to his high school prom. Yet for the first sixteen years of his life, Fricke had closely guarded the secret of his homosexuality. Here, told with insight and humor, is his story about growing up gay, about realizing that he was different, and about how he ultimately developed a positive gay identity in spite of the prejudice around him.

GOLDENBOY, by Michael Nava, $9.00. Jim Pears is guilty; even his lawyer, Henry Rios, believes that. The evidence is overwhelming that Pears killed the co-worker who threatened to expose his homosexuality. But as Rios investigates the case, he finds that the pieces don't always fit together the way they should. Too many people *want* Jim Pears to be found guilty, regardless of the truth. And some of them are determined that Henry Rios isn't going to interfere with their plans.

THE COLOR OF TREES, by Canaan Parker, $9.00. Peter, a black scholarship student from Harlem, takes life too seriously at his new, mostly white boarding school. Things change when he meets T.J., a wellborn but hyperactive imp with little use for clothing. Here, in his first novel, Canaan Parker explores the formation of both racial and homosexual identities, and the conflicts created by the narrator's dual allegiance.

WITHOUT SANCTION, by J.M. Roberts, $9.00. In late-nineteenth-century England, Kit St. Denys has everything he wants: beauty, wealth, and a brilliant acting career. Most importantly, he has the love of the handsome Nick Stuart, a simple country doctor with Puritanical roots. But Kit is running from a hidden, brutal past. Kit's secret demons drive Nick away, across the Atlantic, and into a new life. Kit follows, only to have his past pursue them both with devastating consequences.

THE UNFINISHED, by Jay B. Laws, $10.00. They are the Unfinished. Their lives were interrupted by untimely deaths. Now their terrible predicaments chain them to this earth, jailing them until their business is completed, their stories known. One man hears their cry, but to help them he must put his own life into jeopardy. If he isn't careful, he too may end up ... Unfinished.

STEAM, by Jay B. Laws, $10.00. San Francisco was once a city of music and laughter, of parties and bathhouses, when days held promise and nights, romance. But now something sinister haunts the streets and alleyways of San Francisco, something that crept in with the fog to seek a cruel revenge. It feeds on deep desire, and tantalizes with the false and empty promises of a more carefree past. For many, it will all begin with a ticket to an abandoned house of dreams...

TORN ALLEGIANCES, by Jim Holobaugh, with Keith Hale, $10.00. Jim Holobaugh was the perfect ROTC cadet — so perfect that ROTC featured the handsome college student in a nationwide ad campaign. But as he gradually came to realize that he was gay, he faced an impossible dilemma: to serve the country he loved, he would have to live a life of deceit. His story dramatizes both the monetary waste, and the moral corruptness, of the military's anti-gay policy.

THE MEN WITH THE PINK TRIANGLE, by Heinz Heger, $8.00. For decades, history ignored the Nazi persecution of gay people. Only with the rise of the gay movement in the 1970s did historians finally recognize that gay people, like Jews and others deemed "undesirable," suffered enormously at the hands of the Nazi regime. Of the few who survived the concentration camps, only one ever came forward to tell his story. His true account of those nightmarish years provides an important introduction to a long-forgotten chapter of gay history.

SUPPORT YOUR LOCAL BOOKSTORE

Most of the books described here are available at your nearest gay or feminist bookstore, and many of them will be available at other bookstores. If you can't get these books locally, order by mail using this form.

Enclosed is $________ for the following books. (Add $1.00 postage if ordering just one book. If you order two or more, we'll pay the postage.)

1. ____

2. ____

3. ____

name: ____

address: ____

city: ______________________ state: ________ zip: __________

ALYSON PUBLICATIONS

Dept. J-51, 40 Plympton St., Boston, MA 02118

After December 31, 1994, please write for current catalog.